# Revise A2

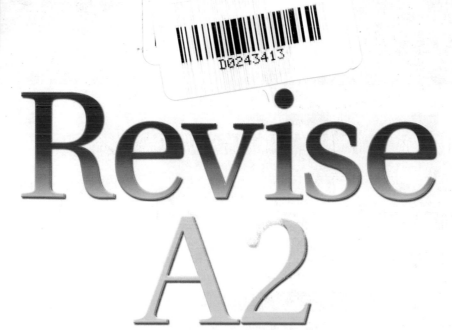

# AQA
# Psychology

Cara Flanagan

# Contents

Part 3 : AQA B Unit 3

Part 4 : AQA B Unit 4

# Specification lists

## AQA A Psychology

| MODULE | SPECIFICATION TOPIC | CHAPTER REFERENCE | STUDIED IN CLASS | REVISED | PRACTICE QUESTIONS |
|---|---|---|---|---|---|
| Unit 3 | Biological rhythms and sleep | 1.1, 1.2, 1.3 | | | |
| | Perception | 2.1 (AS Unit 2.4), 2.2, 2.3 | | | |
| | Relationships | 3.1, 3.2, 3.3 | | | |
| | Aggression | 4.1, 4.2, 4.3 | | | |
| | Eating behaviour | 5.1, 5.2, 5.3 | | | |
| | Gender | 6.1, 6.2, 6.3 | | | |
| | Intelligence and learning | 7.1, 7.2, 7.3 | | | |
| | Cognition and development | 8.1, 8.2, 8.3 | | | |
| Unit 4 — Section A | Schizophrenia | 9.1, 9.2, 9.3 | | | |
| | Depression | 10.1, 10.2, 10.3 | | | |
| | Anxiety disorder – phobias | 11.1, 11.2, 11.3 | | | |
| | Anxiety disorder – OCD | 12.1, 12.2, 12.3 | | | |
| Section B | Media psychology | 13.1, 13.2, 13.3 | | | |
| | The psychology of addictive behaviour | 14.1, 14.2, 14.3 | | | |
| | Anomalistic psychology | 15.1, 15.2, 15.3 | | | |
| Section C | Psychological research and scientific method | 16.1, 16.2 (AS Units 4.1, 4.2 and 7.3), 16.3 (AS Unit 4.3) | | | |

## Examination analysis

The A2 AQA A specification comprises two examination units: Unit 3 and Unit 4.

**Unit 3   Topics in Psychology**                       *1½ hours 50% of A2 (25% of A level)*

*The unit exam is divided into eight sections, each containing one essay-style question. There is one section for each of the topics listed in the table above. Each question is worth 25 marks. Candidates must answer three out of the eight questions. QWC (quality of written communication) will be assessed in each question.*

*The total mark for this paper is 75.*
*Available in January and June.*

**Unit 4   Psychopathology, Psychology in Action and Research Methods**   *2 hours 50% of A2 (25% of A level)*
*The unit exam is divided into three sections:*
- ***Section A** Psychopathology: one essay-style question to be answered from a choice of three (on schizophrenia, depression and anxiety disorder). QWC will be assessed in this essay.*
- ***Section B** Psychology in Action: one question to be answered from a choice of three (one from each topic).*
- ***Section C** Research methods: one compulsory structured question.*

*The total mark for this paper is 85 (Sections A and B are worth 25 marks; Section C is worth 35 marks.) Available in January and June.*

# AQA B Psychology

| MODULE | | SPECIFICATION TOPIC | CHAPTER REFERENCE | STUDIED IN CLASS | REVISED | PRACTICE QUESTIONS |
|---|---|---|---|---|---|---|
| Unit 3 | Section A | **Child Development** | | | | |
| | | Social development | 17.1 (AS Unit 3.1) | | | |
| | | Cognitive development | 8.1, 17.2 | | | |
| | | Moral development | 8.2, 17.3 | | | |
| | Section B | **Applied Options** | | | | |
| | | Cognition and law | 18.1 (AS Unit 2.2) | | | |
| | | Schizophrenia and mood disorders | 9.1, 9.2, 9.3, 10.1, 10.2, 10.3, 18.2 | | | |
| | | Stress and stress management | 18.3 (AS Unit 5.1 and 5.2) | | | |
| | | Substance abuse | 18.4 | | | |
| | | Forensic psychology | 18.5 | | | |
| Unit 4 | | Approaches in psychology | 19.1 (AS Unit 1.1) | | | |
| | | Debates in psychology | 16.1, 19.2 | | | |
| | | Methods in psychology (AS Unit 4.1, 4.2, | 16.2, 16.3, 19.3, 4.3 and 7.3) | | | |

## Examination analysis

The A2 specification comprises two examination units: Unit 3 and Unit 4.

**Unit 3  Child Development and Applied Options**　　　　　2 hours 50% of A2 (25% of A level)

The unit exam is divided into two sections:

- **Section A** Child Development: one structured question to be answered from a choice of three (one from each topic). QWC (quality of written communication) will be assessed in this essay.
- **Section B** Applied Options: two structured questions to be answered from a choice of five (one from each topic). QWC will be assessed in these essays.

The total mark for this paper is 60, divided equally between the three questions.
Available in January and June.

**Unit 4  Approaches, Debates and Methods in Psychology**　　　　2 hours 50% of A2 (25% of A level)

The unit exam is divided into three sections:

- **Section A** Approaches in Psychology: one structured question to be answered from a choice of two. QWC will be assessed in this essay.
- **Section B** Debates in Psychology: one compulsory structured question. QWC will be assessed in this essay.
- **Section C** Methods in Psychology: one compulsory structured question.

The total mark for this paper is 60, divided equally between the three questions.
Available in June only.

# Psychology A level: AS and A2

## AS and A2

All Psychology A level courses are in two parts. Most students will start by studying the AS (Advanced Subsidiary) course in the first year and then go on to study the second part of the A level course (A2) in the second year. To gain the full A level you need to complete both the AS and A2 courses. Some students just do the AS course. Usually the full A level takes two years, allowing one year for AS and one year for A2. But you can take more or less time to complete it.

*Even though you can resit unit exams as often as you like, this information may be passed on by the exam board.*

The Psychology A level is assessed in four unit exams: two are AS and two are A2. These are generally available in January and June every year.

## Assessment objectives

*Psychology is a science subject and, therefore, it shares assessment objectives with all science subjects.*

Following an examination course means that much of your learning is guided by how it will ultimately be assessed. Examination boards set out their 'assessment objectives', which are their criteria for assessing performance. In the A level examinations there are three skill clusters or *assessment objectives*, which, in brief, are **describe** (AO1), **evaluate** (AO2) and **conduct** (AO3). There is also an assessment of the **quality of written communication** (QWC).

### Assessment objective 1 (AO1)

Knowledge and understanding of science and of *How Science Works*. Candidates should be able to:
(a) recognise, recall and show understanding of scientific knowledge
(b) select, organise and communicate relevant information.

### Assessment objective 2 (AO2)

Application of knowledge and understanding of science and of How Science Works. Candidates should be able to:
(a) analyse and evaluate scientific knowledge and processes
(b) apply scientific knowledge and processes to unfamiliar situations, including those related to issues
(c) assess the validity, reliability and credibility of scientific information.

### Assessment objective 3 (AO3)

How Science Works in Psychology. Candidates should be able to:
(a) describe ethical, safe and skilful practical techniques and processes, selecting appropriate qualitative and quantitative methods
(b) know how to make, record and communicate reliable and valid observations and measurements with appropriate precision and accuracy, through the use of primary and secondary sources
(c) analyse, interpret, explain and evaluate the methodology, results and impact of their own and others' experimental and investigative activities in a variety of ways.

### Quality of Written Communication (QWC)

Quality of written communication refers to the use of accurate spelling, punctuation and grammar, and the ability to organise information.

# Types of examination questions used at A2

A2 questions come in three varieties, as shown below.

## Essay-style questions

Essay-style questions are used in AQA A questions only. In such cases the question is not parted. There is a requirement to include description (AO1), evaluation (AO2) and commentary on methodology (AO3). Question examples:
- *Describe and evaluate Piaget's theory of cognitive development. (25 marks)*
- *Discuss **two** biological explanations of schizophrenia. (25 marks)*

## Structured questions

Most A2 questions are structured questions where the question is divided into two or more parts. The parts usually have a common context and often become progressively more demanding as you work your way through the question.
Each part may be wholly description (AO1), for example:
- *Describe psychological research into circadian rhythms. (9 marks)*
- *Describe what Piaget meant by class inclusion. (3 marks)*

Or, each part may be wholly evaluation (AO2), for example:
- *Evaluate research related to circadian rhythms. (10 marks)*

Or, each part may be a mixture of AO1 and AO2, for example:
- *Outline and evaluate biological explanations of addiction. (10 marks)*
- *Discuss the humanistic approach to psychology. (15 marks)*

Some parts may focus specifically on methodology (AO3), for example:
- *Suggest **three** behavioural categories that could be used by researchers in an observational study of friendship in children aged four years. (3 marks)*

In the AQA A exam AO3 marks are combined with AO2 marks. This is because it is difficult to separate AO2 and AO3 in practice, as any evaluation is likely to include reference to methodology (see mark schemes on pages 10–11).

## Stimulus material questions

Some questions begin with a sentence or several sentences to 'set the scene'. The question then follows from this quotation or stimulus material (sometimes also called 'source material'). It is important in such questions to relate your answer to the quotation or stimulus material. This style is used in research methods questions where the details of a research study are outlined, followed by a series of questions.

## Command words

To some extent you can work out what skills are required by the command word at the start of the question. However, there is some flexibility in the way these are used. For example, 'explain' may be all AO1 or may be a combination of AO1 and AO2 marks. The best advice is to just answer the question, but at the same time you should be aware of the meaning *usually* attached to the common command words (shown on the next page).
You can also study the meaning of the command words by looking at the mark schemes published on the AQA website.

**Examples of A2 command words (injunctions)**

| | |
|---|---|
| *Outline, suggest* | To briefly describe without too much detail, identifying the main points. |
| *Describe* | To provide a detailed description. |
| *Explain* | Present an explanation of an issue; this involves more than just describing something; you should also try to make the concept clear or intelligible so that a person can undestand it. |
| *Distinguish between* | Identify and describe differences. |
| *Briefly evaluate* | To evaluate without too much elaboration. |
| *Evaluate (or critically evaluate)* | Present criticisms, which may include positive (i.e. strengths or advantages) and negative (i.e. limitations or disadvantages) points, as well as other means of evaluation, such as applications or implications, and especially methodology. |
| *Discuss* | To include both description and evaluation, including considerations related to research methodology. |

## What are examiners looking for?

In Psychology examiners are looking for evidence of your knowledge, but often there are no 'right' answers. There are a range of correct answers and any of these will receive credit – the examiner is looking for any evidence of your knowledge *as appropriate to the question set*.

The examiners mark your answers *positively*. They do not subtract marks when material is missing. Instead they aim to award marks for any material that is relevant.

## Important information

This book is based on the latest specifications, however, these do change and candidates should always consult the exam board website for the latest versions, and to look at recent mark schemes.

# Mark schemes used at A2

## AQA A A2 marking criteria

### AQA A AO1 mark bands (questions worth 9 marks)

Examiners use marking guidelines similar to the ones on this page and the following pages to assess the AO1, AO2 and AO3 components of extended writing questions.

| | | |
|---|---|---|
| 9–8 marks | **Sound** | Knowledge and understanding are accurate and well-detailed. A good range of relevant material has been selected. There is substantial evidence of breadth/depth. Organisation and structure of the answer are coherent. |
| 7–5 marks | **Reasonable** | Knowledge and understanding are generally accurate and reasonably detailed. A range of relevant material has been selected. There is evidence of breadth and/or depth. Organisation and structure of the answer are reasonably coherent. |
| 4–3 marks | **Basic** | Knowledge and understanding are basic/relatively superficial. A restricted range of material has been presented. Organisation and structure of the answer are basic. |
| 2–1 marks | **Rudimentary** | Knowledge and understanding are rudimentary and may be muddled and/or inaccurate. The material presented may be very brief or largely irrelevant. Lacks organisation and structure. |
| 0 marks | | No creditworthy material. |

In the AQA A A2 exam, all questions are marked out of a total of 25 marks, divided between 9 AO1 marks and 16 AO2/AO3 marks (except for the research methods question).

### A summary table of AO1 mark bands (for questions worth 9 marks)

An examiner decides on which mark to award by first identifying the band that best describes the essay answer. They then decide on the actual mark within the band by considering whether they were more drawn to the band above or the band below, or neither. It is likely that an answer contains elements of several band descriptors but the examiner selects the best fit.

| Marks | Knowledge and understanding | Range of relevant material | Breadth and depth | Organisation and structure |
|---|---|---|---|---|
| 9–8 | Accurate and well-detailed | Selected | Substantial | Coherent |
| 7–5 | Generally accurate and well-detailed | Selected | Evidence | Reasonably coherent |
| 4–3 | Basic/relatively superficial | Restricted | | Basic |
| 2–1 | Rudimentary, muddled and/or inaccurate | Brief or largely irrelevant | | Lacking |
| 0 | No creditworthy material | | | |

### AO1 marks bands (for questions worth 5 marks)

| | |
|---|---|
| 5–4 | Outline is reasonably thorough, accurate and coherent. |
| 3–2 | Outline is limited, generally accurate and reasonably coherent. |
| 1 | Outline is weak and muddled. |
| 0 | No creditworthy material |

## AQA A AO2/AO3 mark bands

If a question is marked out of 10 or out of 6 the same mark bands apply as for questions marked out of 16. The marks are shown in brackets in the column on the left.

QWC refers to quality of written communication.

| | |
|---|---|
| 16–13<br>[10–9]<br>[6] | **Effective**<br>Commentary and evaluation demonstrate sound analysis and understanding. The answer is well focused and shows coherent elaboration and/or clear line of argument.<br>Issues/debates/approaches are used effectively.<br>There is substantial evidence of synopticity.<br>QWC: Ideas are well-structured and expressed clearly and fluently. Consistently effective use of psychological terminology. Appropriate use of grammar, punctuation and spelling. |
| 12–9<br>[6–8]<br>[5–4] | **Reasonable**<br>Commentary and evaluation demonstrate reasonable analysis and understanding.<br>The answer is generally focused and shows reasonable elaboration and/or line of argument is evident.<br>Issues/debates/approaches are used reasonably effectively.<br>There is evidence of synopticity.<br>QWC: Most ideas are appropriately structured and expressed clearly. Appropriate use of psychological terminology. Minor errors of grammar, punctuation and spelling only occasionally compromise meaning. |
| 8–5<br>[5–3]<br>[3–2] | **Basic**<br>Commentary and evaluation demonstrate basic, superficial understanding.<br>The answer is sometimes focused and shows some evidence of elaboration.<br>Superficial reference may be made to issues/debates/approaches.<br>There is some evidence of synopticity.<br>QWC: Expression of ideas lacks clarity. Limited use of psychological terminology. Errors of grammar, punctuation and spelling are intrusive. |
| 4–1<br>[2–1]<br>[1] | **Rudimentary**<br>Commentary and evaluation are rudimentary, demonstrating very limited understanding.<br>The answer is weak, muddled and incomplete. Material is not used effectively and may be mainly irrelevant.<br>If reference is made to issues/debates/approaches, it is muddled and inaccurate.<br>There is little or no evidence of synopticity.<br>QWC: Deficiency in expression of ideas results in confusion and ambiguity. The answer lacks structure and is often a series of unconnected assertions. Errors of grammar, punctuation and spelling are frequent and intrusive. |
| 0 | No creditworthy material is presented |

## A summary table of AQA A AO2/AO3 mark bands (for questions worth 16 marks)

| Marks | Analysis and understanding | Focus | Elaboration | Line of argument | Issues/ debates/ approaches | Synopticity |
|---|---|---|---|---|---|---|
| 16–13 | Sound | Well focused | Coherent | Clear | Used effectively | Substantial evidence |
| 12–9 | Reasonable | Generally focused | Reasonable | Evident | Reasonably effective | Evidence |
| 8–5 | Basic, superficial | Sometimes focused | Some evidence | | Superficial reference | Some evidence |
| 4–1 | Rudimentary, little understanding | Weak, muddled and incomplete | Not effective | May be mainly irrelevant | Absent or muddled/ inaccurate | Little or none |

## Quality of written communication (QWC) marks

| Marks | Structure of ideas and expression | Use of psychological terminology | Spelling, punctuation, grammar |
|---|---|---|---|
| 16–13 | Well structured, clear, fluent | Effectively used | Appropriate |
| 12–9 | Most appropriately structured, clear | Appropriate use | Minor errors that occasionally compromise meaning |
| 8–5 | Lacks clarity | Limited use | Errors are intrusive |
| 4–1 | Lacks structure, often unconnected assertions, confused and ambiguous | | Errors frequent and intrusive |

# AQA B A2 marking criteria

In the AQA B A2 exam all questions are marked out of a total of 20. This is divided up across the different parts of the question. The final part of each question is usually worth 12 marks. This part is marked using the scheme on the right.

The mark scheme below is for those question parts marked out of 12. In such questions there are four AO1 (description) marks and eight AO2 (evaluation) marks. However, the overall mark is determined by a combination of these, as shown in the bands below.

| 12 –10 marks *Excellent answers* | |
| --- | --- |
| AO1 | Thorough description, showing sound and accurate knowledge and understanding. |
| AO2 | Evaluation is full and well-balanced with appropriate analysis. Any references to research are accurate. Evaluative comment is not simply stated but is presented in the context of the discussion as a whole. The answer is well focused, organised and mostly relevant with little, if any, misunderstanding. |
| QWC | The candidate expresses most ideas clearly and fluently, with consistently effective use of psychological terminology. Arguments are well structured, with appropriate use of sentences and paragraphs. There are few, if any, minor errors of grammar, punctuation and spelling. The overall quality of language is such that meaning is rarely, if ever, obscured. |

QWC refers to quality of written communication.

| 9–7 marks *Good to average answers* | |
| --- | --- |
| AO1 | Answer shows knowledge and understanding. |
| AO2 | There is an attempt to present a balanced evaluation. Some analysis is evident and the answer is mostly focused on the question, although there may be some irrelevance and/or misunderstanding. Any references to research are relevant but are perhaps not linked so clearly to the discussion as for the top band. |
| QWC | The candidate expresses most ideas clearly and makes some appropriate use of psychological terminology. The answer is organised, using sentences and paragraphs. Errors of grammar, punctuation and spelling may be present but are mostly minor, such that they obscure meaning only occasionally. |

An examiner decides on which mark to award by first identifying the band that best describes the essay answer. They then decide on the actual mark within the band by considering whether they were more drawn to the band above or the band below, or neither. It is likely that an answer contains elements of several band descriptors but the examiner selects the best fit.

| 6–4 marks *Average to poor answers* | |
| --- | --- |
| AO1 | Answer shows some knowledge and understanding of the area. Answers in this band are likely to be mostly descriptive and there is likely to be irrelevance and/or inaccuracy. Answers constituting reasonable description with minimal focus on the question are likely to be in this band. |
| AO2 | There must be some evaluation in order to gain 5/6 marks. |
| QWC | The candidate expresses basic ideas clearly but there may be some ambiguity. The candidate uses key psychological terminology inappropriately on some occasions. The answer may lack structure, although there is some evidence of use of sentences and paragraphs. There are occasional intrusive errors of grammar, punctuation and spelling, which obscure meaning. |

# Exam advice

## Some dos and don'ts

**Do** answer the question.

- This sounds obvious but, under exam conditions, students can feel very anxious and write about anything they can think of. They don't even read the whole question; they just notice certain key words and start writing.
- Don't regurgitate a prepared answer because you got a good mark for it in class. If it doesn't answer the question, it will not receive any credit.

**Do** use psychological terms and write coherently and legibly.

- This shows the examiner you really have studied psychology, and also boosts your QWC mark. Identify the names of psychologists and use dates if you can (you don't have to be exact – 'the 1950s' is as good as '1953').

**Do** use the mark allocation to guide you in how much you should write.

- A total of 5 marks for a question, for one part of a question, indicates what proportion of time you should spend on that part. If you write a lot for a question with very few marks, you won't get extra credit and you will have less time to answer the other questions.

**Do** take note of the injunctions.

- The injunctions tell you whether you should be describing, evaluating or both. These injunctions are described on page 8.

**Do** elaborate on your answers.

- In many questions you are awarded 1 mark for identifying a point, and a second mark for providing some extra information, such as an explanation, an example, or some research evidence. Elaboration is what makes the difference between a grade A and a grade C.

**Don't** ignore features of a question.

- If the question says 'describe how psychologists have dealt with ethical issues', don't write about ethical issues. Marks would only be awarded, in this case, for writing about *how psychologists deal with* ethical issues.
- If you are unsure what a question means, explain any ambiguities to the examiner in your answer.

**Don't** leave out obvious material.

- It is very easy to think 'the examiner knows that' and think that you don't have to write down the obvious things. However, the examiner cannot be sure that you know it unless you demonstrate it.

**Don't** waste time.

- An examination has a finite length. Don't spend time 'waffling', hoping the examiner might find something relevant in what you say. Examiners award marks only for material that is directly relevant to the question. Spend time thinking and select what you say very carefully. Selectivity is one of the criteria that examiners use when deciding how many marks to award for an answer.

# Four steps to successful revision

## Step 1: Understand

- Study the topic to be learned slowly. Make sure you understand the logic or important concepts.
- Mark up the text if necessary – underline, highlight and make notes.
- Re-read each paragraph slowly.

**GO TO STEP 2**

## Step 2: Summarise

- Now make your own revision note summary:
  What is the main idea, theme or concept to be learned?
  What are the main points? How does the logic develop?
  Ask questions: Why? How? What next?
- Use bullet points, mind maps, patterned notes.
- Link ideas with mnemonics, mind maps, crazy stories.
- Note the title and date of the revision notes
  (e.g. Psychology: Attitudes and prejudice, 3rd March).
- Organise your notes carefully and keep them in a file.

**This information is now in your short-term memory. You will forget 80% of it if you do not go to Step 3. GO TO STEP 3, but first take a 10-minute break.**

## Step 3: Memorise

- Take 25-minute learning 'bites' with 5-minute breaks.
- After each 5-minute break test yourself:
  - Cover the original revision note summary
  - Write down the main points
  - Speak out loud (record on tape)
  - Tell someone else
  - Repeat many times.

**The material is well on its way to long-term memory. You will forget 40% of it if you do not do step 4. GO TO STEP 4**

## Step 4: Track/Review

- Create a revision diary (one A4 page per day).
- Make a revision plan for the topic, e.g. 1 day later, 1 week later, 1 month later.
- Record your revision in your revision diary, e.g.
  Psychology: Attitudes and prejudice, 3rd March 25 minutes
  Psychology: Attitudes and prejudice, 5th March 15 minutes
  Psychology: Attitudes and prejudice, 3rd April 15 minutes
  ... and then at monthly intervals.

# Chapter 1

# Biological rhythms and sleep

## 1.1 Biological rhythms

*After studying this topic you should be able to describe and evaluate:*

- *circadian, infradian, and ultradian rhythms, including the role of endogenous pacemakers and exogenous zeitgebers*
- *the consequences of disrupting biological rhythms, for example, shift work and jet lag.*

## Types of biological rhythm

AQA A ▶ U3

**Biological rhythms** are not the same as *biorhythms* (a pseudoscientific technique that uses biological rhythms to predict a person's behaviour on a given day).

The term **'zeitgeber'** is German for 'time-giver'.

A **circadian rhythm** is one that recurs about once every day (every 24 hours). The word *circadian* comes from two words: 'circa' (about) and 'dies' (day).

The term 'free-running' refers to how the rhythm would function if it is unaffected by any external zeitgebers, such as daylight changes or clocks.

When doctors collect samples of blood or urine for medical testing they record the time of day the sample was taken because some substances fluctuate naturally over the course of the day. This is a further application of research into biological rhythms.

A biological rhythm is a biologically-driven behaviour that is periodically repeated. Biological rhythms may be controlled by **endogenous pacemakers**, i.e. by internal biological mechanisms, or they may be controlled by **exogenous zeitgebers**, i.e. by external factors in the environment, such as daylight.

### Circadian rhythms

#### 1. Sleep/waking cycle

During a 24-hour period we sleep/wake once. Normally our sleep/wake pattern is entrained by external events, such as clocks, meal times and daylight changes.

We also have a free-running daily cycle governed by our endogenous body clock. For example, Michel Siffre (1972) spent six months in an underground cave. His sleep/waking cycle settled down to 25–30 hours.

The endogenous rhythm can only be controlled to a limited amount. Folkard *et al.* (1985) used artificial light to reduce the circadian cycle. Participants coped at a 23-hour cycle, but when it was reduced to 22 hours their bodies reverted to a natural cycle.

#### 2. Temperature

Core body temperature rises and falls during the course of a day (along with heart rate, urine secretion, or any measure that indicates metabolic rate). It reaches a trough around 4am and returns to normal level by about 8pm.

Colquhoun (1970) concluded, from a review of research, that cognitive performance is positively correlated with temperature. Long-term recall is best when body temperature is highest. In contrast, research has found that alertness is best when body temperature is lowest, in the early morning and early evening (Monk and Embrey, 1981).

#### Evaluation

- **Individual differences** – Aschoff and Wever (1976) observed that some people, when isolated from daylight, maintain 24–25 hour cycles, whereas others develop idiosyncrasies such as 29 hours awake and 21 hours asleep. Marks and Folkard (1985) suggested that 'morning' types may peak in their daily rhythms a few hours earlier than 'evening' types.
- **Application** – The field of **chronotherapeutics** aims to match medical treatments to circadian cycles in order to maximise benefits of certain treatments and minimise adverse effects. For example, asthma symptoms worsen during the night, possibly due to increased levels of cortisol. Therefore, some doctors prescribe unequal doses of medication.

'Infra' means 'below; **infradian rhythms** occur less than once every 24 hours, i.e. they are cycles that take longer than one day to be completed.

## Infradian rhythms

### 1. Menstrual cycle

The menstrual cycle occurs once a month. It is controlled endogenously by hormones produced by the pituitary gland. Reinberg (1967) documented the menstrual cycle of a woman who spent three months in a cave, with only dim lighting. Her sleep–wake cycle lengthened slightly and her menstrual cycle became shorter. However, the menstrual cycle can apparently be synchronised by external factors. Russell *et al.* (1980) collected daily samples of women's underarm sweat, mixed it with alcohol and applied this to the upper lip of their female participants. The participants' menstrual cycles began to synchronise, probably due to **pheromones** that acted as exogenous zeitgebers.

**Pheromones** are biochemical substances that act like hormones, except they are secreted into the air and are then transmitted to other animals of the same species and absorbed into their bloodstream.

### Evaluation

* The **purpose of a menstrual cycle** (rather than having constant fertility) is to conserve energy; it is better to restrict periods of fertility and, therefore, there is a need to have endogenous control of the rhythm.
* There are '**side effects**' of the menstrual cycle – pre-menstrual tension has been associated with increased aggressive behaviour in women and has even been used as a defence in criminal trials (Lewis, 1990).

### 2. Circa-annual rhythms

There are various circa-annual rhythms (i.e. occur once a year), for example:

**Migration** – Gwinner (1986) kept wild birds in cages for three years, exposing them to 12 hours of light and 12 hours of darkness. Despite a lack of external stimuli they still showed signs of migratory restlessness, suggesting endogenous control. Migration may also be triggered by the availability of food (exogenous cue).

**Hibernation** – Pengelly and Fisher (1957) artificially controlled squirrels' exposure to light (12 hours on/off) and temperature (0°C). Nevertheless, the squirrels hibernated from October to April.

### Evaluation

* What happens when biorhythms go wrong? **Seasonal affective disorder** (SAD) affects some people during winter. They become depressed, possibly because darkness leads to increased production of melatonin, which affects mood.
* Such understanding has led to **phototherapy** as a treatment for SAD, i.e. exposure to bright lights for several hours a day to reduce the effect of too much darkness/melatonin.

'Ultra' means 'more than'. **Ultradian rhythms** occur more often than once a day, such as heart beats.

## Ultradian rhythms

### 1. Sleep stages

During a night's sleep you pass through different sleep cycles. (These are described on page 19). Each cycle takes about 90 minutes.

### 2. Basic rest activity cycle (BRAC)

During the daytime biorhythms follow this same 90-minute cycle. For example, Klein and Armitage (1979) tested participants' performance on verbal and spatial tasks through the day and found a 96-minute cycle, the same duration as the sleep cycle. Gerkema and Dann (1985) found that smaller animals tend to have more rapid cycles.

### Evaluation

* This 90-minute cycle appears to be controlled by a **different biological clock** to the one governing the circadian rhythm. If the circadian clock is destroyed the 90-minute cycle continues.

## *Control of biological rhythms*

AQA A ▷ U3

The **suprachiasmatic nucleus** (SCN) takes its name because it is located directly above the *optic chiasma* – the place where the optic nerves cross over.

The diagram shows the location of the SCN, the main biological clock.

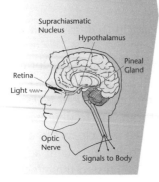

Suprachiasmatic Nucleus
Hypothalamus
Pineal Gland
Retina
Light 〰〰
Optic Nerve
Signals to Body

In animals, such as birds and reptiles, light falls directly on the pineal gland through the skull and affects the production of melatonin.

The concept of **'adaptiveness'** comes from evolutionary theory and refers to the idea that behaviours that persist are likely to be those that promote an individual's survival and reproduction and, thus, the potential survival of their genetic line.

### The role of endogenous (internal) pacemakers

In mammals, the main endogenous pacemaker is the **suprachiasmatic nucleus (SCN)**, a small group of cells in the **hypothalamus** located behind the eyes in the brain. Evidence comes from studies of animals, for example, Morgan (1995) removed the SCN from hamsters and found that their circadian rhythm disappeared. The rhythm could be re-established using transplanted SCN cells. The SCN generates a circadian rhythm but is reset by light from the eyes, even when they are shut. The mechanism underlying this rhythm is an interaction between four proteins: the first two (CLOCK + CYCLE) cause the levels of two other proteins (PERIOD + TIM) to increase, whereas PER + TIM cause CLK + CYC to decrease, so as PER + TIM levels increase, CLK + CYC levels decrease, and as CLK + CYC decreases then so do PER + TIM and then CLK + CYC increases! This produces a rhythm and is the basis of the biological clock (Darlington *et al.*, 1998). Biological rhythms are also endogenously regulated by **hormones**, as in the female menstrual cycle.

There are other regions of the body that produce oscillating rhythms, such as cells in the liver and heart. It has been found that eating times, rather than light, reset some of these other clocks. In fact, research has shown that each cell in the body has an internal ticking clock, affected by a series of clock proteins. There is also evidence that there are separate internal clocks controlling the sleep/waking cycle and temperature. Hawkins and Armstrong-Esther (1978) studied nurses on shift work and found that their circadian rhythms changed, but not their temperature cycles.

Endogenous rhythms are also related to the **pineal gland**. In humans, the pineal gland is regulated by the SCN and leads to changes in levels of **melatonin**. Increases in melatonin are associated with decreases in arousal and sleepiness.

### The role of exogenous (external) zeitgebers

External stimuli may themselves be rhythmic. Day length is the dominant **zeitgeber**. Also important are the seasons, weather, temperature, phases of the moon, tides (in aquatic animals), availability of food, and social stimuli.

Miles *et al.* (1977) studied a blind man who had a 24.9 hour circadian rhythm despite being exposed to a variety of zeitgebers that should have set his 'clock' to 24 hours (such as the radio). He had to use stimulants and sedatives to coordinate his sleep/wake cycle with the rest of the world. This demonstrates that light really is the dominant time-giver. However, light cues can be overcome. Luce and Segal (1966) pointed out that people who live within the Arctic Circle still sleep for about 7 hours, despite the fact that during the summer months the Sun never sets. In this case, social cues are dominant.

#### Evaluation

- It is **adaptive** to have biological rhythms to **govern the biochemical processes** (like the conductor of an orchestra).
- It is also adaptive for these endogenous rhythms to be **reset by external cues** so that animals are in tune with seasonal variations, and daytime/night-time.
- It might be **life threatening** to be solely at the mercy of environmental cues, therefore, endogenous cues are important too.

## Consequences of disrupting biological rhythms

AQA A  U3

Staying up later than normal is an example of phase delay, whereas making yourself go to sleep earlier is phase advance. Most people do find it easier to go to bed late and feel fine the next day, than to get up earlier than normal and feel OK.

It is likely that shift work is a major cause of industrial accidents because these often occur at night. Moore-Ede (1993) estimated the cost of shift worker fatigue in the US to be $77 billion annually. Therefore, this research has important applications.

When external cues (e.g. daylight) change suddenly, we have to re-adjust our internal clock and our ability to cope may be harmed. Generally, **phase delay** (delaying your internal clock) is easier to adapt to than **phase advance** (skipping ahead).

### Shift work

On average it takes about three days to adjust to a 12-hour shift in time (which applies to jet lag as well). Artificial lighting is moderately effective in re-setting the circadian rhythm, but it takes time. Performance is affected because some body clocks are slower to reset and, therefore, the body's rhythms are desynchronised.

### Evaluation

- **Individual differences** – Those people whose circadian rhythms change least may cope best overall (Reinberg *et al.*, 1984).
- **Harmful effects of shift work** – May be caused by other problems, for example, shift workers suffer from sleep deprivation because it is more difficult to sleep during the day (it tends to be noisier than night-time and daylight is disturbing). Shift work also disrupts family and social life, which can lead to depression.
- **Applications** – Dawson and Campbell (1991) exposed participants to a 4-hour pulse of bright light on their first night. This helped their subsequent adjustment as measured by body temperature. Czeisler *et al.* (1982) tested the effects of rotating shifts with the clock (phase delay), rather than against it, so people were doing early shifts and then later shifts. The result was that workers felt better and the management also reported increased productivity and fewer errors.

### Jet lag

Klein *et al.* (1972) found that adjustment was faster for westbound flights (phase delay). Schwartz *et al.* (1995) found that East coast US Baseball teams did better when travelling west than West coast teams travelling east, again showing that phase delay has less effect. On the other hand, on short trips, returning home may be easier than the outward journey because other body clocks haven't changed, meaning that on the return home it may take less time to readjust.

### Evaluation

- **Coping with jet lag.** Redfern (1989) suggested the use of **benzodiazepines** (BZs) to increase melatonin levels and resynchronise the body clock. Webb and Agnew (1971) interviewed regular travellers and found that they used various non-pharmacological approaches, such as a rigid schedule of meals, exposure to light and outdoor activity.
- One of the reasons for jet lag may be that the **temperature clock** is not reset so easily and, therefore, the body is experiencing desynchronised rhythms such as what happens in shift work (see Hawkins and Armstrong-Esther on page 17.)

### Key points from AS

- BZs are also used to decrease anxiety as discussed in *Revise AS Unit 5.2, page 109.*

## Practice essays 1.1

(a) Outline the research studies that have investigated circadian rhythms.

*(9 marks)*

(b) Assess the consequences of disrupting circadian rhythms.   *(16 marks)*

# 1.2 Sleep states

**LEARNING SUMMARY**

*After studying this topic you should be able to describe and evaluate:*

- *the nature of sleep*
- *the functions of sleep, including evolutionary explanations and restoration theory*
- *lifespan changes in sleep.*

## The nature of sleep

AQA A    U3

**Key points from AS**

- The electrical activity of the brain during sleep is recorded using an electroencephalograph (EEG) – see *Revise AS Unit 5.3, page 114* for details.

The phrase 'descending the sleep staircase' is used to describe moving through these sleep stages into decreased consciousness.

Paralysis during REM sleep may serve the useful function of preventing us from acting out our dreams.

Note that dreams also occur in NREM sleep (i.e. stages 1–4).

REM sleep is not found in more primitive animals like reptiles.

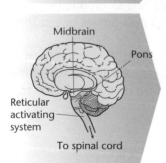
Midbrain
Pons
Reticular activating system
To spinal cord

Sleep is not unconsciousness, it is an altered state of consciousness such that there is a decreased responsiveness to the external environment. It occurs daily (**circadian**) and has distinct stages (**ultradian**).

### Sleep stages

**Stage 1** – Relaxed state, brain waves change from the beta waves characteristic of being awake to **alpha waves**, which are slower (8–12 hertz, i.e. 8–12 waves per second), more regular and have a greater amplitude (i.e. the height of the wave). Alpha waves are seen during meditation. The transition from stage 1 is often accompanied by a **hypnagogic state**, which may include hallucinatory images.

**Stage 2** – Slower, larger brain waves (theta, 4–8 Hz), short bursts of high-frequency **sleep spindles** and **K-complexes** (responses to external stimuli). This is light sleep and the sleeper is easily woken.

**Stage 3** – More slowing down of brain waves and bodily activity (e.g. heart rate). Long, slow delta waves (1–5 Hz) with some sleep spindles.

**Stage 4** – Slow-wave sleep (SWS) with more delta waves than stage 3. It's hard to be woken except by personally significant noises (such as your baby crying). Some physiological activities take place, such as the production of growth hormones. Also, sleep walking and night terrors are experienced in this stage.

**Stage 5 or REM sleep** – Stage 4 sleep is followed by Stage 3, Stage 2 and then Stage 5: **rapid eye movement (REM) sleep**, and active (beta 13–20 Hz) brain waves. Jouvet called this **paradoxical sleep** because of the contradictions: eye movement, heart rate, breathing, etc. are increased, but the body is in a state of near paralysis and it is difficult to wake a person up.

Sleep stages alternate through the night, starting with a rapid descent into deep sleep. Most sleepers complete about five ultradian cycles during a normal night's sleep, with progressively less SWS and more REM activity as morning approaches.

### The physiology of sleep

The brain stem is the area of the brain that controls arousal, alertness and sleep. The brain stem is (in an evolutionary sense) the oldest part of the brain, which controls vital functions. Three neurotransmitters are involved in sleep:

- **Serotonin:** The SCN (see page 17) responds to changes in light and controls production of **melatonin** in the pineal gland which, in turn, leads to production of **serotonin** in the **raphe nuclei** (part of the reticular activating system, **RAS**). Increased levels of serotonin reduce RAS activity and assist the onset of sleep.
- **Noradrenaline** from the **locus coeruleus** (part of the pons) triggers REM sleep.
- **Acetylcholine** is associated with brain activation during wakefulness and REM sleep. It is produced in the **pons** and controls PGO waves that trigger REM.

## The function of sleep

AQA A    U3

Beware of evolutionary arguments that sound as if the animal has made some deliberate choice about behaviour. The 'choice' is made through **natural selection**, a process which has taken place over thousands of years. Behaviours persist only if they are adaptive in some way for the individual. Other behaviours are not selected.

Infant sleep could be explained as an adaptive behaviour to help exhausted parents cope with finding food and other things.

The **EEA** is the environment to which a species is adapted. The selective pressures at that time explain the behaviours that we observe today. In humans it is suggested that our EEA was the period from 1.8 million to 11,000 years ago, when humans lived on the plains in Africa.

There are a few important observations about sleep: (1) All animals sleep, which suggests that sleep serves some important function; (2) Different species have quite different sleep habits, which suggests that sleep patterns are an evolutionary adaptation to environmental conditions; (3) Sleep deprivation studies show that there are some physical effects of both NREM and REM deprivation, but these may be related to motivation as much as some kind of reduced capacity.

### Evolutionary explanations

The evolutionary approach proposes that sleep patterns have evolved because they are adapted to the needs of individual species. Each species has developed different sleep habits and patterns to deal with environmental pressures of predation, energy conservation and foraging requirements.

### 1. Protection from predation (Meddis, 1975)

Meddis suggests that sleep has evolved because it helps keep animals safe from predation. Animals have to gather food (and are then exposed to predators) but at other times they should stay out of harm's way. Siegel (2008) claims that being awake is riskier than being asleep because of the likelihood of injury. Sleep may ensure that animals stay still when they have nothing better to do with their time.

### 2. Energy conservation or Hibernation theory (Webb, 1982)

Sleep is adaptive because it is a means of conserving energy, in the same way that hibernation enhances survival by reducing physiological demands. An animal that is constantly active requires more food, and this is likely to decrease survival. Sleep ensures quietness and energy conservation.

### 3. Foraging requirements

Sleep is also related to the amount of time an animal has to spend finding food. Cows (herbivores) spend a lot of time grazing and, therefore, cannot afford to spend as much time sleeping as, for example, cats (carnivores).

### Evaluation

- It is **difficult to falsify** evolutionary theory.
- There are problems with applying this theory to **human sleep**. In the **environment of evolutionary adaptedness (EEA)**, sleep may have enhanced survival, but this isn't true now.
- Empson (1989) calls ecological theories '**waste of time**' theories because they propose that sleep happens in order to waste time. However, deprivation studies do suggest that lack of sleep has distinct consequences so it can't just be a waste of time. For example, animal studies have shown that sleep deprivation eventually results in death (e.g. Jouvet, 1964). Deprivation of REM sleep results in REM rebound, i.e. an increase in REM sleep on subsequent nights, suggesting that REM sleep may serve a particular function.
- In fact, in Meddis' view, sleep is not just a 'waste of time', but he argues that if an animal has to sleep then it is best to do it **out of harm's way**.
- Support for the evolutionary approach to explaining the function of sleep comes from the fact that it is **present in all animals**, which suggests that it serves some adaptive function.
- Support for the evolutionary approach also comes from the fact that the sleep **patterns of individual species are all different** and can be related to environmental pressures. For example, some dolphins sleep one hemisphere at a time, which may be related to the fact that they will drown unless they surface regularly to breathe.
- Siegel (2008) claims that existing research points to just **one consistent factor** that explains sleep patterns in those species studied – **ecology rather than biology**. He argues that the best strategy for passing on your genes is to be asleep for as long as you can get away with.

## Restoration theory (Oswald, 1980, and Horne, 1988)

Sleep allows various physiological and psychological states to be recovered. For example, infancy is a time of needing high sleep, possibly because of the enormous brain and body growth, and the learning that is taking place.

### 1. Physiological restoration

During slow wave sleep the body makes repairs, waste products are removed, and there is increased production of growth hormone. Stern and Morgane (1974) argue that the normal function of REM sleep is to restore levels of neurotransmitters after a day's activities. Anti-depressants seem to reduce REM activity, possibly because they increase neurotransmitter levels. Cirelli *et al.* (2004) found that genes for proteins, which are involved in adjusting synaptic connections, are switched on during NREM sleep.

### 2. Psychological restoration

Naitoh (1975) reviewed research and found that sleep-deprived individuals described themselves as less friendly, less relaxed, less good-natured, and less cheerful. Berry and Webb (1983) found that when people slept well during the night, their level of anxiety the next day was lower than when they had slept poorly. Also, during REM sleep, memories may be consolidated (according to neurobiological theories of dreams) and emotional experiences may be relived (according to psychological theories of dreams, such as Freud).

### Evaluation

- **Deprivation research** partly supports the restoration view; people do less well when deprived of sleep. In general, memory improves by about 15% after a night's sleep. However, the effects of sleep deprivation may be as much about motivation, i.e. lack of sleep makes people feel less motivated and that's why they don't perform so well.
- However, some studies of sleep deprivation actually suggest there is **little effect from deprivation**. In one famous case study in 1965 Randy Gardner stayed awake for 11 days and simply slept a bit longer when he did go to sleep. However, people deprived of sleep have brief episodes of **microsleep** when some sleep functions may take place. Relaxed wakefulness may also permit some physiological/psychological restoration.
- The idea of **physiological/psychological restoration whilst apparently awake** is supported by recent research with pigeons (Benca *et al.*, 2007). SWS deprivation led to increased slow wave brain activity (as measured by EEG) when awake. Migratory birds can cope for long periods without sleep so they may have evolved a way for parts of the brain to sleep during wakefulness.
- According to restoration theory we would expect to find **increased sleep in relation to increased activity**. Shapiro *et al.* (1981) found that marathon runners did require extra sleep, whereas Horne and Minard (1985) tried to exhaust their participants and found that they went to sleep faster, but not for longer.
- On the other hand, Empson (1989) claims that it is **impossible to go without sleep** and remain fine, and Horne (1988) points out that sleep-deprived participants do show a **rebound effect**, i.e. they sleep longer after deprivation.

### Conclusion

Neither theory accounts for why animals have reduced consciousness when sleeping. It is not necessary for restoration, and from a safety (adaptive) point of view it makes little sense. The fact that all animals sleep means it must perform some restorative function. The fact that each species evolves a particular style suggests an adaptive element as well.

Self-report studies tend to be biased by self-expectations.

It is important to remember, when considering the function of REM sleep, that REM sleep is not the same as dreaming.

Horne (1988) proposed that a distinction should be made between **core sleep** (SWS and REM) and **optional sleep**. During core sleep, brain recovery takes place, whereas bodily processes are recovered during optional sleep and this can also occur during relaxed wakefulness. Therefore, sleep deprivation only requires the recovery of core sleep.

Horne also made the important point that sleep probably serves different purposes in different species. Thus, no single theory of the functions of sleep is likely to be adequate.

The restoration approach provides some views on *why* sleep is important, whereas the adaptive approach also focuses on *when* different species sleep.

## Lifespan changes in sleep

AQA A    U3

**Newborn babies** – Newborn babies tend to sleep for about 2/3 of the day (16 hours in every 24 hours). They display two kinds of sleep: quiet and active sleep, which are immature versions of REM and SWS respectively. At birth there is more active sleep than quiet sleep, but this gradually decreases.

- It has been suggested that babies' sleep is an adaptive mechanism to make their parents' lives easier.
- The greater amount of active/REM sleep may be explained in terms of the considerable learning and brain development that is taking place.

> EEG (electro-encephalograph) is used to measure electrical activity in the brain (see sleep stages on page 19).

**One year** – Over the first year of life there is a gradual maturation of sleep EEG patterns so they begin to look more like the adult form. There is a decrease in active/REM sleep to about 50%, and consolidation of sleep periods: rather than sleeping in short bursts throughout the day, young children sleep through the night and may have one or two naps totalling 10–12 hours of sleep.

**Five years** – Full EEG patterns of sleep are shown by the age of 5, but the frequency is different to adult sleep patterns; there is more REM sleep (about 33% of total sleep time) and less Stage 1 sleep. Most children of this age sleep for about 10 hours, boys sleeping slightly more than girls. There are more instances of **parasomnias** (sleep disorders, such as sleep walking or night terrors – see page 24).

**Adolescence** – At this age, individuals sleep for an average of 9–10 hours per night. The amount of REM sleep is less than in childhood. One distinguishing feature of adolescent REM sleep is that it is sometimes accompanied by orgasm and ejaculation, which is significantly less likely at other ages.

**Middle age** – At this age, parasomnias are very rare but there is an increasing frequency of sleep disorders (such as insomnia and snoring).

**Old age** – Total sleep time remains the same, but the type of sleep differs. REM sleep decreases to about 20% of total sleep time with a corresponding increase of stage 2 sleep (about 60%). The amount of slow wave sleep is also considerably reduced to as little as 5% and may be non-existent for some older people. Older people have more difficulty going to sleep and wake up more frequently (up to six times a night).

Decreases in slow wave sleep are accompanied by decreased production of growth hormones, supporting the view that SWS is important for the production of growth hormone.

### Research studies

Floyd *et al.* (2007) looked at the results of nearly 400 sleep studies and concluded that the percentage of REM decreases with age (decreasing about 0.6% per decade) until the age of about 70, when it starts increasing. This is probably because the total sleep time decreases.

Van Cauter *et al.* (2000) studied data from sleep studies of about 150 men. They found that sleep deteriorates at two points in a person's life – between the ages of 16 and 25 and again between the ages of 35 and 50. Men over 45 have virtually no SWS, which affects hormone production.

## Practice essay 1.2

Describe and evaluate **two** theories of the function of sleep.     *(25 marks)*

# 1.3 Disorders of sleep

*After studying this topic you should be able to describe and evaluate:*

- *explanations for insomnia, including primary and secondary insomnia and factors influencing insomnia, for example, apnoea and personality*
- *explanations for other sleep disorders, including sleep walking and narcolepsy.*

LEARNING SUMMARY

## Insomnia

AOA A — U3

A distinction is made between **primary** and **secondary insomnia**; the former has no known medical, psychiatric or environmental cause, whereas the latter has. Insomnia is diagnosed when:

- a person has been experiencing sleep difficulties for more than one month
- the resulting daytime fatigue causes severe distress or impairs work, social or personal functioning.

> **Insomnia** is characterised by having prolonged difficulties falling asleep and/or remaining asleep, despite the opportunity to do so.

### 1. Causes of primary insomnia

In cases where insomnia has been a lifelong problem, the cause may be due to a brain abnormality involving the sleep circuits (a physical, but not medical condition).

In other cases the cause may be stress. The insomnia should disappear when the source of the stress is dealt with – though sometimes anxiety resulting from insomnia becomes a cause of further insomnia. The person who has difficulty sleeping starts to worry that they can't sleep and this worry in itself becomes the cause of persistent insomnia.

> Some estimates suggest that as many as 50% of all older adults report insomnia problems.

### 2. Causes of secondary insomnia

Causes of secondary insomnia include certain illnesses, such as some heart diseases; mental disorders, such as depression or general anxiety disorder; substances, such as medicine, caffeine, tobacco or psychoactive drugs; and medical conditions, such as hyperthyroidism and Wilson's syndrome. Specific sleep disorders may also be the cause of the problem:

- **Circadian rhythm disorders** are caused when circadian rhythms are disrupted, for example, because of shift work or jet lag.
- **Apnoea** is a disorder characterised by pauses in breathing, which may last a few seconds or minutes and may occur 5–30 times an hour. Normal breathing may restart with a loud snort. The most common cause of apnoea is blockage of the airways (airway collapses), which may occur in people who are overweight. This is called **obstructive sleep apnoea**. **Central sleep apnoea** is less common and occurs because of faulty signals from the brain to the breathing centres.

> The term 'secondary' is used because the insomnia is a side effect (i.e. secondary) to some other problem. Primary insomnia is its own disorder.

**Personality** may be a factor in insomnia, for example:

- Kales *et al.* (1976) gave 124 insomniacs a personality test and found that 85% showed signs of abnormal personality. Kales *et al.* suggest that the emotional arousal associated with 'abnormal personality' is a factor in insomnia.
- Bardwell *et al.* (1999) found that insomniacs scored more highly on anger measures than non-insomniacs.
- Grano *et al.* (2006) found a link between impulsivity and insomnia in men. In women impulsivity was just associated with difficulties getting to sleep.

> **'Sleep hygiene'** is often mentioned as a cause of insomnia, referring to behaviours that affect your sleep for good or bad, e.g. smoking, drinking, napping and exercise. The implication is that people need to improve the hygiene or healthiness of their sleep habits.

## Other sleep disorders

AQA A    U3

Sleep disorders include snoring and restless legs syndrome (an irresistible urge to move your legs because they tingle or burn).

> **Sleep disorders** are medical disorders that interfere with normal physical, mental and emotional functioning.

### 1. Sleep walking (SW) or somnambulism

'Sleep walking' refers to a range of activities that are normally associated with wakefulness (e.g. eating, getting dressed or walking about) and which take place during sleep without the conscious knowledge of the subject. It is most common in childhood, affecting about 20% of children and only about 1–3% of adults (Hublin *et al.*, 1997). Adolescents and adults with SW tend to have an increased prevalence of anxiety and personality disorders.

SW occurs during NREM sleep. The individual usually has their eyes open and may act as if awake, but any speech is nonsensical. In the morning they have no memory of the episode. In severe cases (one or more episodes a night) it may have a considerable effect on a person's life and there may be a risk of injury.

> Some psychologists suggest that NREM parasomnias such as SW, sleep terrors and confusional awakenings are on a continuum and share a genetic cause.

Research has found that SW has a significant genetic component. Evidence comes from familial studies. For example, Broughton (1968) found that the prevalence of SW in first-degree relatives of an affected subject is at least 10 times greater than that in the general population. Twin studies have also been used; Lecendreux *et al.* (2003) report about 50% concordance in identical (MZ) twins compared to 10–15% in non-identical (DZ) twins. They have also identified a gene that may be critical in SW as well as night terrors – the **DQB1*05 gene**.

### 2. Night terrors

Night terrors are a childhood problem. Like SW they occur during NREM sleep and are not related to dreams. The child appears very frightened but, unlike in a nightmare, the child can't be woken and has no memory of the event in the morning.

### 3. Narcolepsy

> Narcolepsy means 'seized with sleepiness'.

Narcolepsy is a disorder of the system that regulates the sleep/wake cycle. It results in sudden and uncontrollable attacks of sleep at irregular and unexpected times, which may last minutes or hours. The most obvious symptom is excessive daytime sleepiness (EDS). The person may appear drunk whereas they are actually just very sleepy, and, after a microsleep, the person may wake without realising they had been asleep.

> The prevalence of narcolepsy is not accurately known. It is significantly under-reported because its severity varies from the barely noticeable to the profoundly disrupting. However, the reported prevalence of narcolepsy in the population ranges from 5 in 10,000 (0.05%) in Europe and North America, to 16 in 10,000 in Japan (www.narcolepsy.org.uk).

The most obvious symptom of narcolepsy is a sudden loss of muscular control (**cataplexy**) triggered by amusement, anger or excitement. Other symptoms that occur when falling asleep or awakening are sleep paralysis (on falling asleep or awakening) and hallucinations (**hypnagogic** when falling asleep and **hypnopompic** when waking up). There may also be moments of trance-like behaviour and interruption of night-time sleep by frequent waking periods.

Narcolepsy usually begins in adolescence and may have a biological basis. It may be the result of a genetic abnormality (related to the HLA complex on chromosome 6), the result of an auto-immune disease or caused by a shortage of the neurotransmitter **hypocretin**.

## Practice essay 1.3

Discuss explanations for **two or more** sleep disorders, including sleep walking and narcolepsy.

*(25 marks)*

# Chapter 2

# Perception

## 2.1 Theories of perceptual organisation

*After studying this topic you should be able to describe and evaluate:*

**AS**

- This unit is covered in *Revise AS Unit 2.1, pages 45–46.*

- Gregory's top-down/indirect theory of perception
- Gibson's bottom-up/direct theory of perception.

**LEARNING SUMMARY**

## 2.2 Development of perception

*After studying this topic you should be able to describe and evaluate:*

- the development of perceptual abilities, for example, depth/distance and visual constancies
- infant and cross-cultural studies of the development of perceptual abilities
- the nature–nurture debate in relation to explanations of perceptual development.

**LEARNING SUMMARY**

### The development of perceptual abilities

AQA A ▶ U3

Depth (distance) perception refers to our ability to perceive that some objects are further away than others.

**The visual cliff**

#### Key points from AS

- Overlap, texture gradient and linear perspective are all cues used in 2D pictures to represent 3D. These cues are discussed in *Revise AS Unit 2.4, page 48.*

### The development of depth/distance perception

#### 1. Evidence that depth/distance perception is innate

Gibson and Walk (1960) used the **visual cliff** (see drawing on left) to test depth perception in infants aged 6–14 months. Most of the infants (92%) refused to crawl over the 'cliff' even if they had a patch across one eye, which showed that (a) they perceived depth, and (b) they were using monocular cues only to perceive depth (since they could see depth with a patch over one eye. Binocular cues depend on the use of both eyes.). However, this may be due to learned rather than innate factors as the infants tested had plenty of sensorimotor experience. However, even younger infants were tested by Campos *et al.* (1978) (and their heart rates were slower then when on the shallow side).

Bower *et al.* (1970) observed even younger infants (6–20 days old) and tested their response to an approaching object. If the infant had no depth perception their response to a large disc stopping further away should be the same as their response to a smaller, closer one because they both create the same retinal image. In fact the infants were so upset by the smaller, closer one that the experiment was abandoned early, without testing all the infants.

#### 2. Evidence that depth/distance perception is learned

Yonas *et al.* (1986) showed that infants' ability to respond to depth cues in pictures emerges rather late. The ability to respond to **overlap** emerged at about 6 months and responsiveness to **texture gradient** and **linear perspective** was only apparent by about 7 months.

Bremner (1994) concluded that the ability to interpret dynamic cues (e.g. as in the study by Bower *et al.*) appears earlier than the ability to use static pictorial depth cues.

Visual constancy enables us to see things as being the same, despite a changing retinal image. For example, a book 'looks' rectangular from any angle despite the fact that the retinal image is usually not rectangular (an example of shape constancy) and a person who is seen in the distance appears the size of a normal person, despite the fact that the retinal image is much smaller (an example of size constancy) – as shown in the picture below.

## The development of visual constancies

### 1. Shape constancy

Bower (1966) conditioned 6–8 week-old infants to turn their heads towards a certain sized or shaped cube by rewarding them with a game of 'peek-a-boo' every time a correct response was made. When he changed the distance or angle (retinal image changes), the infants continued to produce the conditioned response, therefore demonstrating size and shape constancy. If the infant had a patch over one eye, their performance remained the same, but not if they were shown slides. This indicates that they were using **motion parallax** to determine depth.

### 2. Size constancy

Granrud (2006) tested whether 4-month-old infants respond primarily to the physical size of an object or its retinal image size. This was tested by first of all habituating the infants to either a 6cm-diameter disk at a distance of 18cm or a 10cm disk at 50cm. ('Habituation' means they got used to it so it was no longer a novel stimulus and, therefore, would not attract their interest – infants are drawn to look first at something novel). The infants were then tested with 6cm and 10cm disks, presented side by side at a distance of 30cm. For each infant, one test object had a novel physical size but a familiar retinal image size, and the other had a familiar physical size but a novel retinal image size. The infants showed a preference for the object that had a novel physical size, suggesting that they had not developed shape constancy.

### Evaluation

- Testing somewhat **immobile and unresponsive participants** is difficult and prone to subjective interpretation and experimenter bias. For example, many of the studies assess infant perception in terms of which image the infant attends to most – assuming that this means the image is more novel to them.
- Research tends to be **laboratory based** and behaviour is possibly atypical.
- Sensorimotor **learning takes place even before birth**, in the womb, so we can't be sure that abilities present at birth are innate or learned.

Example of stimulus materials used by Fantz.

There are important ethical considerations when using infants as participants, as infants are especially affected by experience and perhaps should not be exposed to any experimental manipulation. Equally, their parents should never be deceived, though briefing parents might bias the research.

## Infant studies of the development of perceptual abilities

The studies described above suggest that perception is due to both nature and nurture. Another area of study has concerned infant face perception. In a classic study Fantz (1961) found that neonates (up to 6-months old) could discriminate certain visual forms (see example 'faces' on the left). The infants preferred more complex patterns to just black and white, and preferred a real face rather than a scrambled set of the same features. This 'facial preference' finding has been replicated in a number of studies, such as Goren *et al.* (1975) who used slightly different heads.

An interest in complexity may be important in stimulating the visual development of the brain. However, the preference for a face cannot be solely due to pattern complexity because the scrambled face was less preferred. It may be due to a liking for things that are symmetrical or it may have adaptive importance: a neonate who can recognise and respond to its own species will better elicit attachment and caring.

### Evaluation

- **Separating maturation from learning** is difficult. Facial preference may develop very early because infants are positively reinforced when they respond to faces.
- **Studies of face perception in adults** provide mixed support for innate perception of faces (see page 29).

## Cross-cultural studies of the development of perceptual abilities

A cross-cultural study is one that makes comparisons across two or more cultures. However, in much of the research this comparison is implicit, i.e. no actual comparison is made between the cultural groups studied and Western norms. In an exam question it may be helpful to make the comparative nature of this work explicit.

### Depth/distance perception

Turnbull (1961) described how a pygmy guide thought that buffalo grazing in the distance were insects. Having lived in a forest all his life, the guide had acquired no knowledge of depth cues, nor of size constancy.

Hudson (1960) tested over 500 children and adults, black and white, from southern Africa. He showed them pictures of a hunting scene or a flying bird and found that the 'school-going' participants interpreted the depth cues correctly whereas the 'non-school-going' participants did not, suggesting that the ability to decode depth cues is learned. Inability to interpret depth cues may be because the pictures are presented on paper. Deregowski et al. (1972) found that the Me'en people in Ethiopia did not respond to drawings of animals on paper, but they did if they were on cloth.

### Interpretation of pictures

An example of a **split style** drawing.

Drawing is not a direct representation of the real world. We learn cultural forms of representation. Aborigines (natives of Australia) use a semi-circle to represent people; a family group is a group of semi-circles around a circle (people sitting round a campfire) (Cox, 1992). The **split-style** drawing technique is used by some Africans (Deregowski, 1972) where objects are represented from above in a flattened form.

### Visual illusions

The **Müller–Lyer illusion**.

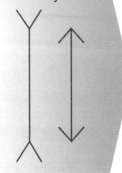

Segall et al. (1963) found that the **Müller–Lyer illusion** would only be perceived by those with experience of a **carpentered environment** (an environment where there are straight lines and rectangles, unlike the round shapes of African dwellings). Rural Zulus did not experience the Müller–Lyer illusion. On the other hand, Allport and Pettigrew (1957) found that Rural Zulus showed the **horizon-ratio effect** to a greater extent than Europeans, presumably because of greater familiarity with large open spaces.

However, Gregor and McPherson (1965) found no differences between Australian Aborigines living in carpentered or open-air environments in terms of Müller–Lyer or the horizon-ratio effect. Cross-cultural differences in perceiving visual illusions may be related more to training and education than environment.

The **horizon-ratio effect** is when two people have the same ratio to the horizon, they appear the same size, but when they have a different ratio to the horizon they appear to be different sizes. This is illustrated in the size constancy drawing on the previous page.

### Evaluation

- Cross-cultural studies are fraught with **difficulties**, such as biased interpretations by observers and limited samples.
- This research has focused on **limited aspects of perception** (e.g. visual illusions) and may tell us little about cultural differences in everyday perception.
- There is a tendency, in psychology, to **confuse 'culture' with 'country'**. A cultural group shares a set of beliefs, values and practices. Within any one country there are many cultural groups. Many so-called cross-cultural studies in psychology actually involve comparisons between different national groups.
- Studies of human neonates (reviewed on the previous pages) suggest that many perceptual abilities are innate. If this view is correct, and abilities such as depth perception are inborn, then we **should find that all people develop these abilities** regardless of their different personal experiences.

## The nature–nurture debate in relation to perceptual development

AQA A U3

Is perception an innate process (nature) or do we have to learn how to interpret sensory data (nurture)?

'Nature' refers to behaviours that are inherited or innate, but this is not the same as behaviours that are present at birth – some biologically-determined behaviours appear later in life, such as changes during adolescence. Additionally, at birth, a young animal has already been alive for some time and environmental factors may have altered behaviour.

'Nurture' refers to behaviours that are the result of experience or environmental influence.

Sensory deprivation has major emotional effects, which could explain the physical effects of such deprivation.

There are some applications of this debate. For example, Banks *et al.* (1975) found that if children with squints are operated on before the age of three, they subsequently develop normal vision. But, if the operation is left any later, the deprivation appears to result in some degree of abnormal binocular vision.

The nature–nurture debate is discussed further on page 183.

Gibson's direct theory proposes that perception is largely innate. James Gibson and his wife Eleanor (Gibson and Gibson, 1955) outlined **differentiation theory** – the view that perceptual development involves learning to differentiate between the distinctive features of different classes of objects. Gregory's indirect theory suggests that perceptual abilities are influenced by learned expectations.

### Evidence for nature

Studies of infant perception show that some abilities are innate (see pages 25 and 26), such as aspects of depth perception and also face perception. Some cross-cultural studies support the idea of innate perceptual characteristics (see previous page). In another cross-cultural study, Rosch (1978) found that members of the Dani (from New Guinea) were quicker at learning the colour name for fire-engine red than other reds, which suggests that this is an innately perceived colour.

Hubel and Wiesel (1962) demonstrated the biological basis of pattern recognition, which is evidence of innate perceptual abilities. They placed microelectrodes in different parts of a cat's visual cortex and found **simple cells** that only fired when the cat was shown a line of unique orientation in a particular part of the visual field. They also found cells sensitive to other features (e.g. a stationary or moving dot, a moving line), and **complex cells**, which responded to several simple cells, and **hypercomplex cells**, which responded to simple patterns or shapes (such as angles). These cells are organised into **functional columns**, which may predispose the brain to be able to make certain comparisons, such as those used in depth perception.

### Evidence for nurture affecting nature

Visual deprivation leads to a loss of innate biological abilities. For example, Wiesel (1982) sewed one eye of a kitten shut. If this is done early enough and for long enough, the eye becomes blind, suggesting that without experience the innate system is not maintained.

Blakemore and Cooper (1970) placed kittens in a drum that had only vertical, or only horizontal, lines. The kittens later had difficulties with depth perception and were virtually blind, except for the contours perpendicular to those they experienced. Examination of their visual cortex showed that there were no cells remaining that responded electrically to the orientation not experienced by the cat. This supports the view that physical degeneration results from a lack of experience during a critical period.

Gregory and Wallace (1963) studied SB, who was blind from birth due to cataracts. In later life the cataracts were removed but SB was never fully able to use his newly acquired sight even though he was not blind. Von Senden (1932) found the same in other cataract patients.

### Conclusions

The conclusion from studies of deprivation is that experience modifies innate abilities. Innate systems are present from birth but require experiential input to be maintained and to adapt to changed circumstances (nature and nurture). The process of differentiation or bottom-up processing (Gibson) may explain innate systems of perception, whereas enrichment or top-down processing (Gregory) is related to those perceptual abilities that are learned. In any one situation the relative contributions of each will vary according to particular circumstances (such as lighting conditions).

## Practice essay 2.2

'Is perception due to nature or nurture, or both?' Discuss the nature–nurture debate in relation to perceptual development. *(25 marks)*

# 2.3 Face recognition and visual agnosias

*After studying this topic you should be able to describe and evaluate:*

- *Bruce and Young's theory of face recognition, including case studies and explanations of prosopagnosia.*

## Bruce and Young's theory of face recognition

AQA A    U3

**Face recognition** is the process by which the brain and mind understand and interpret the human face.

Bruce and Young (1986) developed a model for face recognition, which suggests that there are two different mechanisms for familiar and unfamiliar face recognition.

- The recognition of **familiar faces** involves structural encoding first, followed by face recognition units, person identity nodes, and name generation.
- The **recognition of unfamiliar faces** probably involves recognition of configuration (Yin, 1969). In the Bruce and Young model, recognition of unfamiliar faces involves structural encoding first and then expression analysis, facial speech analysis, and directed visual processing.

The study of face recognition has important applications, for example, in the production of machines that will recognise faces for security, and in assisting police to produce accurate eyewitness records of faces (i.e. identikit pictures).

Face recognition has important survival value because we need to distinguish between friends and foes.

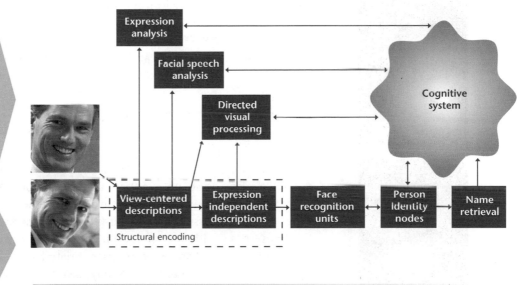

**Prosopagnosia** is a special case of **visual agnosia**, where patients can describe objects in their visual field (including details of colour, texture and shape), but are unable to recognise the objects.

### Research evidence

#### 1. Prosopagnosia

Patients with prosopagnosia cannot recognise faces, but their ability to recognise other objects may be relatively intact. Prosopagnosia is not a unitary disorder – different people show different types and levels of impairment. This supports Bruce and Young's notion that face perception has a number of stages, each of which can be separately damaged.

#### 2. Case studies

Brunsdon *et al.* (2006) studied AL, an 8-year-old with prosopagnosia. The child could not recognise familiar or unfamiliar faces, therefore, the deficit was at the level of structural encoding. However, he could recognise individual features and this ability was used to train him to name familiar faces.

de Haan *et al.* (1991) studied a patient with amnesia, ME, who was good at matching famous faces and names but didn't know any information about them. This supports the separate units of the Bruce and Young model.

Malone *et al.* (1982) studied a patient who was able to recognise photographs of famous statesmen but coped poorly with matching unfamiliar faces, and another patient who could do the opposite.

Young *et al.* (1985) studied normal people and not one of the participants reported being able to put a name to a face without also knowing something else about the person. They could often remember a lot about the person, just not their name.

### 3. Experimental studies

Bauer (1984) showed familiar and unfamiliar faces to patients with prosopagnosia. Despite being unable to identify which faces were familiar, the patients showed a positive **GSR** to the familiar faces, showing an unconscious response.

Thompson (1980) demonstrated the **Thatcher effect** (see left). People find it difficult to detect local feature changes in an upside-down face, but can detect them in an upright face. When a face is upside-down, the configural processing cannot take place, and so minor differences are more difficult to detect. This supports the notion of a unique face processor.

### 4. Neurophysiological evidence

Various studies (e.g. Sergent et al., 1992) have used scanning techniques to identify the areas of the brain that are active when identifying faces. The **fusiform face area (FFA)** is active when processing faces and not as active when identifying other objects, especially in the right hemisphere.

### 5. Infant face perception

Evidence that infants have an innate preference for faces supports the view that face perception is hardwired in a special region of the brain (see pages 25–26).

### Evaluation

- Burton and Bruce (1993) developed a **more precise version** of the Bruce and Young model. The new model has been used in computer simulations. It has no separate store for names, and the familiar face recognition is at the person-identity node rather than at the face recognition unit.
- Some psychologists believe that face recognition is **no different to the recognition of any other complex stimuli.** Faces are simply complex perceptual objects that we become very practised at identifying. Support for this comes from Gauthier *et al.* (2000) who have shown that the FFA is also active when participants are asked to discriminate between different types of birds and cars. This suggests that the FFA may have a general role in the recognition of similar visual objects, rather than just specialising in faces. It is clear that the FFA is important in face recognition but may not be exclusive to it.

**GSR** stands for galvanic skin response, a method of measuring emotional arousal by testing the electrical conductivity of the skin. When a person is emotionally aroused the ANS is activated and sweatiness increases the electrical conductivity of the skin.

The **Thatcher effect** – look at this picture upside-down and you will see that the features are actually in the wrong direction – this is only detected when the face is viewed the right way up.

## Practice essay 2.3

Discuss Bruce and Young's theory of face recognition.     *(25 marks)*

# 3.1 The formation, maintenance and breakdown of romantic relationships

*After studying this topic you should be able to describe and evaluate:*

- *theories of the formation, maintenance and breakdown of romantic relationships, for example, reward/need satisfaction and social exchange theory.*

**LEARNING SUMMARY**

## Formation of romantic relationships

AQA A ▶ U3

This is a **learning theory** account of relationship formation, as it is based on the concept of conditioning (see page 72).

### 1. Reinforcement-affect model (Clore and Byrne, 1974)

- 'Reinforcement' leads us to like (and, therefore, wish to form relationships with) people who reward us (operant **conditioning**). Such reinforcement (rewards) might be someone else acting positively towards us (e.g. smiling or being friendly) or a situation involving someone else rewarding us.
- 'Affect' refers to the positive feelings that are associated with a good experience. This is an example of **classical conditioning** – learning by association. If a particular event or situation (unconditioned stimulus) creates positive feelings (unconditioned response), then a person (neutral stimulus) who is associated with the event becomes a conditioned stimulus producing the conditioned response (positive feelings). Increased 'affect' towards that person leads to relationship formation.

The reinforcement-affect model can be used to explain why politicians like to be seen at award ceremonies. You can also use it to win the affections of your heart throb – appear at events that make them happy (e.g. a football match).

### Research evidence

Veitch and Griffitt (1976) placed participants in a waiting room where they listened to either good or bad news with a stranger present. When they were asked to rate the stranger, the degree of liking was related to the kind of news they had been listening to.

Cunningham (1988) found that men who watched a happy rather than a sad movie later interacted with a female confederate more positively.

Is a simple explanation a bad thing? **Occam's razor** is the principle that one should avoid complex explanations when a simpler one exists. On the other hand, a simple explanation may oversimplify complex behaviours.

### Evaluation

- This is a relatively **simple** model (both an advantage and a disadvantage).
- The research support is rather **contrived and artificial** (Duck, 1992).
- The model does not account for **relationships** where rewards are irrelevant.

### 2. Reward/need satisfaction (Argyle, 1994)

People form relationships because interpersonal relationships satisfy parts of the seven basic human motives or needs: biological (e.g. eating together); dependency (e.g. being comforted); affiliation (seeking company); dominance (establishing social order); sex (reproduction); aggression (interpersonal hostility); and self-esteem (being valued by others).

Evolutionary explanations of human reproductive behaviour (see page 34) can also be used to explain why people form romantic relationships.

### Evaluation

- This explanation is more appropriate to **individualist societies** because the 'needs' are focused on the individual and not the group.

## Maintenance of romantic relationships

AQA A ▶ U3

### 1. Social exchange theory (Thibaut and Kelley, 1959)

'Social exchange' refers to the exchange of rewards between two people, such as being cared for, companionship and sex. Relationships also incur costs, such as money spent or opportunities missed. According to this theory, people wish to maximise their rewards and minimise costs so they receive a profit from a relationship (i.e. satisfaction).

In order to judge the rewards in a relationship people make two comparisons: (1) between actual and expected rewards (called the comparison level, CL), and (2) the comparison level for alternative relationships (referred to as CLalt).

Thibaut and Kelley suggest relationships develop through key stages:
- **Sampling** – Explore rewards and costs directly or indirectly (observing others).
- **Bargaining** – Prospective partners establish sources of profit and loss.
- **Commitment** – Routines are established.
- **Institutionalisation** – Norms and mutual expectations are established.

**Research evidence**

Rusbult (1983) found that 'costs' are only calculated after the honeymoon phase.

Simpson et al. (1990) found that participants who were dating at the time of the study rated members of the opposite sex as less attractive, demonstrating that they closed themselves off from attractive alternatives.

**Evaluation**
- Social exchange theory can be applied to all sorts of relationships, e.g. families, friends.
- **Mechanistic** approach. In reality, relationships are more complex; it is difficult to define rewards or costs and to quantify satisfaction or 'profit'. It also focuses too much on the individual perspective rather than social aspects of a relationship, such as how partners talk with each other and interpret shared events (Duck and Sants, 1983).

### 2. Active maintenance strategies

Relationships are maintained through strategies that couples develop. Rusbult et al. (1986) suggested there are four strategies which can be combined: active or passive, constructive or destructive. For example, loyalty is a passive, constructive strategy where a partner waits for the situation to improve. Dindia and Baxter (1987) found 49 different strategies in their study below.

**Research evidence**

Dindia and Baxter (1987) examined the strategies used by 50 married couples. The strategies ranged from the fairly trivial (e.g. talking about each other's experiences during the day) through to more meaningful strategies (e.g. reminiscing about shared experiences). There were more strategies for maintaining relationships than for repairing them.

Yum (2000) found that partners prefer constructive to destructive strategies.

Dainton (2000) found that those couples who used maintenance strategies reported greater levels of satisfaction in their relationship, supporting the role of strategies in the maintenance of relationships.

**Evaluation**
- This is a **more recent approach** – looking at the interaction between partners rather than the individual's perspective.
- It is a more **qualitative approach** than social exchange theory.

---

Social exchange theory is sometimes called an **economic theory** because it explains relationships in terms of maximising rewards, minimising costs and gaining profits. Such 'economic theories' are more relevant to **individualist** societies rather than **collectivist** ones where people are more concerned with the needs of others.

Social exchange theory can also be used to explain the formation and breakdown of relationships. But, if you do this when answering an essay question, make sure you shape your description to explain formation or breakdown rather than maintenance.

**Equity theory** is a version of social exchange theory, which suggests that balance is achieved more through perceived fairness (equity) rather than exchange. Both over- and under-benefits are not fair.

The maintenance of relationships can be explained more simply in terms of daily routines – such routines provide comfortable predictability and people prefer not to disrupt this.

Much of the early research has been based on studies with college students as participants and, therefore, may explain a certain kind of romantic relationship – one between young people. Long-term, middle-aged relationships may be governed by other factors, such as daily routines.

## Breakdown of romantic relationships

AQA A  U3

Social exchange theory would predict that dissolution is the result of an imbalance in rewards and costs, and/or the existence of a better alternative.

Lee (1984) proposed an alternative stage theory of relational breakdown based on a study of over 100 pre-marital romantic break-ups:

- **Dissatisfaction:** problems recognised.
- **Exposure:** problems identified and brought out into the open.
- **Negotiation:** discussion about the issues raised during the exposure stage.
- **Resolution attempts:** both partners try to find ways of solving the problems.
- **Termination:** if the resolution attempts are unsuccessful.

Felmlee's (1995) 'fatal attraction theory' suggests that the same characteristic(s) that initially caused attraction, ultimately lead to dissolution. Such characteristics might initially be exciting or different but later appear predictable or strange.

### 1. Stage model of relational dissolution (Duck, 1984)

Duck described breakdown in terms of five stages:

- **Breakdown** – Dissatisfaction leads to breaking point. Repair strategy: correct own behavioural faults.
- **Intra-psychic phase** – Thinking about the relationship, at first in private, then with confidants, and finally with partner. Repair strategy: re-establish liking for partner.
- **Dyadic phase** – Deciding whether to break up or repair. Repair strategy: express conflict, clear the air and reformulate rules for a future relationship.
- **Social phase** – Including others in the debate, enlisting support for your 'side'. Repair strategy: outsiders may help patch things up or encourage separation.
- **Grave dressing phase** – Post-mortem for public and private re-adjustment. Repair strategy: decide on a mutually acceptable version of events, and/or attempt to salvage friendship out of the break up.

#### Evaluation

- A **strength** of this model is the inclusion of repair strategies, useful for **marriage guidance** to identify the stage of dissolution reached and strategies appropriate to that stage.
- Duck focused on the processes that take place **after breakdown** and focused less on the early events. This is in contrast with **Lee's model** (see left), which is mainly concerned with events leading up to breakdown.
- Stage models do not explain why breakdown occurs; they are **descriptive**.

### 2. Risk factors (Duck, 1982)

Duck suggested that breakdown can be explained in terms of 'risk factors':

1. **Predisposing personal factors** (dispositional) – distasteful personal habits, change in interests, poor role models (e.g. divorced parents), dissonance (e.g. partners from different religious backgrounds) or poor social skills.
2. **Precipitating factors** (situational) – deception, boredom, relocation, conflict or a better alternative.

#### Research evidence

Rohlfing (1998) found that reduced proximity (a possible predisposing factor) may not lead to breakdown; 70% of students questioned had experienced at least one long-distance romantic relationship (LDRR). Holt and Stone (1988) found that there was little decrease in relationship satisfaction as long as lovers are able to reunite regularly.

#### Evaluation

- These factors offer an **explanation** for dissolution.
- **Many relationships are stable** despite the presence of such factors.
- Some of the factors are **intervening variables**, for example, lower educational levels may be associated with divorce, but are not the cause.

## Practice essays 3.1

(a) Outline **two or more** theories of the maintenance of romantic relationships. *(9 marks)*

(b) Evaluate **one** of the theories you outlined in part (a). *(16 marks)*

# 3.2 Human reproductive behaviour

**LEARNING SUMMARY**

After studying this topic you should be able to describe and evaluate:

- the relationship between sexual selection and human reproductive behaviour
- evolutionary explanations of parental investment, for example, sex differences, parent–offspring conflict.

## The relationship between sexual selection and human reproductive behaviour

Darwin proposed sexual selection as a variation of natural selection. **Sexual selection** is the selection for traits that are solely concerned with increasing mating success. For example, if a peacock's tail increases his chances of being selected as a mate then the trait becomes perpetuated – it has been sexually selected.

Because of **anisogamy** (the fact that each sex has different gametes – eggs and sperm), males (sperm) compete and females (eggs) select.

Any behaviour that increases an individual's reproductive success will be selected and appear in future generations. 'Reproductive success' includes the number of offspring produced, their healthiness, survival and ultimately their reproductive success. In general, each sex behaves differently because of different selective pressures arising from the differences between eggs and sperm (**anisogamy**).

- **Sperm** – males produce millions of sperm and can potentially fertilise hundreds of females at a minimal cost to future reproductive potential. Natural selection will favour strategies that maximise the number of fertilisations, leading to **intrasexual** competition and polygamy.
- **Eggs** – female investment is greater because the egg contains nutrients, which have a physiological cost. Therefore, eggs are produced in limited numbers and females need to be more careful to ensure that each reproduction is successful (e.g. seek good mate, high parental investment and monogamy). Natural selection will favour discrimination in females, which leads to **intersexual** selection strategies.

### Research evidence

The consequence of this is that men should seek partners who have good reproductive potential, whereas females do best with partners who have good genetic potential and are able to provide resources to aid the survival of the young.

Dunbar (1995) found that the male–female patterns shown in personal ads were not shown in gay and lesbian personal ads – presumably because mate choice in these individuals is not driven by reproductive criteria.

Various studies have provided such support. For example, Buss (1989) found that, in 37 cultures, men preferred partners who were young and physically attractive (this indicates good reproductive potential), whereas women valued males with high resource potential, i.e. good financial prospects, ambition, and industriousness. Dunbar and Waynforth (1995) analysed personal ads and found that 42% of males sought a youthful mate, compared to 25% of females. 44% of males sought a physically attractive partner, compared to 22% of women.

However a recent study using speed dating events found no gender differences in the importance placed on physical attractiveness and earning potential (Todd et al., 2007).

### 1. Male (intrasexual) strategies

Males must compete to be selected by females.

**Courtship routines** – The classic example from the animal world is the peacock, who parades in front of a peahen to show off his fabulous tail as an advertisement of his genetic quality. In humans, men buy chocolates and flowers. Miller (1998) suggested that stories, jokes, dance, music and art may all be forms of courtship displays to aid sexual conquests.

**Male size and adornment** – Males evolve weaponry (e.g. antlers) and are bigger for fighting (competition between males for females). Penis size is related to male competition: in species where competition is greatest, penis sizes are larger. In some human groups, men wear penis sheaths to advertise their quality.

Williams (1966) suggested that courtship is a contest between male salesmanship and female sales resistance.

**Sperm competition** – Males also compete at the level of sperm. When females mate with more than one male, a successful male strategy is to produce sperm that will be more successful. As a result, males evolve larger testicles, ejaculate more and produce faster-swimming sperm.

**Sneak copulation** – A non-dominant male discretely copulates when the first male is not looking. Sasse *et al.* (1994) found, in a study in Switzerland, that less than 1.4% of the children's presumed father was not their biological one. Unpartnered males gain from sneak copulation. Women may gain from having varied partners because it increases the quality of their offspring.

**Rape** – Thornhill and Thornhill (1983) controversially argued that men who are unable to mate are driven to select an alternative strategy. Thornhill (1980) cites the behaviour of the male *Panorpa scorpion fly* who inseminates unwilling females by securing the female's wings in an abdominal clamp, showing that rape occurs 'naturally' and, therefore, this suggests that it is an adaptive strategy.

## 2. Female (intersexual) strategies

Females have more to lose because their investment in reproduction is higher. Therefore, females who are 'choosier' have evolved through selective pressure, in particular basing their choice on 'good genes' in order to produce offspring that are fitter (i.e. have a greater chance of survival and reproduction). This choosiness has certain predictable outcomes, as seen, for example, in the runaway process and handicapping theory.

This explanation is also called the 'sexy sons' or 'good taste' hypothesis.

As long as the advantages outweigh the disadvantages, the 'bizarre' characteristic will be perpetuated.

**Runaway process** – Fisher (1930) suggested that females select males with attractive characteristics because they will then produce sons who have inherited those characteristics, increasing the sons' reproductive success (and, therefore, enhancing the continuance of the mother's genes). Initially, the characteristics would have some survival value (e.g. long tail) but, because females actively select mates with this feature, it becomes exaggerated. The classic example of such runaway or bizarre characteristics is the peacock's tail. Miller (1992) argues that the overlarge human brain is an example of the runaway process – our intellectual abilities evolved because of the demands of courtship.

### Evaluation

- Support comes from, for example, Petrie *et al.* (1987) who found that peacocks with the best tails (most eyespots) were most likely to be selected and had the biggest offspring that also survived longest.

Handicapping theory is also called the 'good genes' or 'good sense' hypothesis. 'Good genes' are for survival, as opposed to Fisher's hypothesis where the 'good genes' would be for producing attractive male offspring.

**Handicapping theory** – Zahavi (1975) proposed that females prefer mates with handicaps (such as an over-long tail) because this is evidence of their superior genetic quality. Superior genetic quality is also demonstrated through symmetry and good quality hair/feathers. Møller (1992) suggested that symmetry is a handicap because it requires a great deal of genetic precision. Only good genes can produce a symmetrical body and this explains why symmetricality is attractive.

### Evaluation

The fact that diseases continue to evolve means that this mechanism would be particularly advantageous.

- **Support** comes from, for example, Møller (1990) who studied barn swallows, a species troubled by the blood-sucking mite. He found that parents with longer tails had offspring with smaller mite loads even when they were reared in a foster nest (where the mites could be passed through contact from foster parents with greater mite loads).
- Critics point out that the **same might apply to males who have been injured**, but this 'handicap' would not be heritable and in fact individuals who get injured tend to be weaker to begin with. Females who mated with males handicapped through injury would not provide any genetic benefit for their offspring so this behaviour would not be perpetuated.

## Evolutionary explanations of parental investment

AQA A   U3

Trivers (1972) defined **parental investment** (PI) as 'any investment by a parent in one of her/his offspring that increases the chance that the offspring will survive at the expense of that parent's ability to invest in any other offspring (alive or yet to be born)'.

Who ends up holding the baby? It isn't always females. For example, the male stickleback remains with the eggs he has gathered from a number of females until they hatch; the male seahorse carries fertilised eggs around in a brood pouch.

External fertilisation does not always result in male care, nor does internal fertilisation always lead to maternal care. For example, the female jacana lays a clutch of eggs for each male in her harem and then leaves them for the male to incubate and rear entirely on his own.

### Sex differences in parental investment

#### 1. Eggs and sperm

Parental investment begins with the gametes. Female investment is greater. Either sex may use one of two strategies: r or K.

- **r strategy** – The individual produces many eggs/sperm and devotes little extra care. Survival is ensured through numbers alone, or by having several mates and leaving the partner to care.
- **K strategy** – The individual produces relatively few eggs (female) or mates with one partner, and devotes more energy to ensuring survival.

#### 2. Who provides the care?

Mode of fertilisation may be a way of explaining which sex becomes the carer:

- **Paternity certainty hypothesis** – Ridley (1978) proposed that males are more likely to care for young when fertilisation is external because the care increases the certainty that the offspring are his own. In the case of internal fertilisation the male can desert, knowing (or thinking) that the offspring are his.
- **Order of gamete release hypothesis** – Dawkins and Carlisle (1976) proposed that both sexes prefer not to be left 'holding the baby' because this decreases their future reproductive potential. Internal fertilisation allows the male to get away first; with external fertilisation the female can leave first.
- **Association hypothesis** – Williams (1975) proposed that the adult who is left in close proximity to the embryo tends to care for the young. Where external fertilisation takes place this is the male; with internal fertilisation this is the female.

However, in mammals, shared care is common because, after birth, the young are still quite dependent. The male's investment may be better protected by staying and sharing the care, and protecting the female and young so this behaviour is naturally selected.

#### 3. Parental certainty

Female mammals can be certain that their child is their own, whereas males cannot. The same applies to grandparents – maternal grandmothers are most certain that a grandchild is their own, whereas paternal grandfathers are least certain. Research has supported this. For example, Pollett *et al.* (2007) studied the visiting patterns of grandparents living within 30km of their grandchildren. Over 30% of the maternal grandmothers had contact daily or a few times a week with their grandchildren. In the case of maternal grandfathers, there was on average 25% contact. However, paternal grandparents had much less contact – 15% of the paternal grandmothers and little more than 15% of the paternal grandfathers regularly saw their grandchildren.

#### Evaluation

- **Support** for this comes from Andersson *et al.* (1999), who looked at the investments made by fathers in the college education of their biological children and their stepchildren. The investments were highest when a father was still living with the biological mother of his children, but otherwise investments were the same, which doesn't fit evolutionary theory. Andersson *et al.* suggest that men are willing to invest in stepchildren because it demonstrates to their partner that they are a good provider (a criterion for sexual selection).

### 4. Sexual jealousy

One of the consequences of gender differences in PI is sexual jealousy. Buss (1995) suggests that sexual jealousy has evolved differently in males and females because each sex has different concerns. For a male it is important that his partner is sexually faithful in order to ensure an offspring is his own. For a female, emotional infidelity is more important because she doesn't want to lose her breadwinner and risk more difficulties raising her offspring.

This was supported by a study by Buss *et al.* (1992) who found that American male students indicated more concern about sexual infidelity, whereas female students expressed more concern about emotional infidelity. In addition, the men showed much higher **GSR** responses (indicating distress) when shown pictures of sexual infidelity than emotional infidelity. However, Harris (2003) found this difference did not apply to real-life experiences. When actual reports from men and women about their partner's infidelity were examined there were no gender differences.

**GSR** stands for galvanic skin response, a method of measuring emotional arousal by testing the electrical conductivity of the skin. When a person is emotionally aroused the ANS is activated and sweatiness increases the electrical conductivity of the skin.

The concept of **fitness** is central to evolutionary theory. It describes the reproductive capability of an individual – the fitter you are the more likely you are to reproduce successfully. Fitness is measured by the proportion of the individual's genes in all the genes of the next generation.

## Parent–offspring conflict

Parental investment is not determined solely by parents. Offspring behaviour often influences the process in order to maximise offspring **fitness**. A parent has an equal interest in each offspring, although the amount of resources allocated to each offspring decreases as the child gets older and needs less care to ensure survival. From the offspring's point of view, decreased care is undesirable and this leads to certain behaviours, as listed below.

### 1. Sibling rivalry

In most sexually reproducing species (including humans), individual offspring will want to receive more than their 'fair share' at the expense of other offspring, in order to maximise their own fitness. As a result, sibling rivalries may develop for the attention and available resources of parents. Mock and Parker (1998) document many examples in animals species, for example, egrets who push siblings out of the nest, and shark embryos who eat their embryonic siblings.

Lalumière *et al.* (1996) suggested that human parents cope with sibling rivalry by steering siblings along different developmental paths, maximising each individual's strengths, so that there is reduced sibling competition and also less subsequent competition for the same mates. This might explain why siblings turn out to be so different.

### 2. Parent–offspring conflict before birth

Parent–offspring conflict does not only develop after birth, but begins at the moment a mother's egg is fertilised by the father's sperm (Buss, 1999). High blood pressure in pregnancy (which may lead to the potentially fatal condition called **pre-eclampsia**) may be caused by the foetus secreting hormones when it 'perceives' the need for more nutrition. The higher blood pressure results in more nutrient-containing blood being delivered to the foetus. This mechanism benefits the foetus at the expense of the mother (Haig, 1998).

Research has found that mothers who do have high blood pressure during pregnancy tend to have fewer spontaneous abortions (Haig, 1993) and larger babies at birth (Xiong *et al.*, 2000), both of which suggest that high blood pressure is associated with more healthy foetuses and is, therefore, an adaptive strategy.

## Practice essay 3.2

Discuss the relationship between sexual selection and human reproductive behaviour.

*(25 marks)*

# 3.3 Effects of early experience and culture on adult relationships

*After studying this topic you should be able to describe and evaluate:*

- *the influence of childhood and adolescent experiences on adult relationships, including parent–child relationships and interaction with peers.*

## Influence of childhood experiences on adult relationships

AQA A    U3

### Key points from AS

- John Bowlby's attachment theory, and related research evidence, is discussed in more detail in *Revise AS Unit 3.1, page 53.*

Hazan and Shaver (1987) extended Bowlby's theory to adult relationships. They argued that the **attachment behavioural system** that develops in infancy leads to three aspects of adult behaviour: romantic relationships, caregiving and sexuality.

A lot of research looks at the consequences of being a secure or insecure adult. However, the key question is whether these temperament types are due to childhood experiences or to some other factor, such as the innate temperament of the individual. For the purposes of this section, however, we are only concerned with the link between early experience and later behaviour, rather than the question of whether early experience *caused* later behaviour.

Fraley (2004) concludes that early attachment and later romantic relationships are only moderately related at best.

John Bowlby (1969) proposed that the relationship between a primary attachment figure and his/her infant creates an **internal working model** of relationships. This internal working model creates expectations about future relationships, described as a **continuity hypothesis** – people who are securely attached as infants will continue to form similar relationships throughout life. They are more likely to be sociable and popular with peers, to form lasting romantic relationships and to offer secure attachment to their children.

### Research evidence

#### Friendships

Simpson *et al.* (2007) followed 78 individuals from infancy to their early 20s. Those individuals who were securely attached were more socially competent in school and were more likely to have secure friendships at age 16. In early adulthood these individuals had more positive daily emotional experiences.

#### Romantic relationships

Hazan and Shaver (1987) found that adults who were securely attached as infants believed that love was enduring, and were more mutually trusting, and were less likely to have been divorced. In contrast, adults who had been insecurely attached felt true love was rare, fell in and out of love easily and generally found relationships less easy.

McCarthy (1999) studied women whose attachment types were recorded in infancy. Those who had been classified as avoidant had the greatest difficulty in romantic relationships and those who had been classified as resistant had the poorest friendships. Women who were securely attached as infants had the most successful romantic relationships and friendships.

However, Steele *et al.* (1998) found a correlation of only .17 between secure attachment type at age 1 and at age 20.

#### Caregiving and parenting

Quinton *et al.* (1984) compared a group of 50 women who had been reared in institutions (children's homes) with a control group of 50 'normal' women. When the women were in their 20s it was found that the ex-institution women were experiencing extreme difficulties acting as parents. For example, more of the ex-institution women had children who had spent time in care and more of the ex-institution women were rated as lacking in warmth when interacting with their children.

#### Sexuality

Avoidant romantic attachment is associated with more accepting attitudes of casual sex (Schachner and Shaver, 2002).

# Influence of adolescent experiences on adult relationships

AQA A  U3

## Key points from AS

- You can read a description of Freud's theory and stages of development in *Revise AS Unit 1.1, page 19.*

### Erikson's eight stages of life

*First year* – Trust vs. mistrust

*Second year* – Autonomy vs. shame and doubt

*Third to sixth year* – Initiative vs. guilt

*To puberty* – Industry vs. inferiority

*Adolescence* – Identity vs. identity confusion

*Early adulthood* – Intimacy vs. isolation

*Middle age* – Generativity vs. stagnation

*Old age* – Integrity vs. despair

## Parent–child relationships

Freud suggested that adolescence was a period of identity formation and the development of independence (the **genital stage**). Erik Erikson (1968) developed Freud's ideas, proposing that adult intimacy could only be achieved if earlier crises in development had been successfully negotiated. Erikson suggested that there were eight crises or 'tasks' that occurred during a person's life (see left). Negative outcomes in one stage make successful resolution of the developmental crisis of the next stage more difficult. In early adulthood, intimacy is the main task but this stage cannot be resolved if earlier stages had a negative outcome. This includes attachment experiences in the first year (trust versus mistrust) and also includes, most importantly, the identity crises during puberty. Erikson suggested that a young person who cannot establish their own identity will have problems with intimacy because the individual fears loss of identity if they commit to others.

Erikson's view has been supported by research, for example, Kahn *et al.* (1985) found that students assessed as being low in identity development later had less success in relationships (e.g. men likely to not be married, women more likely to be separated). There may, however, be a gender difference in the link between intimacy and identity. Erikson believed that the relationship between identity and intimacy was different for men and women. He suggested that female identity development was different – for a woman, identity depends on finding a partner first so identity comes *after* intimacy. For males, identity comes *before* intimacy. This may be a gender bias or a real difference.

More recent research has also showed that warm and close parental relationships (attachment) during adolescence are important for the development of autonomy (which is important for adult relationships). This has been called '*inter*dependence' or '**connectedness**' (Coleman and Hendry, 1999).

## Interaction with peers

Ainsworth (1989) suggested that peers were important in adolescent emotional development because they provide attachment relationships and also feedback about social behaviour.

Peers provide an emotional way-station on the way to adulthood; in order to become independent, young people transfer their dependence from parents to peers (Steinberg and Silverberg, 1986). However, there is a different view, which is that peer attachments don't replace parental attachments, they are simply different. Peer relationships are more symmetrical, i.e. each person in the relationship is equal. At the same time, parental relationships during adolescence also change and become more like the new peer relationships – more symmetrical and less critical (Hendry *et al.*, 1993).

Peers also provide opportunities for practising adult romantic relationships; too much practice or practice in poor quality adolescent relationships may negatively impact on young adult relationships. Meier *et al.* (2005) used data from the US National Longitudinal Study of Adolescent Health and found that both adolescent relationship type and the quality of those relationships contribute to the type and quality of young adult relationships.

# Practice essay 3.3

Discuss the influence of adolescent experiences on adult relationships, including parent–child relationships and interaction with peers. *(25 marks)*

# Chapter 4

# Aggression

## 4.1 Social psychological approaches to explaining aggression

### After studying this topic you should be able to describe and evaluate:

**Aggression** refers to behaviour that is intended to cause harm or pain.

- *social psychological theories of aggression, for example, social learning theory, deindividuation*
- *explanations of institutional aggression.*

**LEARNING SUMMARY**

## Social psychological theories of aggression

AQA A ▷ U3

**Vicarious reinforcement** occurs when you observe someone else being reinforced for certain behaviour (e.g. on TV). This increases your own expectation of future rewards and punishments.

See page 72 for an explanation of operant conditioning.

'Social' learning is learning that involves other people – therefore it is 'social'.

### Key points from AS

- **Social learning theory** is discussed in more detail in *Revise AS Unit 1.1, page 17.*

More evidence of the effects of indirect reinforcement on aggression can be found in Chapter 13 on media psychology, see page 125.

You are more likely to imitate (or '*model*') your behaviour on someone you admire or respect (e.g. rock stars, parents, teachers, friends) because you *identify* with them. **Modelling** and **identification** are important concepts in SLT.

### 1. Social learning theory (SLT)

Aggression is learned:

- **Indirectly** – through **observational learning** (you observe what others are doing). Such behaviour is only repeated if **vicarious reinforcement** occurs.
- **Directly** – when a behaviour is performed, it may be directly reinforced and, therefore, more likely to be repeated. If it isn't reinforced, the probability that it will be repeated is decreased.

Both indirect and direct reinforcement are examples of **operant conditioning**.

An individual learns (a) the value of aggressive behaviour (thus increasing tendency to aggress) and (b) to imitate specific acts of aggression.

Albert Bandura first outlined SLT. He suggested that there are four steps in the **modelling** process:

- **Attention** – If a person (model) is attractive, prestigious, or similar you will pay more attention.
- **Retention** – Actions must be remembered (i.e. cognitive processes involved).
- **Reproduction** – Vicarious reinforcement is not enough, imitation can only occur if the person possesses appropriate skills.
- **Motivation** – Imitation is related to direct and indirect reinforcements and punishments.

### Research evidence

Bandura *et al.* (1961, 1963) showed that, if children watched someone else behave aggressively towards a Bobo doll (punching it, shouting at it and hitting it with a hammer), they were more likely to be aggressive themselves later on, and also imitated specific actions when they were placed on their own with the doll (after being mildly frustrated). Later variations found that a filmed version was as effective as a live model, and also that imitation was even more likely if:

- The model was **rewarded**. When the model was punished children did not imitate the behaviour. This shows that observational learning only results in imitation when it is vicariously reinforced.
- The child **identified** with the model. For example, a favourite hero or heroine on TV, or same sex model.
- The participant had low **self-esteem**.

Aggressive video games provide an opportunity to observe the effects of models on behaviours (see page 26).

Aggression can also be explained in terms of **disinhibition** (see page 125) – seeing someone else behave aggressively may reduce one's own inhibitions about behaving in this way.

### Key points from AS

* Social explanations of aggression can be evaluated by considering the relative strengths and limitations of biological explanations. See, for example *Revise AS Unit 1.1, page 13*.

See biological explanations of aggression on pages 43 and 44.

**Deindividuation** describes the loss of a sense of personal identity that can occur when, for example, in a crowd or wearing a mask. It is associated with a reduced sense of personal responsibility and increased anti-social behaviour.

In Zimbardo's view, deindividuation results in anti-social behaviour. Prentice-Dunn and Rogers propose a 'normative' view – deindividuation results in people following groups' norms rather than going against them.

### Key points from AS

* Zimbardo's classic *Stanford Prison study* involved deindividuated behaviour from both prisoners and guards. It is described in *Revise AS Unit, page 123*.
* Obedience studies are described in *Revise AS Unit 6.1, page 128*.

### Evaluation

* Research findings may be due to **demand characteristics** in an unfamiliar social situation (the children had to look for cues of what to do with Bobo).
* SLT can explain **media influences** on anti-social behaviour (see page 125).
* SLT can explain the influence of **coercive home environments**. Parents solve disputes aggressively and children model their behaviour on this (Patterson *et al.*, 1989).
* People are not consistently rewarded for aggression. Often they are punished, which suggests that SLT may be an **oversimplified** account.
* Research doesn't include the effects of **emotional factors or biological factors**, although Bandura acknowledged that biological factors are part of any account. For example, the urge to be aggressive is biological; what is learned (indirectly and directly) is how and when to express the aggression.
* It can explain **individual differences** (people behave differently because of different indirect and direct reinforcement experiences), and can explain **cultural differences** (different cultures reinforce different behaviours and also model different behaviours).
* It explains the fact that people imitate **specific acts** of violence.

## 1. Deindividuation

**Anonymity** – The presence of a crowd (or group) leads individual members to feel anonymous and act according to a different set of rules than they would normally. Zimbardo (1969) suggested that:

* **Individuated behaviour** is rational, consistent with personal norms.
* **Deindividuated behaviour** is unrestrained, acting on primitive impulses, and leads to anti-social acts.

**Reduced self awareness** – An alternative explanation (Prentice-Dunn and Rogers, 1982) for deindividuation effects is that being in a crowd leads to reduced *private* awareness rather than reduced *public* awareness (i.e. anonymity). Normally, people are aware of their personal morals but within a group they may lose sight of 'private' principles and follow the group.

### Research evidence

Zimbardo (1963) repeated Milgram's (1963) obedience experiments with participants either wearing a name tag (individuated) or in a hood (deindividuated). When wearing a hood, participants gave more shocks.

Diener *et al.* (1976) observed the behaviour of over 1,000 children on Halloween. The house owner asked some of the children to give their names. Those who remained anonymous were more likely to steal some money and/or extra chocolate when briefly left alone (i.e. they were more likely to behave anti-socially).

### Evaluation

* In some instances, deindividuation leads to **increased pro-social behaviour** (e.g. at a peace rally). Johnson and Downing (1979) compared the behaviour of people wearing uniforms either like the Ku Klux Klan or like nurses. The latter gave fewer shocks, i.e. deindividuation did not result in anti-social behaviour.
* As with obedience, an individual can elect whether to behave **autonomously**; deindividuation is not inevitable.
* Understanding deindividuation has led to useful **practical applications**, for example, using video cameras at football matches so that people can see themselves and, therefore, be more publically self-aware.

## Explanations of institutional aggression

AQA A    U3

**'Institutional aggression'** includes:

1. The behaviour of people who belong to institutional groups, such as the military and police (and terrorist groups). In general, this kind of institutional aggression does not involve anger and is likely to be **instrumental aggression** rather than **hostile aggression** (i.e. aggression as a means to another goal).

2. The behaviour of people living in institutions, such as prisoners or people in mental hospitals. In general, this kind of institutional aggression is likely to be hostile (i.e. aggression stemming from feelings of anger).

An **institution** is a structure for a particular social group governed by a set of rules and identified with a particular purpose. It may be an actual place (such as a prison or school) or a conceptual structure (such as the armed forces, the judiciary or marriage). Institutions are social constructions, artifacts of a particular time, culture and society, produced by collective human choice.

Essentially, any explanation of aggressive behaviour could be used to answer essays on this topic as long as you link your answer to institutions.

### Key points from AS

- Zimbardo's Stanford Prison experiment is described in *Revise AS Unit 6.1, page 123.*
- Social identity theory is described in *Revise AS Unit 13.7, page 144.*

## 1. Warfare

Warfare is sometimes seen as uniquely human because it requires a culturally-transmitted technology or political organisation. However, 'wars' are frequently observed between animal groups. One long-term study of wolves (Mech, 1970) found that 25% of all deaths were due to intra-species killing (i.e. within species).

Ardrey (1961) suggested that humans engage in warfare because they have a killing instinct, which evolved because humans are, by nature, carnivorous hunters.

Ehrenreich (1997) proposed the **defence hypothesis of warfare** – that the origins of warfare lie in group defence against predators. She argued that humans survived not just because they hunted but because they protected themselves from being hunted. For example, early Americans defended themselves from uncivilised savages by destroying the Indian nation.

Freud (1930) suggested that wars occurred because humans have a death instinct (**thanatos**), which leads the id to be driven towards self-destruction. The ego diverts this urge towards others so that thanatos becomes a desire to destroy and be aggressive towards others. Freud suggested that the only way to prevent people being aggressive is to redirect these urges into sport or other cathartic activities.

Lorenz (see page 45) suggested that animals evolve safety mechanisms to reduce actual physical harm during intra-species conflict, e.g. displays of strength prior to battle, and signals that indicate defeat. In more modern warfare, humans no longer fight face-to-face and are, therefore, capable of greater destruction.

Watson (1974) looked at the role of deindividuation, such as the use of war paint and uniforms. He examined data from 23 societies and found that of those who behaved most aggressively (killed, tortured, and maimed their enemies), 80% were societies who changed their appearance before going to war.

## 2. Terrorism

Terrorism can be explained in terms of minority influence (Kruglanski, 2003). This applies to women seeking the vote at the turn of the 20th Century, as well as militant groups of today. Terrorists seek to bring about social change by changing majority opinion. They do this by being consistent and persistent in their claims and activities. Initially, opinion change may not be apparent. For example, a secret poll conducted by the Ministry of Defence (2005) found that a majority of Iraqis *supported* terrorist attacks, although this was not the public impression. A psychodynamic explanation would be that our instinctive aggressive impulses are normally controlled by the superego. But, when a cause is morally justified (e.g. for the sake of religious ideals), then the superego encourages aggressive behaviour.

## 3. Behaviour of prisoners

Zimbardo, in his classic Stanford Prison experiment (1973), found that the aggressive behaviour of prisoners and guards was due to situational rather than dispositional factors ('a bad barrel rather than a bad apple').

In contrast, Haslam and Reicher (2006) argue that people do not simply behave according to assigned roles; the behaviour of prisoners and guards can be better explained in terms of **social identity theory**.

## Practice essay 4.1

Outline and evaluate **two or more** social psychological theories of aggression.

*(25 marks)*

# 4.2 Biological explanations of aggression

*After studying this topic you should be able to describe and evaluate:*

- *the role of neural and hormonal mechanisms in aggression*
- *the role of genetic factors in aggressive behaviour.*

**LEARNING SUMMARY**

## The role of neural and hormonal mechanisms in aggression

AQA A ▶ U3

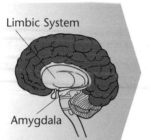

Limbic System

Amygdala

Moghaddom (1998) distinguishes between explanations of aggression which are *normative*, and those which are *causal*. **Normative explanations** explain aggression as being influenced by the norms and rules of particular cultures, i.e. social explanations. **Causal explanations** suggest that aggression is determined by particular factors, such as hormones or hot temperatures, i.e. they are biological explanations.

**Key points from AS**

- Stress response is discussed in *Revise AS Unit 5.1, page 98.*

### Neuroanatomy

Bard (1929) found that cats that had their cortex removed displayed 'sham rage' (i.e. anger without the real emotional content). This suggested that the cortex normally inhibits the **limbic system** (a sub-cortical system including the amygdala, hippocampus and hypothalamus), thus preventing aggression. Later research implicated the **amygdala** in particular. Kluver and Bucy (1939) removed the temporal lobes from monkey's brains and found that they showed little fear or aggression (called the Kluver-Bucy syndrome). Electrical stimulation of the amygdala in animals increases aggression.

Raine *et al.* (1997) used brain scans to demonstrate that murderers were more likely to have abnormalities in their limbic system than normal individuals.

In humans there is evidence that tumours in the limbic system are associated with aggressive behaviour. For example, Charles Whitman, the Texas tower sniper, was found after death to have had a brain tumour that pressed on his amygdala.

### Evaluation

- The link with aggression is **complex**. For example, different areas of the limbic system are associated with offensive, defensive and predatory aggression in rats (Adams, 1986).
- Raine *et al.* point out that brain abnormalities may create a predisposition to be violent but they alone do not **cause** violent behaviour.

### Neurotransmitters

Low levels of **serotonin** are linked to aggression, as shown, for example, by the fact that drugs which increase serotonin reduce aggression (Delville *et al.*, 1997).

### Hormones

**Testosterone** is a male hormone (present in smaller amounts in females). High levels are associated with aggressiveness in animals (e.g. Gilberto *et al.*, 1997), however, some experiments have not shown a relationship between testosterone levels and aggression in humans (Albert *et al.*, 1993).

High levels of **adrenaline** have also been linked to aggression; adrenaline is linked to the fight/flight response.

The female hormones **oestrogen** and **progesterone** increase just before menstruation (creating pre-menstrual tension – see also page 16) and have also been linked to greater hostility (Hoyenga and Hoyenga, 1993).

### Evaluation

- Testosterone has been linked to particular **kinds of aggression** – physical aggression (violence). It may amplify it, but it does not cause it (Simpson, 2001).
- Hormones may be an **effect**, **rather than a cause**, of aggression.

## *The role of genetic factors in aggressive behaviour*

 AQA A ▶ U3

Various lines of research have suggested that higher aggression can be linked to certain genes.

### The Y chromosome

Witkin *et al.* (1976) found an over-representation of **XYY** men in prison populations (i.e. one Y chromosome too many). This has been supported by later research.

> The Y chromosome is the male chromosome. All humans have 23 pairs of chromosomes. In a normal male, one pair is XY, which creates a male. Normal females are XX. (See biological explanations of gender differences, page 59.)

### Criminal families

Mednick *et al.* (1984) found that adopted children whose biological fathers were criminals were more likely to become criminals themselves, than adopted children whose adopted fathers were criminals. This suggests that a tendency to being criminal (and presumably more aggressive) is in your genes.

This line of argument has been used by various criminals, such as Stephen Mobley who killed a man in 1981. His defence was that it wasn't his fault because his family had a history of violence so he had inherited the gene. The court didn't accept his argument and he was sent to the electric chair.

### MAOA gene

The MAOA (monoamine oxidase A) gene is important in eliminating excess amounts of certain neurotransmitters, such as adrenaline and serotonin. Caspi *et al.* (2002) studied over 400 New Zealand men and found that those with low MAOA gene activity *and* who had been abused in childhood were four times more likely to have been convicted of a violent crime by the age of 26.

> Biological data is often from studies of non-human animals, which overemphasises the importance of biological factors. In humans, innate behaviour is more modifiable.

Brunner *et al.* (1993) studied a family of impulsive, aggressive males who also had a mutation in the gene coding for MAOA.

### Selective breeding

The genetic basis of aggression has also been demonstrated in selective breeding programmes. More (or less) aggressive breeds of dogs, bulls or other animals are developed by selecting suitable males and females for breeding.

#### Evaluation

- This research often assumes that being **criminal is equal to being aggressive**. However, many people in prison are there for crimes that are not connected with aggression. It may simply be that certain genes are linked with low intelligence, and less intelligent men are more likely to end up in prison!

#### General evaluation of biological explanations

> You can contrast biological explanations of aggression with social explanations described on pages 40 and 41.

- If hormones or genes are the cause of aggression, they can be used to **reduce aggression/violence**. However, drug therapies have not been found to be successful in the treatment of aggression (Tyrer *et al.*, 2008).
- Biological accounts explain the motivation to be aggressive but **not the methods used or the targets of aggression** (e.g. violence towards other racial groups).
- Biological accounts cannot explain **cultural differences**.

## *Practice essay 4.2*

Outline and evaluate **one** social psychological explanation of aggression and **one** biological explanation of aggression.                    *(25 marks)*

# 4.3 Aggression as an adaptive response

*After studying this topic you should be able to describe and evaluate:*

- *evolutionary explanations of human aggression, including infidelity and jealousy*
- *explanations of group display in humans, for example, sports events and lynch mobs.*

## Evolutionary explanations of human aggression

AQA A ▸ U3

Aggression is a solution to a range of adaptive problems – i.e., solving these problems would have enhanced the survival and reproductive benefits of the actor; hence, this mental module (aggressive response) would have spread through the population.

Lorenz's view is that aggression is an instinct. Freud's theory (page 42) of aggression is also an 'instinct theory', i.e. he suggested aggression is an innate tendency, but he was not considering it from an evolutionary point of view.

A **ritual** is a stylised set of actions which has evolved socially or biologically to communicate information. An example of ritualised human aggression can be seen in Australian Aboriginal structured violence – two combatants are only allowed to cut/stab their opponent in the back (It's very hard to kill a person that way). At the end village elders examine the warrior's wounds to determine the winner.

Konrad Lorenz, in his book '*On Aggression*' (1966), proposed that aggression evolved in all animals (including humans) because it is adaptive – the most aggressive animals control access to resources such as mating, territory and food. Lorenz proposed a **hydraulic model** – certain environmental signals (such as the sight of a rival male) acts as a 'releaser' of 'action specific energy'. Over time this energy builds up (like a cistern of water filling up) and will eventually lead to an outburst of aggressive behaviour if not released earlier in some acceptable way such as engaging in sports (a process called **catharsis**).

A more recent evolutionary approach has been outlined by Buss (2005), where aggression is seen as a means of solving various adaptive problems: getting valuable resources that others possess, defending oneself against exploitation or physical attack, deterring others from aggression against you, climbing up in the dominance hierarchy of a group, inflicting costs on intrasexual rivals, deterring long-term mates from (sexual) infidelity and gaining access to mates.

### Evaluation

- Evolutionary accounts are **determinist**, suggesting that human aggressive behaviour may be inevitable in certain situations.
- The evolutionary approach emphasises the **positive aspects** of aggression and recognises its survival value.
- The evolutionary approach does not account for **cultural differences**.

### Evolutionary stable strategy (ESS)

Maynard-Smith (1982) proposed that uncontrolled violence is not a stable strategy. If all members of a population are violent, they will kill each other. At the other extreme, a population that is totally non-violent (called 'doves' as opposed to 'hawks') will not work – a chance mutation producing one 'hawk' will wipe out the 'doves'. Therefore, in any population, there will be a balance of hawks and doves. This was supported by Barrett *et al.* (2002) who drew on 'Njál's Saga (13th Century Viking blood feuds) to demonstrate that genetic groups are more likely to survive if they have some members who are violent. In the case of the Viking saga, those families who had family members who were **berserkers** (warriors) were more likely to survive than those families who didn't have berserkers in their family group.

### Ritualised forms of aggression

Lorenz also argued that intra-species aggression does not naturally lead to death or injury because this would lead to the extinction of the species. He suggested that ritualised forms of aggression evolve to prevent actual harm taking place. For example, two male stags circle each other, make threatening noises and lock horns but usually one will back down before there is major injury. In humans the lack of face-to-face contact in modern warfare may explain why warfare is lethal, whereas 'naturally' it would not be.

Jealousy concerns something you have and are afraid of losing, especially losing an important relationship to a rival. Envy is the desire for something you haven't got.

Infidelity refers to being unfaithful, but it extends beyond sexual unfaithfulness.

A man whose wife cheats on him is referred to as a cuckold. But no equivalent word exists for a woman whose husband has cheated on her.

You can contrast evolutionary explanations of aggression with social explanations (e.g. social learning theory), discussed on page 40.

## Jealousy

Jealousy is cited as one of the top three causes of murders. From an evolutionary perspective, there are various ways to explain why jealousy is a source of murder and aggression.

### 1. Infidelity

Evolutionary theory predicts a different response to infidelity in men and women because for each gender the loss of a partner has different consequences. Men are more concerned with sexual infidelity because they cannot be certain that any child is theirs unless their partner is sexually faithful and, from an evolutionary point of view, men (and their genes) do 'best' by preventing sexual infidelity. Women on the other hand, are more concerned in the resources a partner can provide and do 'best' if they do not share these with other women. Women, therefore, have evolved a greater concern with emotional infidelity. This was supported in a study by Buss *et al.* (1992, see page 37). Daly *et al.* (1982) found the same was true for relationship violence – men were more violent when their partner was sexually unfaithful.

### 2. Male-to-male rivalry

Males compete with other males to gain access to females. Such competition arises because females tend to be the ones who choose and males compete with each other to be chosen (see page 34). This male-to-male competition can be seen in contests between males, and is supported by research that has found that male-to-male violence is prevalent among young males in virtually all societies (Daly and Wilson, 1988). The universal nature of such behaviour supports the evolutionary perspective.

### 3. Female-to-female rivalry

Males prefer to mate with physically attractive females because physical attractiveness is linked to fertility (see Buss, 1989, page 34). This leads to female-to-female rivalry. As predicted by evolutionary theory, Buss and Dedden (1990) found that women were more likely than men to verbally belittle the physical appearance and promiscuity of their same sex rivals, a tactic that would reduce the attractiveness of a rival.

### 4. Sibling rivalry

Siblings are often jealous of each other. Parental investment theory (see page 36) suggests that sibling rivalry (and jealousy) has evolved in order for each child to try to maximise the resources allocated to that child inevitably at the expense of any other offspring. Harris (2004) suggests that this may be a better explanation of the origins of jealousy rather than infidelity.

### Evaluation

- Violence is **not necessarily a natural outcome of jealousy**. If it was, then rates of uxoricide (murdering one's wife) would be constant across cultures, whereas Daly and Wilson (2006) report that the rates of uxoricide are twice as high in the US compared to the UK, but considerably lower than they were 20 years ago.
- Harris (2003) also found that the gender difference existed in imagined scenarios (as in Buss *et al.'s* research, see page 37). But, when she examined **actual reports** from over 100 men and women about a partner's infidelity the gender difference disappeared. Both men and women were more concerned with emotional infidelity.
- Harris also found **cultural differences** – European and Asian men are less likely than American men to say sexual fidelity is worse. This suggests that cultural factors are more significant than innate factors.

## Explanations of group display in humans

> Group displays are related to dominance in terms of mating and territorial possession.

Group display is a ritualised form of aggressive threat, akin to the ritualised aggression suggested by Lorenz (see page 45).

### Sports events

**War dances** – A number of national sports teams have adapted native war dances to use in opening ceremonies. The New Zealand rugby team starts each match by performing the *haka*, a traditional Maori war dance. The Tongans also perform the *Kailao*. War dances are performed by warriors before battle to proclaim their strength and intimidate the enemy, and also to motivate the warriors and show their obedience, skill and weapons. War dances involve fierce facial expressions and the waving of weapons. Other examples of group display include cheerleading and the Mexican wave, both of which may relate to war dances. Such group displays motivate fans and increase social identity.

> Evolutionary stable strategies are described on page 45.

**'Owner wins' strategy and territorial behaviour** – Group displays may be related to territorial behaviour. They are a means of staking out a group territory and thus increasing confidence in winning. Sports teams are more likely to win home games – and the same is true in the animal kingdom where 'owner wins' is an evolutionary stable strategy (Maynard-Smith and Parker, 1976). The group display is an attempt to declare ownership, which is particularly important for visiting teams.

**Ritual behaviour** – Marsh (1982) argued that sporting events serve as occasions for 'ritual confrontations' between fans. This involves verbally abusing rival fans, threatening them with attack, and general horseplay. His views were based on extensive observations of football fans. He concluded that these confrontations are relatively harmless and are just symbolic displays of aggressive energy. They are highly structured and predictable, and serve to control the extent to which people are aggressive. Marsh believed that if the aggressive behaviours associated with football were suppressed, the rates of violent crime and fighting behaviour in non-sport settings would increase.

### Evaluation

- Some believe (e.g. Dunning *et al.*, 1988) that Marsh's account **underplays the amount of violence** that does occur at football matches.
- An alternative account is that young men are socialised to value displays of aggression and masculinity, which **emphasise their social identity** (i.e. the groups they belong to that increase their self-esteem).

> A **lynch mob** is a group of people who have assembled with the intention of inflicting violence on another person, which results in the death of that person. It is an example of an aggressive mob; another example is a riot mob – a highly emotional crowd (temporary collection of people) that pursues some violent or destructive goal.

### Lynch mobs

Le Bon (1903) presented an influential account of mob behaviour. He proposed that people behave in an extreme way in crowds because they lose their sense of identity (deindividuation). Anti-social behaviour spreads through a crowd like a disease – a process termed **'social contagion'**. An alternative view was presented by Turner and Killian (1957). Their **emergent norm theory** is related to social identity theory (see page 42) and suggests that distinctive behaviours emerge as a crowd interacts, creating norms for that group. In this account the behaviour of the crowd is seen as rational rather than irrational, and it also allows for the fact that not all members behave in the same way.

## Practice essays 4.3

(a) Outline explanations of group display in humans. *(5 marks)*

(b) Outline and evaluate evolutionary explanations of human aggression.

*(20 marks)*

# Chapter 5

# Eating behaviour

## 5.1 Eating behaviour

LEARNING SUMMARY

*After studying this topic you should be able to describe and evaluate:*

- *factors influencing attitudes to food and eating behaviour, for example, cultural influences, mood, health concerns*
- *explanations for the success or failure of dieting.*

### Factors influencing attitudes to food and eating behaviour

AQA A    U3

Our eating behaviour is due to a mix of both nature and nurture, i.e. innate factors (discussed on page 50) and acquired/learned factors, which are discussed on this page.

The term **culture** refers to all the rules, customs, morals and ways of interacting that bind together members of a society or some other collection of people. We learn all these rules, customs, etc. through the process of socialisation. Different social classes have different attitudes to, among other things, attachment and also eating behaviour, and therefore, might be regarded as different 'subcultures'.

The appearance, smell, taste and texture of food are probably the most important determinants in food preferences (Hetherington and Rolls, 1996). Other factors are also important, such as the price of food and a person's socioeconomic status, ethical concerns and hunger.

#### 1. Cultural influences

Chrisler (1997) suggested that cultural factors moderate individual differences in eating behaviour, i.e. they modify innate preferences (see page 51).

**Social learning** – We model our behaviour on what we see other people doing, especially when they are rewarded (vicarious reinforcement) and when the models are people we identify with (e.g. parents, siblings). Therefore, we learn to like eating the same things that we see other people enjoying. Equally, we learn to avoid eating things that we see other people disliking.

**Mere exposure** – People like things which are familiar (Zajonc, 1968). Research shows that the more frequently a food is tasted, the more it is liked. Rozin (1987) claims that mere exposure is the overriding factor in acquired food likes.

**Social context** – Eating is often a social occasion and is likely to be affected by family food rules at a younger age as well as later learning experiences.

#### 2. Mood

'Emotional eaters' are individuals who eat to comfort themselves. This may lead to bulimia, an eating disorder where overeating is subsequently compensated for by purging (for example, by self-induced vomiting or laxative use). Depression may cause people to overeat because low levels of the neurotransmitter **serotonin** are linked to depression.

Emotional distress may also lead to undereating because joy and anger can inhibit hunger contractions.

#### 3. Health concerns

Many people today consider what they eat in terms of the healthiness of the food, for example, choosing low fat items or fresh vegetables. People who rate nutrition as important prefer healthy foods (McFarlane and Pliner, 1997). However, healthy food may sometimes have a negative effect. For example, a Finnish study (Kähkönen and Tuorila, 1998) found that young men had a lower expectation in terms of tastiness of low fat Bologna sausages compared with regular ones.

**Evaluation**

- Such accounts **don't explain why children** typically avoid certain adult foods such as mushrooms and tomatoes. A full account includes nurture and nature.
- Understanding health-based choices is **useful in designing programmes** to encourage healthy-eating lifestyles.

## Explanations for the success or failure of dieting

AQA A    U3

### Success

See page 72 for an explanation of operant conditioning.

**Operant conditioning** – A small degree of success will act as a reinforcer, encouraging a person to continue dieting. This may explain why diet plans often start with a rigorous first few weeks, which should result in significant losses.

On page 54 an evolutionary explanation is presented for anorexia, which suggests that some people may be genetically programmed to respond in the opposite way to food restriction.

**Social support** – The success of the organisation *Weight Watchers* is explained in terms of the support provided by other members. Such self-help groups (as distinct from individual dieting regimes) provide successful role models, vicarious reinforcement and a social identity that empowers individuals. Miller-Kovach *et al.* (2001) showed that a *Weight Watchers* programme was more successful than using an individual self-help method over a period of two years. Lowe *et al.* (2004) reported that weight losses are reasonably well maintained even after five years; an average of 71.6% of participants maintained a loss of 5% or more.

### Failure

Traditional dieting strategies tend not to work for emotional eaters because the psychological aspects of weight management aren't fully addressed by most plans.

**Hormones** – Cummings *et al.* (2002) studied the hormone **ghrelin**, which is produced in the stomach. Low levels of ghrelin stimulate appetite. They found that it increases by an average of 24% when people are on low-calorie diets, therefore, making people even more hungry! The researchers concluded that severe food restriction results in a physiological response of increasing appetite to avoid starvation. The result is that weight loss is made more difficult. Interestingly, patients who had stomach reduction surgery experienced reduced levels of ghrelin because there is less stomach to produce the hormone, which may explain part of the success of such operations.

Research into the success and failure of dieting has grown in popularity because of the recent epidemic levels of obesity and also the obsession by many men and women to become thinner.

**Cognitive factors** – Williams *et al.* (2002) linked failure in dieting to cognitive factors. They measured eating behaviour (using the Dutch Eating Behaviour Questionnaire) and attention, and found that people who have difficulties with sustained attention are less successful at dieting.

**Personality factors** – A number of studies compare high and low 'restrainers'. High restrainers are individuals who diet by restraining the amount they eat, as opposed to 'low restrainers' who find it easy to simply restrict their food intake. Mensink *et al.* (2008) suggest that high restrainers are very sensitive to food cues and, therefore, find it more difficult to resist food. In order to diet successfully they have to make bigger efforts to resist food than low restrainers and so they are more likely to fail. For example, Stirling *et al.* (2004) looked at the effects of forbidden food on subsequent eating behaviour in restrained and unrestrained normal-weight women. Despite being told not to eat some chocolate, the high restrainers consumed a small quantity of the forbidden food.

The evidence related to diet failure can be turned around and used to discuss dieting success.

**Type of diet** – Low-fat diets may be counter-productive and lead to diet failure because such diets can lead to anxiety, depression and other mental health problems (Food and Mood Project, 2008). This can create a vicious cycle because low mood then leads to overeating. For example, Nolen-Hoeksema (2002) found that 80% of women who coped with low mood by binge eating went on to develop full-blown depression within five years.

Biological explanations of eating behaviour can help understand the success and failure of dieting. These are discussed on the following pages. In addition, explanations of obesity (on pages 57 and 58) are relevant.

### Evaluation

• Diet success and failure is likely to have **multi-causal explanations**.

## Practice essays 5.1

(a) Discuss **two** factors that influence attitudes to food / eating behaviour.

*(10 marks)*

(b) Discuss **two** explanations for the failure of dieting.   *(15 marks)*

# 5.2 Biological explanations of eating behaviour

*After studying this topic you should be able to describe and evaluate:*

- *the role of neural mechanisms involved in controlling eating and satiation*
- *evolutionary explanations of food preference.*

## Neural mechanisms involved in eating and satiation

AQA A   ▶ U3

**Satiation** refers to feeling full.

The **hypothalamus** is part of the **limbic system** which is generally concerned with emotion and homeostasis (maintaining a steady state).

Diagram of hypothalamus and the LH and VMH.

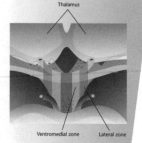

Thalamus

Ventromedial zone    Lateral zone

See page 43 for an illustration of the limbic area.

**Serotonin** is a neurotransmitter that is generally associated with mood. Levels of serotonin are commonly low in depressed people and anti-depressants often work by increasing serotonin levels. The same treatment has been used with anorexics to increase their appetite.

Understanding how non-biological factors interact with, and can override, physiological satiety signals and promote overeating, is important in successful diet control.

### 1. Hypothalamus

The hypothalamus is the hunger centre of the brain, located in the midbrain. It regulates eating, acting like a thermostat to start/stop eating:

- The **ventromedial hypothalamus (VMH)** is associated with cessation of eating, i.e. hunger is suppressed in response to body signals of satiation.
- The **lateral hypothalamus (LH)** is stimulated by low serotonin levels and creates sensations of hunger, which leads to eating.

Animals that overeat (**hyperaphagia**) or undereat (**aphagia**) have been found in post-mortem examinations to have damaged VMH and LH respectively. Recent naturalistic studies of animals by de Araujo *et al.* (2006) confirmed the role of the LH as the most important brain region for hunger motivation. This is confirmed by human studies, for example, Reeves and Plum (1969) performed a post-mortem examination of a patient who had doubled her body weight in two years. They found a tumour in the VMH. Quaade (1971) found that electrical stimulation of the LH in obese patients led to reports of feeling hungry.

### 2. Other regions of the limbic system

Other parts of the limbic system have also been implicated in hunger/satiation, such as the **orbitofrontal complex** and **hippocampus**. Wang (2006) found that these two regions were activated by signals from the stomach, indicating fullness. The involvement of the limbic system indicates the complex set of information involved in hunger because this brain region is not just linked to emotional behaviour but also to learning and memory, movement, and the processing of sensory information.

### 3. Blood-glucose levels

**Glucostatic theory** suggests that the brain monitors blood-glucose levels; glucoreceptors may be located in the VMH. One source of glucose comes from the intestine, which produces **cholectystokinin (CCK)** in response to the presence of food. CCK causes the liver to produce glucose and to signal the brain.

### 4. Lipids (fats)

**Lipostatic theory** suggests that reduced fat levels may create sensations of hunger. **Leptin** is a hormone derived from fat. London and Baicy (2007) found that leptin reduces activation in regions of the brain linked to hunger, whilst enhancing activation in regions linked to inhibition and satiety.

### Evaluation

- The **brain alone is not responsible** for eating behaviour. However, the stomach does not play a major role in hunger because people with no stomach still feel hungry.
- Fullness (satiation) may also be explained by **cognitive factors** ('I have eaten, therefore, I am full') and **activity in the stomach** (stretch sensors in the stomach report fullness, which is why liquids make you feel full).

## Evolutionary explanations of food preference

AQA A ▸ U3

Food preferences evolved because liking particular kinds of food is adaptive (i.e. it prompted survival and thus, reproduction). Such preferences can be observed in terms of eating behaviours that are innate; if they are innate they are likely to be adaptive.

The **EEA** (environment of evolutionary adaptiveness) is the environment to which a species is adapted. The selective pressures at that time explain the behaviours that we observe today. In humans it is suggested that our EEA was the period from 1.8 million to 11,000 years ago when humans lived on the plains in Africa.

The term **'sauce béarnaise syndrome'** was coined by Martin Seligman after he had eaten a sumptuous dinner including the rich sauce béarnaise, followed by a concert with music by the composer Wagner. Later that night he developed stomach flu resulting in nausea and a lot of vomiting. For the next 10 years he felt very queasy any time he smelled sauce béarnaise. This led him to reflect on the acquired association. He had also spent the evening listening to Wagner but did not feel queasy when he heard that music again. This led him to suggest that we have an innate predisposition to learn links between tastes and nausea.

### Sweet foods

Davis (1928) looked at eating behaviour in three infants and found an innate preference for sweet foods. A liking for sweetness might be adaptive: our evolutionary ancestors in the EEA often experienced food shortages, so a preference for high-calorie (sweet) foods would be adaptive. In addition, sweet foods are generally not poisonous, making them doubly valuable to primitive humans. This explanation is supported by Araujo's (2008) research with mice, which showed a preference for the calorie content of foods, rather than sweetness.

### Variety

Davis (1928) also found an innate liking for a variety of food. Research has in fact found an interest in new foods that is coupled with a fear of them. This reflects the risks and benefits of new foods. Liking for variety and newness would be important, from an adaptive viewpoint, in order to ensure a plentiful food supply. However, there is also the risk that new foods might be poisonous, so some cautiousness is important and adaptive.

### Meat

Young children generally don't like eating meat; it is a taste acquired later. Dunn (1999) claims that human beings are not instinctively attracted to eating live or dead meat in nature. If a child was given an apple and a live chicken, they would instinctively play with the chicken and eat the apple. If a cat was presented with the same choice, their natural impulse would be the opposite.

### Salt

Salt (sodium chloride) is vital for survival because if a person is deprived of salt, their body becomes dehydrated, resulting in death. Research shows that people innately respond to sodium deficiency by eating saltier foods (Beauchamp *et al.*, 1983), which would be important in maintaining sufficient amounts of sodium in the body. Desor *et al.* (1975) found that preferences for salt emerge in infants at about 4–6 months rather than being present at birth. This is due to maturation of the nervous system.

### Bitter and sour tastes

Bitter/sour tastes are avoided because of their linkage to poisonous plants. However, Liem and Mennella (2003) demonstrated that children have a greater liking for sour tastes than adults. This might be because they have a greater interest in trying new foods than adults, which would have adaptive advantages. By adulthood, learned preferences have overtaken innate tendencies.

### Distate-nausea linkage

Seligman and Hager (1972) suggested that animals have an innate predisposition to learn associations between foods that cause nausea and avoidance. This has been called the **sauce béarnaise syndrome** (see left). This kind of one trial learning would have an adaptive advantage especially when the food is novel (i.e. tasted for the first time). The effect was demonstrated by Bernstein (1978) in children receiving chemotherapy. Those who were given ice cream flavoured with Maple syrup prior to chemotherapy avoided the ice cream subsequently.

### Evaluation

- **Testing neonatal preferences is problematic.** Research is based on the infants' facial expressions when offered different foods and may not produce reliable results.

## Practice essay 5.2

Discuss evolutionary explanations of food preference.　　*(25 marks)*

# 5.3 Eating disorders

*After studying this topic you should be able to describe and evaluate:*

Note that the specification states you only have to study one eating disorder. This book covers all three of the listed disorders and you should select one of them.

* *psychological explanations of one eating disorder, for example, anorexia nervosa, bulimia nervosa, obesity*
* *biological explanations, including neural and evolutionary explanations, for one eating disorder, for example, anorexia nervosa, bulimia nervosa, obesity.*

LEARNING SUMMARY

## Anorexia nervosa: psychological explanations

AQA A ▷ U3

**Anorexia nervosa**
literally means a 'nervous lack of appetite'. The main characteristics are:
* *Severely underweight* due to deliberate and prolonged restriction of calorie intake.
* Intense *fear of gaining weight*.
* Anorexics have a *disturbed body image* and usually continue to see themselves as overweight despite large weight loss.

### Key points from AS

* The study of individual differences at AS level included three psychological approaches to explaining abnormality: the psychodynamic, behavioural and cognitive approaches. These approaches are used here to explain anorexia. You can use the evaluations of these approaches when considering the explanations of anorexia – see *Revise AS Unit 7.1, pages 153–155.*

See page 72 for an explanation of classical and operant conditioning.

### 1. Psychodynamic explanations

**Family systems theory** – Minuchin *et al.* (1978) suggested that anorexics' families are enmeshed. The members don't have a clear identity and the family finds it hard to resolve conflicts. This leads to anxiety, which may be projected onto the 'ill' child, i.e. the eating disorder arises as a means of dealing with family conflict. Humphrey *et al.* (1986) did find that families who had a child with an eating disorder have more negative and fewer positive interactions than 'normal' families.

**Autonomy** – Anorexics tend to be somewhat obsessive personalities, with low self-esteem and a fear of their own autonomy. Bruch (1987) suggested that certain mothers wish their daughters to remain dependent and, therefore, encourage anorexia. Equally, the daughters wish to remain children. Anorexia develops as a means of asserting autonomy by exerting control over the body. The fact that most anorexics come from middle-class families where there are high expectations supports this.

### Evaluation

* The role of autonomy could explain why anorexia is especially **common during adolescence**. Blos (1967), a psychodynamic theorist, proposed that adolescence is a time of reindividuation.
* Psychodynamic theories cannot explain the **recent increase** in anorexia.
* Parental conflict may be an **effect rather than a cause** of anorexia.
* The accounts are difficult to prove wrong (**falsify**).

### 2. Behavioural explanations

**Classical conditioning** – Leitenberg *et al.* (1968) suggested that anorexics have learned that eating is associated with anxiety, because eating too much makes people overweight and unattractive.

**Operant conditioning** – Weight loss is reinforcing because people praise it and the individual has escaped from an aversive stimulus.

**Social learning theory (SLT)** – Feminine stereotypes in the media and the current emphasis on dieting promote a desire to be thin, which is exaggerated by vulnerable individuals.

### Evaluation

* Unlike biological explanations, SLT can account for **increased incidence** of anorexia. Becker (1999) found that the introduction of television in Fiji was associated with an increased incidence of eating disorders in young Fijian girls.
* SLT can also explain **cultural differences**, though Hoek *et al.* (1998) claim that rates of anorexia are fairly constant across cultures.
* Conditioning theory can explain how the disorder is **maintained**.

Adolescence may be a prime time for anorexia because it is the time that girls (especially) are aware of making themselves attractive. They also often put on weight with puberty and this triggers slimming.

- **Behavioural therapies have been successful** in treating anorexia, e.g. through rewards for attaining and maintaining target weight (Sue *et al.*, 1994). This supports learning theory as an explanation.
- **Social factors alone** cannot explain anorexia because otherwise more people would suffer from it. This can be explained in terms of the diathesis-stress model (see next page).

### 3. Cognitive explanations

**Distortion of body image** – Garfinkel and Garner (1982) found that anorexics typically overestimate their body size compared with 'normal' controls. This distorted thinking may explain why they wish to lose more weight than other individuals.

**Females more than males** – Fallon and Rozin (1985) found that females rated their ideal body weight as significantly lower than the weight males thought most attractive, whereas males rated their ideal body weight as higher than their actual weight.

### Evaluation

- The disordered thinking may be an **effect rather than a cause** of anorexia.

It is worth reading through the explanations of bulimia and obesity, on the following pages to gain further insights into explanations of eating disorders.

## Anorexia nervosa: biological explanations

AQA A    U3

MZ twins share the same genes, whereas DZ twins are only as similar as any siblings – they share 50% of the same genes.

### 1. Genetic explanations

**Twin studies** – Holland *et al.* (1984) found a 55% concordance rate for identical (MZ) twins compared with only 7% for non-identical (DZ) twins. This suggests that there is a significant genetic component in anorexia.

**Obsessive-compulsive personality type** – Klump *et al.* (2000) suggest that people with anorexia and their parents have an obsessive, compulsive personality disorder that produces perfectionist behaviour. This can be seen in their obsessive interest in food. What drives obsession? One possibility is that it is **serotonin**, and abnormal levels of serotonin could be genetically caused.

### Evaluation

- The fact that not all MZ twins develop the disorder means that genetic transmission **cannot be the sole explanation.**
- However, the diathesis-stress model proposes that **genetic vulnerability** must be part of the explanation, though there also needs to be some trigger ('stress').
- Biological explanations can't explain the **recent increases** in cases of anorexia.

**Key points from AS**
- A general outline of biological explanations of abnormality can be found in *Revise AS Unit 7.1, pages 151–152.*

The role of the LH and VMH is hunger and satiety. (See page 50).

### 2. Neural explanations

**Hypothalamus** – Gorwood *et al.* (1998) suggest that genes may cause abnormal levels of abnormal development of the **hypothalamus**. The **lateral hypothalamus (LH)** may be innately damaged, resulting in undereating because no feelings of hunger are produced, and the **ventromedial hypothalamus** (VMH) continues to send signals to suppress hunger.

**Serotonin** – There is considerable evidence that increased serotonin activity in the brain is associated with a suppressed appetite and also with increased anxiety, obsessive behaviour, phobias and even vomiting – all characteristics of people with anorexia. It may be that restricted food intake alleviates related problems because, if no food is eaten, a substance called **tryptophan** is produced and body serotonin levels drop. Therefore, people with anorexia feel better by starving themselves.

**Adrenaline and cortisol** are produced at times of stress and they reduce appetite. When stress dies down, appetite should return to normal. But, it's possible that this does not happen in people with anorexia since they lack the hormone to switch the appetite back on (**AVP**) (Collier *et al.*, 1999).

It is preferable to talk about individuals with anorexia rather than use the term 'anorexics' because the latter term makes it sound as if the disorder overwhelms the whole person. There is more to an anorexic person than anorexia. However, it is convenient shorthand to use when writing about the disorder.

**Key points from AS**
- The activity of the sympathetic nervous system suppresses hunger. See *Revise AS Unit 5.1, page 98.*

This means they remain in a state of suppressed appetite. A key characteristic of anorexia is that they can resist the need to eat, and this explanation accounts for this.

**The hippocampus** regulates production of **cortisol**, which then has the effect of shrinking the size of the hippocampus, causing further cortisol to be produced. This could explain why people with anorexia get stuck in a vicious cycle and can't start eating again even when they want to.

### Evaluation

- It isn't always possible to distinguish **cause and effect**. For example, which comes first – stress or hippocampal shrinkage?
- The cycle of non-eating caused by hippocampal shrinkage explains why it is **hard to break out of anorexic behaviour** once weight loss has started.

## 3. Evolutionary explanations

**Starvation strategy** – Guisinger (2004) has suggested that anorexia evolved as a consequence of the problems faced by nomadic populations in the EEA (see page 51). Such populations would frequently experience scarcity of food and starvation. Normally animals respond to starvation by feeing intensely hungry and having low activity levels. In contrast, individuals who have a genetic tendency toward anorexia react to starvation by feeling no hunger and feeling full of energy. This would enable such individuals to cope better with starvation because they would move on to find food, whereas 'normal' behaviour (feeling hungry and sluggish) would actually be counter-productive to survival. This anorexic reaction is triggered when an individual loses a significant amount of weight, which explains why anorexics find recovery so difficult – once they have lost a key amount of weight this turns off their hunger.

**Intrasexual competition** – Abed (1998) proposed that eating disorders are related to competition between females. Thinness is an important factor in female attractiveness, especially because it distinguishes younger women (who are more fertile and, therefore, preferable to men for mating) from older women. In modern society older women are now often quite thin (called 'pseudo-nubile women'), which increases female competition for mates causing 'runaway' female intrasexual competition whereby the originally adaptive strategy spirals out of control in response to a range of environmental factors.

### Evaluation

- Starvation theory is **supported by research**. For example, Kron *et al.* (1978) has noted that anorexic patients have a tendency towards hyperactivity and compulsions to move.
- The intrasexual competition explanation can account for the fact that **eating disorders affect mainly young females**, and decline with advancing age.

## 4. Diathesis-stress model

The most significant criticism of all psychological models is that they cannot explain the biological evidence, and vice versa (biological models cannot explain psychological evidence).

The diathesis-stress model offers a good compromise position. It suggests that people are born with a genetic vulnerability (diathesis) to develop certain disorders. However, a disorder like anorexia nervosa will only surface if events in the person's life (stressors) trigger it. Such stressors include emotional difficulties at home or school (e.g. bullying) and/or exposure to thin role models. The diathesis-stress model explains why one MZ twin may develop anorexia but the other may not.

Both psychological and biological explanations are **determinist** – suggesting that a person's behaviour is determined by factors outside their own control.

An important strength of all evolutionary explanations is that they are **ultimate explanations**, i.e. why people are predisposed to develop certain behaviours. All other psychological explanations are **proximate** – they explain the immediate events around the acquisition of a behaviour and ignore the underlying value of such behaviours.

You can read more about sexual selection on page 34.

The importance of all explanations is that they highlight the *best route to recovery*. In the case of evolutionary explanations the suggestion is that the biological block to eating needs to be overcome.

You can evaluate explanations of anorexia with those for bulimia and obesity on the following pages.

# *Bulimia nervosa: psychological explanations*

AQA A ▶ U3

There is a considerable degree of overlap in the explanations offered for anorexia nervosa and bulimia nervosa, so reference should be made to pages 52–54, especially when considering evaluations.

## 1. Psychodynamic explanations

**Family conflicts** have also been identified in families with bulimics (see notes related to anorexia on page 53).

**Abuse** – Individuals deal with being abused by repressing such memories and then repressed feelings are expressed through the symptoms of bulimia. Bulimia is a means of punishing the body, and expressing self-disgust. Gender differences can be explained because females are more likely to turn blame inwards and are, therefore, more likely to develop bulimia. On the other hand, an abused male becomes hostile towards others and is less likely to develop bulimia. Abuse is probably more common in girls.

**Conflict** – Chassler (1998) suggests that bulimia represents conflicting wishes for merger and autonomy. Bingeing is an attempt to regain a momentary experience of the mother and merge with the engulfing maternal object. However, the terror of engulfment results in purging, rejecting this 'bad' object.

### Evaluation

- A number of bulimics have experienced abuse (McLelland *et al.* (1991) report that about 30% have). However, not all people who are abused develop bulimia, and not all bulimics have been abused, so this **can only explain some cases.**

## 2. Behavioural explanations

**Conditioning** – Rosen and Leitenberg (1985) suggest that bingeing causes anxiety. Purging reduces that anxiety. This is a cycle that is reinforcing.

**Social learning theory** – Lee *et al* (1992) related the lack of bulimia among Chinese girls to socio-cultural factors, such as cultural attitudes to being fat (fat is desirable and, therefore, overeating doesn't create anxiety) and the rarity of dieting (therefore, lack of role models). Such factors support the view that social learning determines whether or not dieting and bulimia occur.

### Evaluation

- Research evidence supports the influence of cultural factors. For example, Nasser (1986) found that 12% of Egyptian women who were studying in London developed bulimia compared with no cases in Cairo.

## 3. Cognitive explanations

**Disinhibition hypothesis** – Ruderman (1986) suggested that dieters who have rigid cognitive styles respond to situations of overeating by going over the top (becoming disinhibited). Once they have overeaten, they purge in order to rectify their mistake.

**Distorted body image** – Cooper and Taylor (1988) reported that bulimics usually show a substantial discrepancy between their estimation of their true body size and the size they would ideally like to be. This distorted thinking would encourage the desire to lose weight.

**Coping style** – Vanderlinden *et al.* (1992) suggested that bulimics have a tendency to perceive events as more stressful than most people, and use binge/purge as a means of coping with the stress or gaining a sense of control.

### Evaluation

- Distorted cognitions may be a **cause rather than an effect** of eating disorders.

---

**Bulimia nervosa** literally means 'hungry as an ox'. It is a more common problem than anorexia and probably more related to dieting. The main characteristics are:

- Periods of *compulsive bingeing*, which often involves eating enormous amounts of *high-calorie food.*

- Bingeing creates guilt so it is followed by forced vomiting or the use of laxatives (*purge*).

- Occurs *more than 2 times a week* for over 3 months

- *Weight obsession,* though it is usually nearer normal than anorexics.

- *Secondary problems* arise from the persistent vomiting, for example, tooth decay from the acid of the vomit.

### Key points from AS

- The study of individual differences at AS level included three psychological approaches to explaining abnormality: the psychodynamic, behavioural and cognitive approaches. These approaches are used here to explain bulimia. You can use the evaluations of these approaches when considering the explanations of bulimia – see *Revise AS Unit 7.1, pages 153–155.*

It is worth reading through the explanations of anorexia and obesity, on the previous and following pages to gain further insights into explanations of eating disorders.

## Bulimia nervosa: biological explanations

AQA A U3

### Key points from AS

- A general outline of biological explanations of abnormality can be found in *Revise AS Unit 7.1, pages 151–152.*

Binge–purge is the key characteristic of bulimia that distinguishes it from anorexia and, therefore, explanations should focus on both of these behaviours.

It is estimated that bulimia affects up to 10% of the female population, and some males.

It is preferable to talk about individuals with bulimia rather than use the term 'bulimics' because the latter term makes it sound as if the disorder overwhelms the whole person. There is more to a bulimic person than bulimia. However it is a convenient shorthand to use when writing about the disorder.

The role of the LH and VMH in hunger and satiety is discussed on page 50.

See page 54 for evolutionary evaluations of anorexia.

### 1. Genetic explanations

Kendler *et al.* (1991) found a concordance for bulimia of 26% for MZ twins and 16% for DZ twins. Bulik *et al.* (2000) concluded that bulimia is 83% genetically influenced, whereas anorexia nervosa is 58% genetic.

Lilenfeld *et al.* (2000) suggested that inherited factors may predispose some individuals to impulsivity and that such individuals develop bulimia.

#### Evaluation

- The fact that there is not 100% concordance for MZ twins supports the **diathesis-stress model** (see below).
- One of the difficulties in studying anorexia and bulimia is the **reliability in diagnosis**. All studies rely on identifying characteristics of a disorder and, inevitably, different criteria may be employed, leading to different rates of diagnosis.

### 2. Neural explanations

**The ventromedial hypothalamus** (VMH) may be damaged. The lateral hypothalamus (LH) stimulates eating and the VMH usually stops eating. But if the VMH is damaged then there is no sense of satiety and overeating occurs. In an individual who wishes to be thin, overeating is controlled as far as possible but then may result in an excessive binge, which further results in compensation through purging.

**Serotonin** is linked to this process because it helps to regulate the feeding centres of the hypothalamus. Low levels of serotonin stimulate the LH (Galla, 1995). Serotonin either predisposes an individual to develop bulimia, or perpetuates the disorder, or both.

#### Evaluation

- This makes sense because **bulimics have an enhanced rather than absent appetite**. They overeat and then feel guilty because of the desire to be thin.
- Further evidence **links serotonin and bulimia**. People with bulimia suffer specifically from carbohydrate craving (Turner *et al.*, 1991) and increased consumption of carbohydrates increases production of serotonin. This has led to the use of selective serotonin reuptake inhibitors (SSRIs) to treat bulimia.

### 3. Evolutionary explanations

**A strategy for dealing with food shortage** – In the **EEA** (see page 51) nomadic humans would have to cope with intermittent periods of food shortage. One physiological adaptation would be to prepare for a coming famine by increasing baseline weight and appetite. Dieting may activate this system resulting in overeating (bingeing), especially craving carbohydrates for quick weight gain and energy.

**Intrasexual competition** as an explanation of anorexia has also been applied to bulimia. Faer *et al.* (2005) suggest that in the case of bulimia it has been proposed that competition is for mates, whereas for anorexia it is for status. However, the research evidence collected from their questionnaire did not support this.

#### Evaluation

- This explanation can be **contrasted with the evolutionary explanations for anorexia and obesity.**

### 4. Diathesis-stress model

See page 54.

## Obesity: psychological explanations

AQA A   U3

**Obesity** is when a person is carrying too much fat for their height and sex. It is associated with many illnesses, such as cardiovascular disease and diabetes.

Obesity rates are set to increase dramatically in the coming years to become an epidemic.

### Key points from AS

- Obesity is discussed in *Revise AS Unit 1.1, page 21*.

See page 72 for an explanation of classical and operant conditioning.

### Key points from AS

- The study of individual differences at AS level included three psychological approaches to explaining abnormality: the psychodynamic, behavioural and cognitive approaches. These approaches are used here to explain obesity. You can use the evaluations of these approaches when considering the explanations of obesity – see *Revise AS Unit 7.1, pages 153–155*.

Obesity can be measured in terms of **BMI (body mass index)**. It is calculated by dividing your weight (kg) by your height (m). A BMI of over 30 is classed as obese.

It is worth reading through the explanations of anorexia and bulimia, on the preceding pages to gain further insights into explanations of eating disorders.

CBT stands for cognitive-behavioural therapy.

### 1. Psychodynamic explanations

The psychodynamic explanation is that obese individuals have experienced some serious disturbance during the oral stage of psychosexual development, i.e. when their libido was focused on their mouth and the infant sought oral gratification. It could either be a case of emotional deprivation or a case of overindulgence, which would mean that the libido remains locked into that form of gratification.

There may be other factors that lead to obesity, such as depression or low self-esteem. Psychodynamic explanations of such factors, therefore, can be used to explain obesity (see pages 90 and 108).

#### Evaluation

- All psychological explanations have **important implications** for treatments (weight loss programmes). It is not just a matter of reducing weight but targeting the root cause of the emotional disorder.
- Factors such as depression or low self esteem may be the **effects of obesity** rather than the initial cause, but either way they may serve to perpetuate the problem.

### 2. Behavioural explanations

**Operant conditioning** – In our society, food is one of the key reinforcers. Children are given sweets for being good and we are often encouraged to reward ourselves by having an edible treat. Such reinforcement encourages weight gain.

**Classical conditioning** – Food is naturally associated with a sense of pleasure; a person can be trained to dislike food if it is associated with something unpleasant.

**Social learning theory** – There are some stereotypes that encourage obesity, for example, fat men are regarded as 'jolly' and mother figures are portrayed as being rotund. Such role models may encourage overeating.

#### Evaluation

- **Cultural differences** in obesity are likely to be related to differential reinforcement, which is derived from social norms. In the UK, about 22% of the adult population are classed as obese; slightly more women are obese than men. In some countries there is a very significant difference between men and women, for example, in Egypt 45% of women are obese compared to 22% of the men. Gender differences may be biological as well as cultural.
- **Acceptance of fatness** is also related to social norms. Data from the Framingham heart study followed over 30,000 children for 32 years and found that BMI change was linked to BMI changes in family and friends, even when they lived far apart. This suggests that the key factor in a person's weight was the attitudes shared by people around them.
- **Behavioural therapies may work in the short term** but in the long-term attention is needed to emotional and cognitive factors.

### 3. Cognitive explanations

Cognitive explanations focus on information-processing biases for food-relevant stimuli. Braet and Crombez (2003) studied 34 children and found that obese children showed a greater sensitivity to food words than control children. Such hypersensitivity may initiate or maintain dysfunctional eating behaviour.

#### Evaluation

- The **success of CBT** suggests that cognitive factors are important.

## Obesity: biological explanations

AQA A ▷ U3

**Key points from AS**

- A general outline of biological explanations of abnormality can be found in *Revise AS Unit 7.1, pages 151–152*.

Compulsive overeating is a form of addictive behaviour, so explanations of addiction can be applied here (see pages 133–134).

Genetic linkage is never 100%, which means that environmental factors continue to be important. In addition, some people with, for example, two copies of the FTO gene are not obese. Therefore, genetics cannot be the whole explanation.

The role of the LH and VMH in hunger and satiety is discussed on page 50. The roles of ghrelin and leptin are also discussed on pages 49 and 50 respectively.

See pages 54 and 56 for evolutionary evaluations of anorexia and bulimia respectively.

## 1. Genetic explanations

There are a number of genetic conditions (such as Prader-Willi syndrome) where obesity is a classic symptom, suggesting that there is a genetic link to obesity.

Wardle *et al.* (2008) analysed 5000 twins aged 8–11 years and compared them in terms of BMI and waist circumference (a measure of abdominal fatness or adiposity). They found a heritability figure of 77%, with a relatively small environmental factor, half of which was due to shared environmental effects (i.e. same home, same upbringing) and the other half due to non-shared effects.

Frayling *et al.* (2007) researched the FTO (fat mass and obesity) gene, finding that people who possessed two copies of this gene had a 70% increased risk of obesity; people with one copy had a 30% increased risk. Price *et al.* (2008) also found an association between the FTO gene and obesity when comparing about 600 extremely obese women with normal controls, and with non-obese sisters.

### Evaluation

- Wardle *et al.* (2008) suggest that the **obesity epidemic is clearly due to environmental factors** (e.g. changing availability of food, attitudes to eating) because genes have not altered. However, Musani *et al.* (2008) argue that there is support for the view that genes may be changing. For example, moderately obese people are more fertile and this would increase the gene pool for obesity.

## 2. Neural explanations

The **hypothalamus** regulates hunger. Lesions in the ventromedial hypothalamus (VMH) caused massively obese rats. Two hormones, **leptin** and **ghrelin** provide important information to the hypothalamus. Leptin is produced by adipose (fat) tissue and signals the presence of fat reserves. Its effect on the hypothalamus is to release appetite-suppressing substances; lack of leptin leads to feelings of extreme hunger. Some fat people may lack leptin because of a faulty gene.

### Evaluation

- Early research on leptin was with mice and the effects are **not as straightforward as in humans** (Paracchini *et al.*, 2005).
- Use of leptin in **obesity treatment** has not been found to be effective.

## 3. Evolutionary explanations

**Thrifty gene hypothesis** – Some ethnic groups may be more prone to obesity because of this gene. In the **EEA** (see page 51) there would have been periods when food was scarce. This gene enables an individual to make use of periods of abundance and store energy efficiently. People with greater adipose reserves are more likely to survive famine.

### Evaluation

- This explanation can be **contrasted with the evolutionary explanations for anorexia and bulimia**.

## 4. Diathesis-stress model

See page 54.

## Practice essay 5.3

Discuss **two or more** biological explanations for **one** eating disorder.
Include neural and evolutionary explanations in your answer. *(25 marks)*

# Chapter 6

# Gender

## 6.1 Biological influences on gender

After studying this topic you should be able to describe and evaluate:

- the role of hormones and genes in gender development
- evolutionary explanations of gender roles
- the biosocial approach to gender development.

LEARNING SUMMARY

## The role of hormones and genes in gender development

AQA A    U3

Many people use the terms 'sex' and 'gender' as if they refer to the same thing, whereas this is not true.

**Sex** is a biological fact, the fact of whether someone is male or female.

**Gender** refers to what it is to be male or female.

X and Y chromosomes.

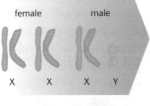

female        male

X    X    X    Y

The term foetus refers to the stage of development before birth.

Evidence of cultural similarities supports biological (innate) explanations of gender roles (page 67).

### Genes

Typical sex chromosome patterns are XX for a female and XY for a male, so-called because of their shapes (see illustration on the left). The Y chromosome carries very little genetic material. There is usually a direct link between chromosomal sex and gonads (i.e. the vagina/womb or penis/testicles). However, there are exceptions, for example, the case of the Batista family. Four children were born with normal female genitalia but at puberty male genitalia appeared. They were genetically XY but had not developed male genitalia because of insensitivity to the male hormone **testosterone**. During puberty, massive amounts of testosterone are produced and this caused the male genitalia to appear. The girls seemed to accept their change of sex without difficulty.

### Hormones

Chromosomes determine a person's sex, but most sexual development and activity is governed by hormones. During prenatal development all embryos start developing the same genital structures, then male hormones such as **testosterone** cause the female parts to be absorbed and the male parts to develop. However, even though testosterone may not have affected the development of genitalia it may have a significant masculinising effect on the developing brain in the foetus. For example, testosterone promotes development of the areas of the brain associated with spatial and mathematical skills, whereas **oestrogen** is thought to do the same in the areas of the brain associated with verbal ability (Brosnan, 2004).

**Research evidence**

Dörner (1974) injected female rats with male hormones during pre-natal development and they showed male behaviours.

Money and Ehrhardt (1972) demonstrated the effects of testosterone on female development by using a group of 25 normal XX girls whose mothers had been prescribed drugs containing **androgen** (a male hormone) during pregnancy to reduce the risk of miscarriage. The androgenised girls were not more aggressive than a control group but preferred vigorous outdoor activity and boys' sports and had less interest in playing with dolls or playing games involving mothering-roles.

Berenbaum and Hines (1992) studied 60 girls with **congenital adrenal hyperplasia** (see page 64) and found that they were more aggressive and more interested in male-type activities than their sisters, which could be due to the effects of androgen on the brain during foetal development.

**Evaluation**

- The evidence clearly shows the **importance of biology** (genes and hormones).
- **Social factors** are important too.

## Evolutionary explanations of gender roles

AQA A ▶ U3

The **EEA** is the environment to which a species is adapted. The selective pressures at that time explain the behaviours that we observe today. In humans it is suggested that our EEA was the period from 1.8 million to 11,000 years ago when humans lived on the plains in Africa.

In the **EEA** males and females faced different adaptive problems, which led to different gender role behaviours.

### Mating strategies

The most basic difference between men and women lies in their method of reproduction. Men produce millions of sperm and can potentially fertilise hundreds of females at a minimal cost to future reproductive potential. This means their most successful strategy will be to reproduce as frequently as possible with the most fertile women. Women make a greater investment in each reproduction because each egg contains nutrients, which has a physiological cost and they carry the baby during prenatal development and nurse their infants for a considerable time after. Therefore, women do best by being choosy about mates.

Several gender differences arise from these differences:

The key to evolutionary explanations is that any behaviour that increases an individual's reproductive success will be selected and appear in future generations, and is, therefore, adaptive.

- Men seek signs of fertility in potential mates (e.g. full lips, rosy cheeks and a thin waist all signal youth and fertility) whereas women seek mates who will provide a good home (e.g. have money and power). Analysis of personal ads by Waynforth and Dunbar (1995) has supported this prediction (see page 34).
- Males will compete with other males to be chosen, which increases the likelihood of inter-male competitivess and aggression. Females also compete to be seen as the most attractive.
- Males are more likely to be sexually indiscriminate (because this maximises the genes they pass to the next generation). Females are more likely to be choosy and also coy (coyness is a strategy to allow a female time to make her choices).

### Interpersonal orientations

'Caringness' is also related to moral understanding (see page 162).

The stereotype of female caringness may be based on evolved differences due to different adaptive problems faced by ancestral males and females. In the EEA, work was largely segregated between the sexes with men hunting and women being responsible for child care. In situations of threat (stress) it would have been adaptive for men to respond with the **fight or flight response** and women to respond with tend and befriend in order to care for themselves and their offspring. The tend and befriend response is associated with the hormone **oxytocin**. The female hormone **oestrogen** enhances the effects of oxytocin, whereas the male hormone **testosterone** reduces its effects (McCarthy 1995). Research shows that women are, in fact, more likely to seek the company of others in times of stress, compared to men (Tamres *et al.*, 2002).

These evolutionary explanations can be evaluated by contrasting them with social explanations for gender roles.

### Adaptive advantage of sex roles

Kuhn and Stiner (2006) argue that humans (*homo sapiens*) had the evolutionary edge over Neanderthals (*homo neanderthalensis*) because they developed different sex roles. The Neanderthal diet was mainly animals, and men and women both hunted. There is evidence for this from the fact that male and female skeletons showed injuries that occurred during hunting, and also there is a lack of evidence of reliance on subsistence foods; Neanderthals were large and needed high-calorie foods. When hunting was unsuccessful the groups starved. In human groups a division of labour evolved – men were the hunters while women engaged in subsistence farming and skill-intensive crafts (e.g. milling grain, making clothing and shelter). This enabled human groups to avoid starvation and live at higher population densities. The result was the beginning of complementary sex roles related to a division of labour that provided a strong adaptive advantage for *homo sapiens*, and may explain why Neanderthals disappeared.

A criticism of the evolutionary approach is that it is **determinist**. In the case of gender differences it suggests that such differences are inevitable.

## The biosocial approach to gender development

AQA A ▶ U3

The **biosocial** approach proposes that gender is determined jointly by biological and social factors, and most importantly takes the view that they cannot be separated. Biological and social factors combine to produce masculine and feminine behaviours and identities.

Dr John Money believes that social factors override biological ones in shaping gender identity, which is a **behaviourist** view. According to Money, assigned gender is more crucial than biological factors. However, the data that Money gathered to support his views is now treated with some degree of skepticism as he may have allowed his expectations to affect his observations.

Social influences on gender role are considered on page 65, including the effects of parents, peers and the media – these are all examples of social factors.

### The contribution of biological factors

On page 59 we examined the contribution of biological factors to gender development. Support for the importance of biological factors comes from a classic case study begun by John Money (1972). He documented the case of twin boys, one of whom accidentally had his penis cut off when he was being circumcised (due to an infection) in infancy. Money believed that gender is entirely determined by socialisation in the early years of development, so he advised the boy's parents to deal with the absence of his penis by raising him as a girl (called Brenda). Brenda knew nothing about this gender re-assignment until her mid-teens. When she did discover, she/he elected to return to her/his biological gender and become a man (Diamond and Sigmundson, 1997).

#### Evaluation

*   This case study suggests **that biology does have a significant role to play**. Other case studies support these findings. For example, Reiner and Gearhart (2003) studied 16 genetic males who were born with no penis and were reassigned as females at birth. All showed relatively male interests and attitudes and 10 of them elected to become males again by the time they were 16.
*   However, other case studies show that **biological sex does not need to match gender identity**. See, for example, Goldwyn (1979) on page 64. Indeed, Money (1991) reported 250 cases where people were content with their gender reassignment.

### The contribution of social factors

There are various explanations for the contribution of social factors:

**Indirect reinforcement** – Children identify with certain people (e.g. parents, peers, pop stars and the media generally) and model their gender behaviours on them, most particularly if the behaviour is seen to be rewarded (vicarious reinforcement). See evidence on page 65.

**Direct reinforcement** – When a child experiences vicarious reinforcement it leads them to repeat such behaviours. If their own behaviour is then rewarded (reinforced) this will increase the likelihood of future similar behaviour, whereas if it is punished the likelihood will be decreased.

#### Evaluation

*   Social learning theory explains **cultural differences** (see page 67) and accounts for the influence of **stereotypes**.
*   **Variable reinforcement** – reinforcements are **not sufficiently consistent** to explain all observed differences, but gender appropriate behaviours are clearly reinforced.
*   Children **do not imitate (model) every behaviour they observe**. For example, boys observe girls' behaviour being rewarded but don't imitate it. This shows that social learning isn't just passive but is also related to cognitive factors (see cognitive-developmental theories on page 62). Perry and Bussey (1979) found that children only imitate those behaviours that fit their gender stereotypes, which means that they actively organise the effects of vicarious reinforcement.

## Practice essay 6.1

Describe and evaluate evolutionary explanations of gender roles.

*(25 marks)*

# 6.2 Psychological explanations of gender development

*After studying this topic you should be able to describe and evaluate:*

- *cognitive developmental theory, including Kohlberg, and gender schema theory*
- *explanations for psychological androgyny and gender dysphoria, including relevant research.*

**LEARNING SUMMARY**

## Cognitive developmental theories of gender development

AQA A    U3

The essence of the **cognitive approach** is that it is what you *think* which has the greatest influence on your behaviour. The cognitive-developmental approach is concerned with how thinking develops. In this case we are looking at the development of thinking about gender.

### 1. Kohlberg's theory

Kohlberg (1966) argued that we acquire our gender concepts through interactions with the environment (social learning), mediated by maturational cognitive factors.

- Different stages of gender identity develop only after a child's way of thinking has aged (matured) to the right point.
- Gender identity is the result of a child's active structuring of his/her own experience (a cognitive process), not just the passive product of social learning.

Kohlberg proposed three stages:

(1) **Basic gender identity** (2–3½ years) – Children recognise their gender but this is based on outward appearance and can easily be changed. Therefore, they have no gender identification with the gender and no need to acquire gender-appropriate behaviours.

(2) **Gender stability** (3½–4½ years) – Awareness that gender is fixed across time ('I will become a man'), but children still think that dressing like a girl makes you a girl, and dressing like a boy makes you a boy.

(3) **Gender constancy** (4½–7 years upwards) – Recognition that superficial changes do not alter gender; that gender is consistent across time and situation. This is similar to the conservation skills that Piaget described in general cognitive development (see page 82). It is only after stage (3) that a child can begin to acquire gender concepts appropriate to his/her own gender.

According to the cognitive approach, children attend to same-sex models because they have already developed a consistent gender identity, not vice versa. The social learning approach takes the opposite view (see page page 65).

### Research evidence

Thompson (1975) showed that gender identification was more accurate in 3 year olds (90% correct) than in 2 year olds (76%).

Slaby and Frey (1975) asked children questions about gender stability, such as, 'Will you be a mummy or a daddy when you grow up?' Children did not know the correct answer until the age of 3 or 4.

Slaby and Frey (1975) also showed pre-school children a film with men on one side and women on the other. Those children who had previously been rated as having gender consistency watched more same-sex models. This shows how they actively seek information that will help them develop gender-appropriate behaviour.

### Evaluation

- This approach **combines social learning** with some aspects of **biological** development.
- This view assumes that **development proceeds in stages**, and that gender identity is mediated by cognitive factors. This may not be universally true.

A **schema** can be described as an organised packet of information or a cluster of related concepts. It is a bit like a stereotype.

### Key points from AS

- **Social identity theory** is described in *Revise AS Unit 1.1, page 19*. It proposes that comparisons are made between groups in order to increase self esteem, and we all have a need to increase our self-esteem. **Ingroup favouritism** and **outgroup negative bias** enhance social and personal esteem, and lead to biased perceptions of ingroup and outgroup members.

## 2. Gender-schema theory

Martin and Halverson (1981) presented an alternative view to Kohlberg's, but which was still a cognitive view of gender development. Their theory emphasises the importance of **schema**; as soon as a basic gender identity develops, children are then motivated to learn more about their gender and will incorporate this information into a gender schema. Like all schemas, this serves to organise relevant information and attitudes and will influence behaviour.

Early gender identity leads to the formation of **ingroup schemas**, i.e. attitudes and expectations about your own gender. The child also develops outgroup schemas. Such ingroup/outgroup schemas lead to **ingroup favouritism** – being more positive about your own group as a means of boosting your own self-esteem. These schemas also mean that children spend more time with their own group (same-sex peers) and reject opposite-sex peers. This will reinforce their gender stereotypes because they spend time within their own group and are exposed only to same-sex concepts.

### Research evidence

Martin and Little (1990) found that pre-school children had very little gender understanding, yet they had strong gender stereotypes about what boys and girls were permitted to do.

Masters *et al.* (1979) showed that children aged 4–5 years were more influenced in their choice of toy by the gender label (e.g. 'It's a girl's toy') than by the gender of the model seen playing with the toy.

Martin and Halverson (1983) found that when children were asked to recall pictures of people, children under 6 recalled more of the gender-consistent ones (such as a male firefighter or a female teacher) than gender-inconsistent ones (such as a male nurse or a female chemist).

In Kohlberg's theory, a child must recognise the permanence of their gender *before* they can begin to acquire gender schema. In gender schema theory, gender schemas begin to be formed much earlier. As soon as the child recognises that there is a difference between men and women, gender appropriate attitudes and behaviour are learned.

### Evaluation

- The theory offers a **middle ground** between social learning and cognitive-developmental explanations.
- It explains how **gender stereotypes persist**, because people are more likely to remember information that is consistent with their schemas.
- It explains how gender behaviour occurs **before gender identity**.
- It lacks mention of **biological factors** and assumes that all gender behaviour is mediated by cognitive factors.

## Compromise position

Stangor and Ruble (1989) have proposed a way in which both approaches (Kohlberg and Martin and Halverson) can be combined: gender constancy and gender schema may relate to different aspects of development.

Bem's theory (on the next page) can also be described as a gender schema theory because she proposes that it is psychologically healthier to be gender non-schematic, i.e. hold schemas that are not based on fixed ideas of maleness or femaleness.

- Gender constancy is related to motivation. Once you realise you are always going to be a girl you are *motivated* to find out about this role and this will be associated with things like activity choice.
- Gender schemas are concerned with organisation of information and, therefore, should affect cognitive variables, such as memory.

Stangor and Ruble tested children aged 4–10 years and found that: (a) preference for same-sex toys increased with increased gender constancy (therefore, supporting gender constancy theory); and (b) memory for gender-consistent pictures increased with age (therefore, supporting gender schema theory).

## Explanations for psychological androgyny and gender dysphoria

AQA A ▶ U3

Androgyny refers to the mixing of masculine and feminine traits. The word androgyny literally means male-female.

### Psychological androgyny

Sandra Bem (1976) suggested that traditional views of gender emphasise gender difference – you are a boy or a girl. Bem proposed that it is psychologically more healthy to have a mixture of male and female traits (**androgyny**) because it allows a person to select the best and most appropriate behaviours for them. Bem (1983) reformulated her approach in terms of gender schema theory, suggesting that androgynous people have a different cognitive style to a traditionally sex-typed person. An androgynous person, when faced with a decision as to how to behave in a particular situation, responds independently of any gender concepts (**gender aschematic**), whereas a traditionally sex-typed person determines what would be appropriate for their gender using gender schemas (**gender schematic**).

### Research evidence

The BSRI is different to other measures of gender behaviour because it allows a person to select both male and female options. Forced choice scales (having to select male or female) may have produced false information about gender inclinations.

Bem designed the Bem Sex Role Inventory (BSRI) to test her ideas. Bem (1975) found that 34% of the male participants and 27% of the female participants in her study were androgynous. Bem and other researchers (e.g. Flaherty and Dusek, 1980) have found that androgynous subjects are more adaptable in different situations, have higher self-esteem and a greater sense of emotional well-being.

### Evaluation

- Other research has **not been so supportive**. For example, Whitley (1988) found that masculine identity led to greater self-esteem than androgyny.

### Gender dysphoria

Gender dysphoria is a condition where an individual feels uncomfortable with the gender they have been assigned at birth and may wish to change gender. It is also called **gender identity disorder**, **gender incongruence** or **transgenderism**.

**Psychological explanations** – Freud suggested that 'normal' gender development involves identification with your same-sex parent (in the phallic stage).

**Biological explanations** – A person's genetic sex (XX or XY) may not accord with aspects of their gender (as determined during prenatal development). Such mismatches can be caused by additional hormones in the mother's system, or by the foetus's insensitivity to the hormones, known as **androgen insensitivity syndrome (AIS)**, which results in female genitalia, despite having male genes. There are other rare conditions, such as **congenital adrenal hyperplasia (CAH)**, where abnormally high levels of male hormones are produced in a female foetus, causing enlarged female genitals, which may mean that the baby is assumed to be male when she is born.

It is estimated that 1 in 4000 people in the UK are receiving medical help for gender dysphoria. It is also estimated that 1 in 2000 people are born with anomalous genitals (external genitals do not match biological sex) and may be given an erroneous gender assignation (Colapinto, 2000).

### Research evidence

Rekers (1995) examined over 70 boys with dysphoria and found no evidence of biological causes but did find a general absence of appropriate male role models. In cases of AIS, female reassignment may not lead to dysphoria. Goldwyn (1979) described the case of Daphne Went, an XY individual with AIS who was content with her female role and adopted two children. Further gender-anomalous case studies are described on pages 60 and 61.

This view of gender identity is similar to John Money's approach to understanding gender – social factors have greater importance than biology.

### Evaluation

- Many transgender people do not regard their cross-gender feelings and behaviours as a disorder. They argue that **gender characteristics are socially constructed** and, therefore, naturally unrelated to biological sex.

## Practice essays 6.2

(a) Discuss **one** explanation of psychological androgyny. *(10 marks)*

(b) Discuss **one** cognitive developmental theory of gender development.
*(15 marks)*

# 6.3 Social constraints on gender role

*After studying this topic you should be able to describe and evaluate:*

- *social influences on gender role: for example, the influence of parents, peers, schools and the media*
- *cross-cultural studies of gender role.*

**LEARNING SUMMARY**

## Social influences on gender role

AQA A ▶ U3

The research in this section represents the **social learning** approach to understanding gender development – the influence of our social world on our gender development.

Parents, peers, teachers and the media provide indirect (vicarious) reinforcement of gender behaviours. Parents, peers and teachers directly reinforce gender behaviours.

The evidence on this page demonstrates the importance of social factors in the development of gender roles. But, there is a lot of evidence to support the other side of the coin – the importance of biological factors (see pages 60 and 61) and also the way that children think about their own gender (see pages 62 and 63).

Maccoby and Jacklin (1974) undertook a massive review of more than 1500 studies of gender differences and concluded that the differences observed were minimal and that most popular gender-role stereotypes are 'cultural myths', which are perpetuated by social influences.

### The influence of parents

Parents have expectations (stereotypes) about gender behaviour and these will affect their patterns of reinforcement. For example, Smith and Lloyd (1978) gave mothers a set of feminine, masculine and neutral toys. When a 6-month-old baby was dressed and named as a boy, the mothers encouraged more physical activity and gave masculine toys to the baby.

Parents also provide direct reinforcement and reinforce their children's behaviour differentially. For example, Eccles et al. (1990) found that parents encouraged their children to play with gender-appropriate toys, i.e. girls to play with dolls and engage in housekeeping games, and boys to play with cars and do sporting activities. Fagot et al. (1992) found that parents who showed the clearest differential reinforcement had children who were quickest to develop strong gender preferences, indicating that differential reinforcement is effective.

There are differences between mothers and fathers. Ruble (1988) found that fathers reinforced gender stereotypes more than mothers. Idle et al. (1993) found that fathers reacted more negatively than mothers when their sons played with girls' toys.

### Evaluation

- Maccoby (1998) argued that **peers, not parents**, are the prime socialising influence on gender development
- However, other researchers (e.g. Santrock, 1994) suggest that **parents are the primary influence** during the important early years.

### The influence of peers

Peers act as role models. Children are more likely to imitate same-sex role models. Slaby and Frey (1975) found that this was more likely in children with higher levels of gender constancy (see page 62), i.e. after they had begun to identify with their own gender.

Peers are important in reinforcing existing stereotypes. Lamb and Roopnarine (1979) found that pre-school children generally reinforced peers for sex-appropriate play and were quick to criticise sex-inappropriate play. Bussey and Bandura (1972) found that 3–4 year olds disapproved of gender-inconsistent behaviour by peers (e.g. boys playing with dolls).

### Evaluation

- **Direct instruction may override peer influence**. Martin et al. (1995) found that boys would imitate girls' toy choice *if* the toys were labelled 'boys' toy' (and the same was true for girls). The label acts as a form of direct instruction.
- Peers are likely to be **important in middle childhood** but not in the first few years of life when important aspects of gender development are taking place. In early life, parents and family may be more important.

## The influence of schools

In school, peers will have an effect on gender development, but teachers may moderate this influence by presenting more gender neutral reinforcement.

However, there may also be the reverse trend, where teachers are more likely to reinforce gender-stereotypical behaviour. For example, they may encourage male students to dress traditionally (no earrings, short hair), whereas peers might encourage anti-stereotypical behaviour (Johnson and Workman, 1994).

### Evaluation

Children may respond selectively to reinforcement. Fagot (1985) found evidence that teachers tend to reinforce 'feminine' behaviours in both boys and girls, such as quiet, sedentary activities but only girls acquire them, which supports the cognitive approach.

## The influence of the media

Media influences are discussed in chapter 13 (see page 125 onwards)

Stereotypes abound in the media. For example, Hodges *et al.* (1981) found that men on television are more likely to be shown as being in control, whereas women are more at the mercy of others. Meehan (1983) found that 'good' women are portrayed as submissive, sensitive and domesticated, whereas 'bad' women are independent and rebellious. Women are generally characterised as being younger than men (Elasmar *et al.*, 1999).

The media (especially television) is linked to sex stereotyping behaviour in children. For example, Williams (1985) found that the children's sex role attitudes became more traditional and sex-stereotyped after two years of exposure to television in a town called 'Notel', which previously had no television. McGhee and Frueh (1980) found that children who watched more television had more stereotypical gender role expectations.

Television is not the only source of media influence. Books also create and reinforce stereotypes. Crabb and Bielawski (1994) found that gender stereotypes in books had been changing in a review of children's books between 1938 and 1989.

Two theories have been used to explain media effects:

- **Social learning theory** – children model the stereotypes presented on television.
- **Cultivation theory** – the more time spent watching television, the more the individual's picture of the world will reflect what they see on television.

### Evaluation

- Some research **overestimates the influence of the media** on gender development. Children under the age of 4 are probably not very affected by the media, yet that is an important time for gender development. Television probably has most influence during adolescence, but the effects may just be to reinforce existing stereotypes, rather than to create them.
- The media can be used to **change gender stereotypes**. Pingree (1978) found that gender stereotyping was reduced when children were shown advertisements with women in non-stereotypical roles. Similarly, Johnston and Ettema (1982) found that children modelled non-traditional behaviours on a television series called *Freestyle*, and such changes were noticeable nine months later.
- There has been a **reduction in gender stereotypes** on television (Signorelli, 2001) thus, reducing the effects that the media has on children's stereotypes. For example, women are portrayed in a less negative way on television. They are more often employed outside the home and their jobs are more prestigious. In the 1970s, women were more often seen in traditional female occupations (nursing, teaching, etc). However, the reverse trend has been slower (men portrayed in traditional female jobs/activities).

## Cross-cultural studies of gender role

AQA A ▸ U3

The influence of social factors can be seen when making cross-cultural comparisons. The existence of cultural differences in gender roles supports the view that social factors are important, whereas the existence of cultural similarities emphasises the role of innate, biological factors.

### Cultural differences

Margaret Mead (1935) conducted a classic cross-cultural study of gender differences in Papua New Guinea (an island in the south Pacific). She studied three primitive societies:

- **Arapesh** – the men and women were peaceful in temperament.
- **Mundugumor** – both the men and women were war-like in temperament.
- **Tchambuli** – the men spent their time decorating themselves while the women worked and were the practical ones, the opposite of traditional Western cultures.

Mead concluded that gender roles were culturally determined (**cultural determinism**). However, later (1949), she supported cultural relativism – the view that some behaviours are innate and universal. In all three societies, all the men were more aggressive in comparison with the women, though both sexes of the Arapesh were not aggressive and both sexes of Mundugumor were aggressive.

More recent studies support the existence of cultural differences. For example, Sugihara and Katsurada (2002) found differences between traits considered desirable in Japan and America; Japanese men do not seek to be 'macho' types like Americans but instead value being well-rounded in the arts.

### Cultural similarities

Williams and Best (1990) explored gender stereotypes in 27 different national cultures, finding many similarities across cultures. Participants were given a list of 300 psychological characteristics and asked to identify which were more frequently associated with men or women. There was a broad consensus across countries about the different characteristics common in each gender. Men were seen as more dominant, aggressive and autonomous, whereas women were more nurturant, deferent and interested in affiliation. This suggests that there are universal gender stereotypes about male–female roles.

Interestingly, Williams and Best also asked children to rate the characteristics and found the same patterns as in adults, which seems to support a biological source to the perceived differences in gender stereotypes.

Williams and Best also investigated expectations about gender roles in 14 countries using the sex role ideology (SRI) scale. In 12 of the countries, men expressed more traditional views about how women should behave, whereas women were more egalitarian (e.g. they thought men and women should share household duties).

A **collectivist** society is one where individuals share tasks and belongings and value interdependence, unlike **individualist** societies, which emphasise individuality, individual needs and independence.

### Evaluation

- Mead's early conclusions about **cultural relativism** seem to be supported.
- Williams and Best (1992) found that **consensus about stereotypes** was strongest in collectivist societies and weaker in individualist societies, where gender equality is more influential.
- In recent years there has been a **reduction in the differences** between male and female gender roles, which suggests that social influences may override biological predispositions. People have become more flexible in how different roles are allocated in a society.

## Practice essays 6.3

(a) Describe social influences on gender role.                    *(9 marks)*

(b) To what extent can gender development be explained in terms of social factors?                    *(16 marks)*

# Chapter 7

# Intelligence and learning

## 7.1 Theories of intelligence

**After studying this topic you should be able to describe and evaluate:**

- *theories of intelligence, including psychometric, information processing, Gardner's theory of multiple intelligences and learning approaches.*

**LEARNING SUMMARY**

### Theories of intelligence

AQA A    U3

**Intelligence** refers to mental abilities, such as the ability to reason, to solve problems, to think abstractly, to learn, etc. Intelligence is also an adaptive trait, particularly among our ancestors, because individuals who are more intelligent are more likely to survive and reproduce.

The term **psychometric** refers to techniques that measure some aspect of human behaviour, such as personality tests or intelligence tests.

**Factor analysis** is a statistical technique used to identify the variables that explain correlations between scores on tests of different abilities. Imagine that you give various mental tests to a large group of people. You then correlate the scores of each test with the scores of every other test in turn, producing a **correlation coefficient** for each pair of tests. If there is a strong correlation between any two tests this suggests that they share a common variable or factor.

### 1. The psychometric approach

One approach to explaining intelligence is to identify the factors that underlie successful performance on IQ tests, using a method called **factor analysis**.

**Spearman's two-factor theory** – Spearman (1904) found that children's scores on different mental tests were positively correlated and concluded that there was one general mental ability (the *g* **factor**) which underlies performance on lots of different mental tasks. He suggested that there are also specific factors (*s* **factors**). The differences between individuals is largely due to the g factor but s factors explain why a person does not do equally well on all tasks.

**Thurstone's primary mental abilities (PMAs)** – Thurstone (1938) also did a factor analysis of performance on IQ tests but found no single factor; he identified seven distinct primary mental abilities: spatial ability, perceptual speed, numerical reasoning, verbal meaning, word fluency, memory, and inductive reasoning (generating rules from a set of observations). Thurstone regarded g as an average of these PMAs. The PMAs are independent and are not correlated, so g will vary depending on which mental tests are used and which PMAs they tap.

**Vernon's hierarchical model** – Vernon (1950) proposed that g is what all tests measure. **Major group factors** are what some tests measure, **minor group factors** are what particular tests measure, and **specific factors** are what particular tests measure on specific occasions. This reconciles the Spearman and Thurstone models.

**Cattell's fluid and crystallised intelligence** – Cattell (1963) again used factor analysis and concluded that g could be divided into **fluid intelligence (gf)** and **crystallised intelligence (gc)**. Fluid intelligence is basically abstract reasoning and is innate (for example, selecting problem-solving strategies appropriate to the problem). **Crystallised intelligence (gc)** encompasses knowledge that comes from experience (for example, vocabulary).

#### Evaluation

- Factor analysis produces **objective statistical facts**.
- However, the factors that are identified are just **arbitrary categories** and different methods produce different factors (as shown above). Therefore, it is in fact a **subjective approach**.
- Many of the theories are based on **rather restricted samples**. For example, Spearman and Vernon used mainly schoolchildren. It is unlikely that crystallised intelligence would have been found in such samples.
- Recent evidence from Duncan *et al.* (2000) supports the existence of g. **PET scans** assessed the mental activity of participants while they completed three types of general intelligence test (spatial, verbal, and perceptual-motor). They showed that, despite the diverse tests, one region (the lateral prefrontal cortex) was missing when participants were engaged on high g tasks, but not the control tasks.

The information-processing approach is based on computer analogies – input, output, storage, programmes, routines and so on. Information-processing theories assume that one person is more intelligent than another because they can process information more efficiently.

### Key points from AS

- Working memory is discussed in *Revise AS Unit 2.1, page 30*

Sternberg's view is that there are three subtheories that explain an individual's intelligence. Traditional theories overlook the key interaction between the three subtheories or components: intelligence (analytic skills), context (practical skills) and experience (creativity).

## 2. The information processing approach

**Case's information-processing theory** – Robbie Case (1992) suggested that information-processing ability is related to the use of **mental space** (M space). M space is a concept rather similar to 'working memory'. There is a limit to the amount of information that can be held in M space at any one time, but processing efficiency increases with age because:

- **The brain matures** – Changes in the myelin sheath (a fatty protective layer around the nerves, which increases) leads to faster neural transmission rates.
- **Cognitive strategies develop** – As children get older the amount of M space needed for well-practised mental tasks is reduced, thus increasing the amount of available space.
- **Metacognitive skills** (thinking about thinking) – Important for efficient use of M space, for example, being aware of which words you don't understand when reading something, monitoring your own progress on a mental task, etc.

**Sternberg's triarchic theory** – Robert Sternberg (1988) incorporated information-processing into a broader theory of intelligence. He felt that intelligence consists of three aspects, rather than the traditional view that it is concerned just with analytic skills.

- **Componential** (analytical) subtheory – the individual's internal world. Intelligence comprises reasoning ability and metacognitive processes that control the strategies and tactics used in intelligent behaviour.
- **Contextual** (practical) subtheory – the individual's external world. To be intelligent you have to be able to apply your skills in everyday life and adapt to changing conditions – in work, relationships, etc. It is a kind of streetwise knowledge, such as knowing how to manipulate others for their own good, or working out the quickest way to get from A to B using public transport.
- **Experiential** (creative) subtheory – an individual's past experiences link the internal and external world. Intelligence is being able to produce new ideas from previously unrelated information based on past experience, i.e. being creative.

According to Sternberg, a complete explanation of intelligence must entail all of these three subtheories. Conventional notions of intelligence miss this important interaction between components, context and experience.

### Evaluation

- A strength of the information-processing approach is that it is concerned with **how people actually solve complex problems**, whereas the psychometric approach provides a **description** of the human intellect.
- Information processing theory also goes beyond psychometric theories and identifies a **wider range of skills** that contribute to intelligence.
- Case's theory **lends itself to research investigation**, which is a strength. For example, Chi (1978) tested M space by comparing the ability of children who were chess experts with adults who had no chess experience. The task was their ability to remember chess board positions. The children could recall more, presumably because they had developed relevant strategies through experience.
- Case's theory **can be used to measure intelligence** by assessing the capacity of M space.
- Both theories can be **applied to education**, for example, by training students in metacognitive skills.
- Information processing theories link theories of intelligence (in the domain of individual differences in psychology) with the **domain of cognitive psychology** (see Piaget's theory of cognitive development, page 81).

## 3. Gardner's theory of multiple intelligences (MI theory or MIT)

Howard Gardner (1983, 1995) also regarded the traditional view of intelligence as too limited. He suggested that just because a person is not good at maths it doesn't mean that person has low overall intelligence. According to MIT, each person has a unique 'cognitive profile' based on eight different intelligences:

- **Linguistic** – Communicating well (e.g. poet, orator).
- **Logical-mathematical** – Handling logical arguments (e.g. scientist).
- **Spatial** – Able to sense your position in relation to other things (e.g. sailor, sculptor, surgeon).
- **Bodily-kinesthetic** – Using your body well (e.g. dancer, athlete, surgeon).
- **Musical** – Performing and composing music (e.g. musician, composer).
- **Interpersonal** – Sensing other people's feelings (e.g. sales person, teacher, politician).
- **Intrapersonal** – Self-awareness (e.g. therapist).
- **Naturalistic** – Recognising patterns in nature (e.g. biologist, naturalist).

> **Key points from AS**
>
> - Autism is discussed in *Revise AS Unit 7.3, page 166.*

Gardner drew up this list after extensive research involving case studies of unusual people, such as child prodigies or autistic savants. Steven Wilshire is an example of an autistic savant, a young man who has an exceptional artistic ability and photographic memory but has profound social and learning disabilities (autism). Evidence also comes from studies of people with brain damage who continue to function normally in some areas of mental activity, but not others. Studies of the brain also provide evidence for **localisation** of function in the brain – particular abilities (or intelligences) are associated with specific areas of the brain. Finally, Gardner based his theory on the evolutionary relevance of certain capacities and data from subtests on intelligence tests.

> **Key points from AS**
>
> - There is a discussion of brain localisation in *Revise AS Unit 5.3, page 112.* For example, language centres are normally located in the frontal and temporal cortex on the left side of the brain, whereas the motor centre is in the frontal lobe.

Gardner has considered other intelligences. **Spiritual** and **moral intelligences** were excluded because the evidence (from sources listed above) does not suggest that they are separate entities. **Existential intelligence** (the ability to think philosophically) meets most of the criteria, except it is not linked to any specific region of the brain.

### Evaluation

> An empirical approach is one where data has been collected through direct observation or experience.

- Many psychologists attack the theory because they say it is based on **intuition more than empirical data**. A recent review (Waterhouse, 2006) concluded that there was little hard evidence for the theory; it is a line of rational argument rather than a science.
- A second key criticism is that the term 'intelligences' is misleading. For example, Eysenck (1994) claims that Gardner is talking about nothing more than **talents and abilities**. However, Gardner's response is that if spatial or musical ability must be called a 'talent', then language and logic must be called merely a talent as well.
- The approach is actually rather similar to **Thurstone's and Vernon's** multifactor models (see page 68).
- It is a **popular approach with some educators**. Schools traditionally emphasise logical and linguistic intelligence, which means that students who have other talents/intelligences are not valued and Gardner's approach challenges this. The educational value is supported by research, for example, Kornhaber (2004) looked at 41 American schools that based their curriculum on MIT and concluded that it led to high quality work.

The **learning approach** is related to the **behaviourist approach**, which is concerned with observable behaviour rather than anything that might be going on inside a person's mind.

## 4. The learning approach

Intelligence can be defined as the capacity of an organism to learn to adjust successfully to novel or difficult situations, and to solve new problems drawing on past experience, i.e. it is the capacity to learn. This approach is not concerned with how we think, but instead concerned with measurable outcomes – what a person has learned.

The learning approach applies to human and non-human intelligence. Psychologists are interested in how one individual differs from another in terms of intelligence, but are also interested in how one species differs from another in terms of intelligence. For example, Warden (1951) tested animal intelligence using plates. First, the animal learns that if it steps on a plate it will be rewarded (a cage door opens and the animal can get food). Next, a second plate is introduced and the animal must now learn to step on the two plates in the correct sequence in order to get the reward, then a third plate is added and the animal must learn to step on all three in a given order, and so on. The limit reached is a kind of intelligence score – for guinea pigs it's one plate, for rats it's two plates, for cats seven plates, and for some monkeys 22 plates.

The learning approach to intelligence has similarities with the experiential aspects of Sternberg's theory (previous page), which was concerned with a person's ability to solve new problems based on past experience, i.e. to learn.

Another widely used test of animal (and human) intelligence involves **discrimination**. For example, you show the animal three objects, of which two are the same. Food is hidden under the different object and the animal is expected to be able to learn the principle of identifying the odd one out in order to get the reward. Monkeys learn this quickly but rats don't, suggesting that rats have 'low intelligence'.

It is important to distinguish between simple reflex learning (as in classical conditioning) and higher order learning, where complex links have to be acquired (as in Warden's study). The latter is related to intelligence.

However, when testing animal intelligence, it is important to test them under the right circumstances. In the case of the rats mentioned above, further research showed that they were not as dim as it seemed. Langworthy and Jennings (1972) had the bright idea to test rats using objects that smelled (two smelled the same and one was different). The rats then coped well because they have a well-developed sense of smell but a less well-developed visual ability (see also instinctive drift, page 74).

Animal learning often involves **trial and error**, whereas primates and humans display **insight learning** – a more intelligent approach. Köhler (1925) gave a classic demonstration of insight learning with a chimpanzee called Sultan. Sultan was in a cage and a banana was placed outside the cage, just out of reach. Inside the cage were a stick and some boxes. Sultan first tried to reach the fruit with his hand. He sat down and gazed around. Suddenly he grabbed the stick and got the fruit. Sultan had solved the problem without any reinforcement, though he may have been applying his experience from previous situations and, therefore, demonstrating intelligence.

### Evaluation

- The learning approach **contrasts with all other theories**, in focusing on behaviour rather than mental activity. This is also a limitation because mental states are an important part of intelligent behaviour.
- On the positive side, it enables the focus to be on observable behaviour and thus provides a useful means of **measuring intelligent behaviour**.

## Practice essays 7.1

(a) Describe **one or more** information processing theories of intelligence.

*(9 marks)*

(b) Evaluate **one** of the theories you described in part (a).     *(16 marks)*

# 7.2 Animal learning and intelligence

*After studying this topic you should be able to describe and evaluate:*

- *the nature of simple learning (classical and operant conditioning) and its role in the behaviour of non-human animals*
- *evidence for intelligence in non-human animals, for example, self-recognition, social learning, Machiavellian intelligence.*

**LEARNING SUMMARY**

## The nature of simple learning

AQA A     U3

Classical and operant conditioning are the basics of learning theory or the **behaviourist** approach. Social learning theory was a later development (sometimes called neo-behaviourism), which added cognitive and social factors.

Pavlov was the first to demonstrate classical conditioning, producing a salivation response in dogs to the sound of a bell.

Guthrie (1935) suggested that, in fact, all learning takes place on a single trial. The reason it appears to take more trials is because a large number of simple components are being acquired.

### Classical conditioning

Classical conditioning involves learning to **associate** a stimulus with a response. Before conditioning takes place an organism has an innate link between a stimulus and reflex response, such as the smell of food leading you to salivate, or a puff of air to the eye causing you to blink. Classical conditioning involves acquiring (learning) an association between a **neutral stimulus (NS)** and the **unconditioned stimulus (UCS)**, so that the neutral stimulus will produce the **unconditioned response (UCR)**. The NS is now called a **conditioned stimulus (CS)** and the UCR is now the **conditioned response (CR)**.

| food | response | salivation | bell | response | no salivation | bell + food | response | salivation | bell | response | salivation |

| Unconditioned stimulus | Unconditioned response | Neutral stimulus | No conditioned response | | Unconditioned response | Conditioned stimulus | Conditioned response |

- **One-trial learning** – Usually the NS and UCR have to be paired more than once for learning to take place, but under some conditions one trial is sufficient. For example, one fearful incident in childhood may lead to a lifelong fear of dogs.
- **First-order conditioning** – Initially, conditioning acts on reflex responses.
- **Higher-order conditioning** – The CS from the original (first-order) conditioning series is used as the UCS in a new series. For example, a bell might be the first CS, which can then be associated with a time of day.

### Operant conditioning

Operant conditioning is learning a behaviour because of its **consequences**.

Skinner (1938) placed a pigeon in a 'Skinner box'. If it pecked a lever, a door would open and food (a **reinforcer**) was delivered. The pigeon first pecked randomly around the box as part of its natural exploratory behaviour. Accidentally, it pecked the lever (stimulus) and received food (response). Each time it does this the S–R link is strengthened or 'stamped in' and also any unrewarded behaviour is 'stamped out' (i.e. when pecking elsewhere no food appears). So, behaviour has been brought under stimulus control.

If the pigeon learns to peck at a button whenever it is lit, in order to get food, it is learning to discriminate between different states of illumination of the button (a discriminative stimulus).

Skinner described operant conditioning in terms of ABC: **A**ntecedents (the situation beforehand); **B**ehaviour (what the pigeon does); and **C**onsequences (the probability of a behaviour being repeated depends on strengthening or weakening S–R links).

**1. Positive reinforcement** (receiving something pleasant) increases the probability of a response recurring because the response is pleasurable. For example, receiving a smile when you give someone a kiss.

**2. Negative reinforcement** (escape from an unpleasant stimulus) is pleasurable and increases the probability of the same response in the future. For example, finding that a smile stops your mother shouting at you.

**3. Positive punishment** (punishment by application), receiving something unpleasant, decreases the probability of a future behaviour. For example, being told off for smiling at an inappropriate moment.

**4. Negative punishment** (punishment by removal), removing something desirable, also decreases the probability of future behaviour. For example, not being allowed a dessert because you didn't finish your main course.

Any **reinforcer** results in a pleasurable state of affairs and *increases* the likelihood that the behaviour will be repeated. This applies to positive *and* negative reinforcement. Any **punisher** *decreases* the likelihood that the behaviour will be repeated.

Some people argue that classical and operant conditioning are actually the same thing. In the classical conditioning experiment is food a UCS or a reward? The bell is a signal that the food is coming; salivating is an anticipatory response to food. If the bell comes immediately after the food it should still result in conditioning (backward conditioning) but such conditioning is rare, which suggests that the food is a reward and this paradigm is operant conditioning.

## Features of conditioning

- **Generalisation** – Animals respond in the same way to stimuli that are similar.
- **Extinction** – The new response disappears because it is no longer paired or reinforced.
- **Shaping** – Animals gradually learn target behaviour by being reinforced for behaviours that are closer and closer to the target.
- **Reinforcement schedules** – Partial reinforcement schedules are more effective than continuous reinforcement, and are more resistant to extinction.

### Evaluation

- It is a very **reductionist and determinist explanation** of behaviour – behaviour is determined by the environment and cannot be controlled by free will. The use of behaviourist principles to determine the behaviour of others (as in some prisons and psychiatric institutions) could be considered **unethical**. Both Watson and Skinner (see his book 'Walden Two') had a desire to use their principles to produce a better society.
- Behaviourism ignores influences on behaviour such as **emotion**. It also ignores **cognitive factors** and cannot explain behaviours such as the use of cognitive maps (mental representations of the environment used, for example, in navigation).
- Learning theory also cannot explain **innate influences**. For example, Seligman (1970) suggested that a species is biologically predisposed to acquire certain conditioned responses more easily than others (see next page for more details).
- Skinner believed in **equipotentiality** – that any response could be conditioned in any stimulus situation. However, Breland and Breland (1961) showed that learning is constrained by innate capabilities (see next page for details).

**Key points from AS**

- For more evaluations of the behaviourist approach, see *Revise AS Unit 1.1, pages 15 and 16*.

## The role of learning in the behaviour of non-human animals

AQA A ▸ U3

On the previous two pages we looked at how classical and operant conditioning can be used to explain the behaviour of non-human animals. On this page the focus is on applying these principles to learning in the natural environment.

**Biological preparedness** is considered again on page 113 and taste aversion is discussed on page 51.

Avoidance behaviour also involves operant conditioning as outlined by Mowrer (see page 114).

The BBC reported that the RSPCA has recently started playing CDs of birdsong to birds in their care before releasing them back into the wild so they can sing the right songs. Birds reared in captivity don't learn to sing the right songs.

Conditioning is in itself an innate characteristic. All animals are 'hardwired' to be conditioned by experience, i.e. to learn to respond to their environment. Being conditionable is an adaptive behaviour, i.e. being able to respond to the particulars of your environment.

### Classical conditioning in the natural environment

It is likely that animals learn fears through classical conditioning, and even one-trial learning. For example, Garcia and Koelling (1966) demonstrated that rats soon learned to avoid a sweet-tasting liquid when it was accompanied by an injection of a substance that made them ill. In this case, the UCS–UCR is the injection that produces nausea, the NS is the sweet-tasting liquid that has become associated with the UCS and, thus, becomes a CS producing the CR of nausea.

Seligman's concept of **biological preparedness** suggests that some animals have an innate tendency to acquire certain conditioned responses more easily than others because they are adaptive. In this case it would be adaptive to learn to avoid anything linked to nausea. When Garcia and Koelling paired the injection with an electric shock the rats did not acquire an aversion to the sweet liquid – presumably because there is not an innate tendency to avoid things linked to electric shocks.

### Operant conditioning in the natural environment

Trial and error learning is an example of operant conditioning. Errors act as punishers and decrease the likelihood of a response being repeated. Gradually, an animal learns to produce the appropriate response. For example, a predator learns which prey are easiest to catch through trial and error (reward and punishment).

Animals cannot be conditioned to acquire just any response. This was demonstrated by Breland and Breland (1961) who tried to train a pig to insert a wooden token into a piggy bank for a reward. But the pigs handled the token like any object – tossing it up and rooting with it. What animals learn tends to resemble their instinctive behaviour (**instinctive drift**).

### Social learning in the natural environment

Bird species vary in the extent to which their song development is innate. Some birds have almost no facility for learning and the full adult song is present even in birds raised in isolation, for example, the Alder Flycatcher. However, most birds need to hear the adult song to develop their innate version, therefore, they are learning through imitation.

Slater (1981) showed that chaffinches produce only a very basic song repertoire if they are hand-reared, and are strongly inclined to copy the song of any bird they hear. Some birds have a highly developed ability to learn by imitation, for example, parrots and mynah birds can imitate sounds produced by other species.

Social learning involves **mentalistic processes** and is, therefore, also included as evidence of intelligence (see next page).

#### Evaluation

- The lower you go down on the phylogenetic scale, the less an animal's behaviour is affected by learning. There is an **important trade off** – instinctive responses mean that an animal can deal with its environment reasonably well because an adaptive behavioural repertoire has evolved to fit its environmental needs. Instinctive behaviours ensure a quick response, rather than one that has to be learned through trial and error. However, instinctive repertoires are also fixed and mean that an animal cannot respond to changing conditions. The ability to modify behaviour in the light of unpredictable environmental changes is a sign of intelligence, and gives such animals a selective advantage, but at some cost.

## Evidence for intelligence in non-human animals

AQA A ▶ U3

Mentalistic abilities are those that involve some form of mental activity or 'intelligence'. Conditioning is a non-mentalistic ability.

Lewis and Brooks-Gunn (1977) used the mirror test to demonstrate that infants of a certain age had developed a self-concept (see page 90).

In order to imitate a behaviour, the animal who is observing must understand that the particular behaviour is linked to the particular outcome. This requires some form of intelligence.

A 'tutor' probably needs to have some idea of what the learner is thinking, which involves a theory of mind. Deception also requires a theory of mind – a concept which is discussed on page 91. It is not a formal psychological theory (like Bowlby's theory or Piaget's theory), but a collection of ideas that an individual has when trying to understand what is going on in another animal's mind.

Theory of mind is likely to be favoured by natural selection, insofar as it promotes social relationships.

### Self-recognition

If a person can recognise him/herself, this implies the possession of a self-concept, which is a **mentalistic state**. Gallup (1971) used the mirror test to demonstrate self-recognition. A red mark is placed on an animal's forehead (when anaesthetised). Comparison is then made between how often the animal touches this mark without and with a mirror. Gallup (1977) found that chimpanzees and orangutans are capable of self-recognition, but other primates and non-primate animals are not.

However, Epstein *et al.* (1981) found that pigeons can learn to use a mirror to help them remove bits of paper stuck to their feathers. This suggests that they have self-recognition and leads us to question whether the mirror-test really does demonstrate mentalistic abilities because pigeons are not generally regarded as being 'thinking animals'.

### Social learning

Kawai (1965) observed Japanese snow monkeys on a small island. Sweet potatoes were left on the beach for the monkeys, one of whom (Imo) 'invented' the idea of washing the sand off the potatoes in the sea. Soon, other monkeys imitated her, thus evolving a new kind of behaviour, which was passed to subsequent generations. Imo also invented a way of washing wheat. However, Nagell *et al.* (1993) suggested that the behaviour in Kawai's study could be explained in terms of **stimulus enhancement** (non-mentalistic behaviour), rather than imitation. When the other monkeys observed Imo washing potatoes this simply drew their attention to both the potatoes and the water, and enhanced their ability to solve the same problem.

Imitation is a passive process where the individual animals don't deliberately perform an action so it can be imitated. **Tutoring** is an active process where the tutor modifies its behaviour to accommodate the needs of the learner. Boesch (1991) observed tutoring in chimpanzees. Mothers sometimes intervened when offspring were having difficulties cracking open nuts. The offspring were imitating what they had seen but not getting it right. The mother might leave a 'hammer' nearby (stimulus enhancement) or might place the nut in a better position (tutoring).

### Machiavellian intelligence

Machiavellian intelligence refers to the ability to intentionally deceive another individual. In order to intentionally deceive another individual, you have to have an understanding of what they know, or don't know.

Whiten and Byrne (1991) compiled a record of 250 naturalistic examples of deception, such as a vervet monkey making a fake alarm call.

Experimental evidence was produced by Premack and Woodruff (1979) who arranged for a chimpanzee to see a trainer place food under one of two containers that were out of reach. A second trainer entered the room in a green coat (the chimpanzee was trained to know that he was co-operative) or a white coat (known to be competitive). On most trials, they manipulated both trainers to obtain food – they helped the cooperative trainer and deceived the competitive one. The chimpanzee knew that the competitive trainer would act on their false information, which is evidence of Machiavellian intelligence.

## Practice essay 7.2

Discuss the nature of simple learning (classical and operant conditioning) and its role in the behaviour of non-human animals.                   *(25 marks)*

# 7.3 Evolution of intelligence

*After studying this topic you should be able to describe and evaluate:*

- *evolutionary factors in the development of human intelligence, for example, ecological demands, social complexity, brain size*
- *the role of genetic and environmental factors associated with intelligence test performance, including the influence of culture.*

**LEARNING SUMMARY**

## Evolutionary factors in the development of human intelligence

AQA A ▶ U3

> **Intelligence** is the ability to deal effectively and adaptively with the environment. An animal that can respond more effectively to environmental challenges will be more likely to survive and reproduce.

### Ecological demands

The ecological approach suggests that aspects of an animal's environment (ecology) demand intelligent behaviour. In particular, being a good forager (obtaining food) requires intelligence, therefore, intelligence would have increased survival and been naturally selected. Hunting and finding food requires memory, planning, co-ordination and tool use, which all involve considerable intelligence. A good forager is more likely to be chosen as a mate, thus enhancing reproduction of such genes.

> Foraging is an ecological (environmental) demand.

Dunbar (1992) suggested that the evolution of human intelligence can be explained in terms of the change from a leaf-eating diet to fruit-eating. Leaf-eaters (**foliovores**) have a small home range and less difficulty managing their food source, whereas modern humans became fruit-eaters (**frugivores**) and had to remember the location of their food supply, evaluate the ripeness of fruits, develop a harvesting plan and so on. Individuals who were more successful were naturally selected.

### Social complexity

Animals live in groups because there are advantages (e.g. for foraging, reproduction and predation), but group living also presents problems (e.g. conflicts, inter-relationships between group members, managing cooperation). An individual who can solve social problems is more likely to survive and reproduce.

One particular facet of sociality is the ability to understand the intentions of others (**theory of mind**) and the ability to cheat (**Machiavellian intelligence**) and detect cheats. Both are evidence of intelligence (see previous page).

Another outcome of sociality is communication between species' members in order to coordinate social activity. Humans are the only species to have developed language, which is probably the outcome of intelligence rather than cause of it. However, once language evolved, it then had a significant effect on the further development of intelligence. Vygotsky (see page 82) proposed that it is language that transforms elementary mental functions (possessed by all animals, such as attention) into higher mental functions.

### Evaluation

> The **Wason four card selection task** requires a participant to decide which of four cards needs to be turned over in order to prove a logical statement right or wrong (such as 'If a card has a vowel on one side, then it has an even number on the other side.'). The cards have the letters/numbers A, D, 4 and 7 on them.

- Cosmides (1989) showed that participants, when doing the **Wason four card selection task**, cope better with a concrete example that involves social relations rather than an abstract version because our intelligence is adapted to cope with such problems.
- Dunbar (1993) found no relationship between the size of the **neocortex** (part of the brain involved in higher order thinking) and environmental complexity in a range of different primates, but did find a **strong correlation between size of neocortex and group size**, as an indication of the complexity of social relationships. This supports the social complexity explanation for the evolution of human intelligence.

## Brain size

Large brains have evolved:

(1) in bigger animals to coordinate bigger bodies

(2) to cope with the demands for greater intelligence (such as social complexity).

Having a large brain incurs a cost because it requires more energy and makes birth more difficult. Therefore, it is likely that there is some adaptive advantage to a proportionately bigger brain.

**Comparative studies** of different species support the role of brain size in intelligence. Rumbaugh *et al.* (1996) *tested primate intelligence by training them* on two tasks: if one set of learning facilitated the second task then this was taken as evidence of intelligence. They found that primates with proportionally larger brains did best. However, poorer performance may be because an animal is asked to perform a task that comes less naturally to them (consider instinctive drift, page 74), rather than because they are less intelligent.

When conducting comparative studies it is necessary to take account of body size. Jerison (1978) developed the **encephalisation quotient** (EQ), where the actual brain mass of a species is divided by its 'expected' brain size for that body size. Using this scale, humans have the highest EQ (7) of any animal. Other primates score around 2.34 and dolphins score 4.5.

**Human studies** indicate a small but significant correlation between brain size and intelligence. Early studies found no correlation between brain size and intelligence but that may be because they couldn't measure brain size accurately (they used skull size). Willerman *et al.* (1991) used brain scans and correlated IQ scores of college students with brain size, finding a positive correlation of 0.51 between IQ and brain : body ratio. A further study by Andreasen *et al.* (1993) used a more representative sample (advertising through a newspaper) and found a lower but significant correlation.

**Sexual selection** – Miller (1992) argues that the rapid change in human brain size (trebling in the last three million years) can be best explained in terms of sexual selection because it directly selects for reproductive success. Intelligence is a runaway sexy trait. The cost of a large brain is outweighed by its selective advantage. This view explains why people list intelligence as one of the most important characteristics in a prospective partner. It also explains why men have larger brains relative to body weight.

## Evaluation

- Some research suggests that relative brain size **may not be related to intelligence**. The spiny anteater has a comparatively larger neocortex (taking body size into account) than a human, yet it does not have a greater intelligence.
- Research also shows that the **relationship between brain size and IQ is not a simple one**. For example, Sassaman and Zartler (1982) studied nearly 200 children with microcephaly (an abnormally small brain). About 40% were not retarded and 7% were of average IQ. Skoyles (1999) suggests that the problem may be that IQ tests measure a particular aspect of intelligent behaviour. He believes that **'expertise'** is not important in IQ tests but this would have had an adaptive advantage and may be the factor that is related to increased brain size.
- **Organisation** may be more important than size. Albert Einstein's brain, when examined at postmortem, showed no size advantage but there were some differences in terms of organisation, such as more tightly packed neurons in his prefrontal cortex. Holloway (1979) claims internal structural complexity is more important in the evolution of intelligence.

Sexual selection is explained on page 34 and runaway process is explained on page 35.

Miller (1998) points out that this theory can explain why men have historically been more creative in the arts, because this allows them to demonstrate their intelligence.

It is impossible to know whether such brain organisation is a cause or an effect of intelligence. Human brains are more highly organised than the brains of other animals.

## Intelligence test performance

 AQA A ▶ U3

This section looks at intelligence test performance (i.e. IQ tests) rather than intelligence. This is because psychologists can only investigate the relationship between intelligence and other factors by operationalising intelligence, i.e. using IQ tests.

Monozygotic (MZ) twins share the same genes, whereas dizygotic (DZ) twins share 50% of the same genes. If MZ twins have more similar IQs this suggests that IQ is inherited.

A **gene** is a unit of inheritance. Studies of genetics aim to show that IQ is inherited.

It is probably best to think of genetic factors as a '**reaction range**'. They provide a potential which is very much dependent on environmental influences as to whether it is maximised or minimised. This is similar to the concept of diathesis-stress described on page 54 (genetic vulnerability related to life experiences determine an individual's behaviour).

### The role of genetic factors

**1. Twin studies** – Research shows that MZ twins (genetically identical) have more similar IQs than DZ twins. For example, Bouchard and McGue (1981) reviewed a number of studies and found an MZ correlation of .85 and a DZ correlation of .58. Even when MZ twins are reared apart (which means IQ similarity can be due to a shared environment) they have very similar IQs. Pedersen *et al.* (1992) reported on the Swedish Adoption/Twin Study of Ageing (SATSA), that MZ twins reared apart or together had IQ correlations of about .79; DZ twins reared apart were .32 and DZ twins reared together were .22. This suggests that about 80% of IQ is inherited.

#### Evaluation

- If intelligence was entirely inherited, the **MZ correlations should be 100%**; the fact that scores are lower shows a significant environmental component.
- The **assumption that MZ twins are identical is wrong.** Allen *et al.* (1976) found constitutional differences based on different birth and intrauterine experiences, and found that these could be related to different parental perceptions and expectations of the twins.

**2. Familial studies** – Bouchard and McGue (1981) surveyed over 100 studies looking at familial correlations of IQ, and found that the closer the genetic link, the higher the correlation between IQs. For example, siblings reared together had a correlation of .45 and adopted siblings had a correlation of .31.

#### Evaluation

- This would seem to support the genetic position, but it could be taken equally as **evidence for environment**.
- Comparisons from one study to another (**meta-analysis**) involve grouping together many different tests which may not be comparable.

**3. Adoption studies** – Skodak and Skeels (1949) followed 100 adopted children and their natural mothers. At age 4 their IQs were correlated by .28. At 13 it had risen to .44, i.e. genetic effects became stronger. Plomin (1988) followed children involved in the Texas Adoption Study, and found that correlations between adoptive parents and their adopted children fell from .15 to .02 at age 10. This again suggests that genetic factors are ultimately more significant.

#### Evaluation

- Adoptions are often made to **similar environments**.
- Adoption studies can also be used to **support the environmental position** (see next page).

**4. Gene mapping studies** – Various studies have identified genes related to IQ test performance. For example, Chorney *et al.* (1998) identified a gene (IGF2R) found in 33% of 'super-bright' children but only 17% of 'average' IQs. Dick *et al.* (2007) found a link between the gene, CHRM2, and performance IQ, which involves a person's ability to organise things logically.

#### Evaluation

- Since intelligence is determined by many genes (polygenic), **an array of genes are involved.** No individual set of genes will create high IQ.
- Gene mapping studies have important **ethical implications**. Such research evidence might be used to classify the potential abilities of individuals, which would overlook the role of environmental factors in determining a person's actual intelligence.

**5. Indirect genetic influences** – The effects discussed so far are direct effects of genes on IQ. Indirect genetic effects occur in several ways. Genetically-determined characteristics create a child's **microenvironment**, which then influences development. For example, a child who has an innately pleasant temperament gets on better with people, and increased social contacts may enhance mental development. Indirect influences also include the fact that genetically more intelligent parents may well create a more stimulating home environment, which increases the IQ of their children.

## The role of environmental factors

**1. Adoption studies** – Scarr and Weinberg (1977) found that, on average, adopted children have IQs that are 10–20 points higher than those of their natural parents.

**Evaluation**

- Adoptive families are generally wealthier and better educated than natural families, which would **cause environmental factors to appear stronger**.
- Early adopted children do better, favouring the idea that **environment is important under suitable circumstances**.

**2. Family influence** – Parent–child interactions affect the development of IQ. Yarrow (1963) found a correlation of .65 between IQ at six months and the amount of time the mother spent in social interaction with her child.

Family influence can also be seen in the fact that birth order is related to IQ, presumably because first born children get more parental attention that children born later. Zajonc and Markus (1975) examined the IQ data of 40,000 Dutch males born in 1944, finding that IQ declines with family size and birth order. In larger families, each child has a smaller share of parental attention, less money and more physical deprivation.

**3. Diet** – IQ scores in Japan have increased by an average of 7.7 points over the last ten years, whereas IQ has only increased by 1.7 points in the US. This can only be explained in terms of improved environmental factors, probably diet (Lynn, 1986). Harrell *et al.* (1955) gave low-income, expectant mothers supplementary diets. When their children were tested at age 3 they had higher IQs than those whose mothers had been given **placebos**.

**4. Enrichment** – **Operation Headstart** (started in 1965) resulted in initial IQ gains, but these turned out to be small and short-lived, and the costs were high. Follow up studies, such as Lazar and Darlington (1982), found that participants were less likely to become pregnant, to need welfare assistance or become delinquent. They were more likely to complete high school, to be employed after high school, and/or to continue in further education. This shows some benefit from the enrichment programme. Ramey *et al.* (1999) reviewed 10 studies that randomly allocated children to treatment and no-treatment groups (improving on the original design where children were not randomly allocated) and concluded that there was firm evidence that Headstart did boost IQ.

**The Milwaukee Project** – Heber *et al.* (1972) worked with newborn infants and their low-social-class black mothers who had IQs below 75. Half the group were 'controls' and received no extra treatment. The mothers in the experimental group were given help with job-related skills, parenting and housekeeping, and their children were involved in a regular day-care programme from the age of 3 months. By the time the children entered school, the experimental group had a mean IQ of 124, whereas the control group's mean IQ was 94. By the age of 10 there was still a 10 point IQ difference.

You can use research on environmental factors to evaluate genetic explanations, and vice versa.

The question of whether genetic or environmental factors contribute most to IQ is one of the best examples of the **nature–nurture debate** (see page 183). It isn't just a theoretical debate but is highly relevant to decisions about who to educate and how.

**Placebos** are substances that have no pharmacological effects but the person taking them thinks they are the real thing. This means you can separate the psychological from the physical effects of being given a drug treatment.

If IQ was genetically fixed then enrichment programmes would not be effective.

Any study that looks at IQ has the potential for being socially sensitive research.

## The influence of culture

Culture refers to the rules, customs, morals and ways of interacting that bind together members of a society or some other collection of people. The concept of culture embraces all aspects of an individual's environment: methods of child-rearing, diet, education, etc.

1. **Culture bias in tests** – Almost all IQ tests have been designed by white, middle-class Westerners, and have been standardised on similar populations. Inevitably, people from other cultures do less well on 'our' IQ tests, although alternative explanations may be offered for their poorer performance (such as race or social class).

2. **Race and IQ** – Jensen (1969) sparked off a controversy when he suggested that black people have innately lower IQs because, on average, they scored 15 points less than white people.

   This finding may be due to test culture bias. This was demonstrated by Dove (1968) who created **Dove Counterbalance General Intelligence Test** to show that if you asked a set of questions that were based on black culture then white people perform poorly.

   Poor test performance by certain racial groups may also be due to lower stimulation, social deprivation, etc.

   Mackintosh (1986) compared white and West Indian children in England. When the groups were unmatched in terms of environmental factors, such as family education, there was a 9 point difference but when matched there was a 2.6 point difference, showing that environmental factors are important.

What is intelligence? People from different cultural backgrounds would define, and assess, it differently.

3. **Social class** – Bernstein (1961) introduced the notion of **restricted language** (code) as opposed to **elaborated code** (a richer form of language). Children from low social classes learn a limited form of language which lacks, for example, abstract concepts and limits their cognitive development and verbal intelligence. Labov (1970) rejected this idea and claimed that Bernstein was confusing social and linguistic deprivation, and had failed to recognise the subtleties of non-standard English.

   Sameroff *et al.* (1987, 1993) conducted the Rochester Longitudinal study, following over 200 children since birth. They found a clear negative (about .60) association between number of risk factors and IQ; risk factors include parental mental health, education, occupation, family support, stressful life events, and family size (all of these are related to social class). They also found that, at age 4, high-risk children were 24 times more likely to have IQs below 85 than low-risk children. When a child is not exposed to risk factors, genetic factors will be important in determining intelligence. When there are risk factors, these will be of more importance than the inherited ones.

4. **Motivation** – Lower class children may have less desire to do well. Zigler *et al.* (1973) found that such children improved their test performance by 10 IQ points if they had a play session with the tester beforehand to increase familiarity and decrease anxiety, whereas middle class children only gained 3 IQ points.

### Evaluation

- It is impossible to conduct definitive research on race because we cannot **define race** nor can we exclude the **effects of deprivation**.
- The concept of 'race' is in itself problematic as it is not true that, for example, whites and blacks form separate biological groups. There is **more genetic variation within** any so-called racial group than **between** racial groups.
- Such research raises important **ethical issues** and is socially sensitive.

## Practice essay 7.3

Discuss evolutionary factors in the development of human intelligence.

*(25 marks)*

# Chapter 8

# Cognition and development

## 8.1 Development of thinking

*After studying this section you should be able to describe and evaluate:*

- *theories of cognitive development, including Piaget, Vygotsky and Bruner*
- *applications of these theories to education.*

LEARNING SUMMARY

## Piaget's theory of cognitive development

AQA A ▸ U3
AQA B ▸ U3

**Cognitive development** is the study of how mental abilities develop.

The term **'schema'** is used in many areas of psychology; it is a cluster of related concepts that represent particular aspects of the world.

**'Equilibration'** means the desire for balance or equilibrium.

An **'operation'** is an internally consistent, logical mental rule, such as the rules of arithmetic.

Piaget's theory is sometimes called an *'ages and stages theory'* because of the concept of stages. However, the structure of the intellect and the way development takes place (through disequilibrium and accommodation) is just as important.

**Horizontal décalage** describes the fact that not all aspects of the same stage appear at the same time, for example, the ability to conserve number and volume. Uneven cognitive performance is probably due to different learning experiences.

Jean Piaget (1896–1980) developed the most influential theory of cognitive development. It has two important assumptions:

- There are **qualitative** differences between child and adult thinking, thus, there is a sequence of distinct stages in development.
- It is a **biological** approach: biological readiness is the prerequisite for change.

### The structure of the intellect

Variant cognitive structures, which develop with age: **schemas** and **operations**.

Invariant cognitive structures: **assimilation** (information taken in) and **accommodation** (schema adjusted). The process is 'driven' by **equilibration**.

### Stages in cognitive development

**Sensorimotor stage** (0–2 years) – Early reflex activities, circular (repetitive) reactions co-ordinate sensory and motor activity.

**Pre-operational stage** (2–7 years) – Development of the use of symbols to represent experience (e.g. language). Thought processes lack adult logic (they are not 'operational'), e.g. egocentric thought and animism (i.e. the belief that inanimate objects have human feelings). This stage is subdivided into the pre-conceptual stage (i.e. when concepts are not fully formed) and the intuitive stage (i.e. when appearance, not reality, is important).

**Concrete operational stage** (7–11 years) – The child has developed adult (internally consistent) logic, but only in concrete situations. Problem solving is random rather than systematic.

**Formal operational stage** (11+ years) – Abstract and systematic thought.

**Research evidence**

**Object permanence** (sensorimotor stage) – The realisation that objects continue to exist even when they cannot be seen. Piaget claimed that this developed after the age of 8 months. Bower (1981) showed that infants aged 5–6 months old showed surprise when an object that had been hidden behind a screen was no longer there. Baillargeon and DeVos (1991) used the rolling car task to show that 3–4 month old infants were aware of object permanence (see page 159).

**Reality-appearance distinction** – Pre-operational children focus on the appearance of things and not the reality (i.e. they lack internal consistency). DeVries (1969) showed children a cat, and then hid the cat's head behind a screen while strapping on a dog's head; 3 year olds thought it was a dog even though they saw the transformation; 6 year olds were able to distinguish appearances from reality.

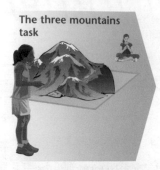

**The three mountains task**

Piaget's methods involved naturalistic observation and semi-structured interviews, using small samples – often his own children. He did spend over 50 years amassing a detailed record of individual behaviour (an **idiographic approach** – see page 185). Piaget also conducted research with Inhelder of a more experimental nature, which did involve large samples of children.

Critics tend to take Piaget's model too rigidly, and supporters suggest it should be viewed as a metaphor. The stages are not fact but a useful structure for understanding behaviour and generating research.

**Class inclusion** – McGarrigle *et al.* (1978) showed that the class-inclusion (centration) questions don't make sense in the pre-operational stage. However, if they asked children, 'Are there more black cows or more sleeping cows?' instead of Piaget's 'Are there more black cows or more cows?' the percentage who answered correctly moved from 25% to 48%.

**Egocentrism** – Piaget and Inhelder (1956) used the **three mountains task** to show that pre-operational children couldn't take the perspective of another – they tended to describe what the doll saw in terms of what they actually saw. However, when Hughes (1975) used a more realistic task with a toy policeman, pre-operational children did better.

**Conservation** (concrete operational stage) is the ability to understand that quantity is not changed even when a display is transformed so it looks bigger. Piaget used counters, beakers and balls of clay to demonstrate that children under 7 cannot conserve. Samuel and Bryant (1983) found that younger children coped better with one question, but there were still age differences. McGarrigle and Donaldson (1974) used 'naughty teddy' to create the transformation and young children did better, though Moore and Frye (1986) suggested that this is because naughty teddy unduly distracted the children.

**Formal operational thinking** – Bryant and Trabasso (1971) showed that difficulty on transitive inference tasks may be due to memory failure rather than lack of ability. Piaget and Inhelder's (1956) beaker problem showed that formal thinkers are systematic. Shayer and Wylam (1978) found that only 30% of 15–16 year olds had achieved formal operational thinking.

### Evaluation

- Piaget's theory was the **first comprehensive account** of cognitive development. It changed the traditional view of the child as **passive**, and stimulated research.
- The evidence largely supports the **stage sequence**, though Piaget's tasks may have confused children and created demand characteristics.
- The influence of **language** and **social and emotional** factors were overlooked.
- If Piaget was right and cognitive development depends on maturation then **practice should not matter**. However, some studies show that practice can improve performance. For example, Hughes (1975) found that 90% of pre-operational children could cope with the three mountains task when their errors were explained to them.
- Piaget suggested that **disequilibrium** would be the driving force in cognitive development. However, conflict does not tell a child how to solve the problem.

## Vygotsky's theory of cognitive development

| AQA A | U3 |
| AQA B | U3 |

Vygotsky was born in pre-Revolutionary Russia but his work was not known to the West until it was published in English in 1962.

An 'expert' is anyone with greater knowledge.

An important way to evaluate any theory is by how it might be applied to everyday life. Page 85 has information about how all three theories of cognitive development can be applied to educational practice.

Lev Semenovich Vygotsky (1896–1934) produced a theory that contrasted with the dominant Russian view (stemming from Pavlov) that learning was a product of passive conditioning. He suggested that cognitive development is the outcome of:

- The **social construction** of knowledge.
- The **social environment** (language and other cultural symbols, and experts).

### The structure of the intellect

**Elementary mental functions** are innate capacities, such as attention and perception, possessed by all animals. These will develop to a limited extent through experience.

Cultural influences transform elementary functions into *higher mental functions*. Culture teaches children what to think and how to think.

'Sociocultural' refers to the social and cultural context in which learning takes place.

## Stages in cognitive development

- **Pre-intellectual, social speech** (0–3 years).
- **Egocentric speech** (3–7 years). Language controls one's own behaviour.
- **Inner speech** (7+). Language serves for thought and social communication. Since social processes shape language, they also shape thought.

The **ZPD** is the distance between a child's current and potential abilities. The aim of instruction is to stimulate those functions that lie waiting in the ZPD.

## The process of sociocultural influence

Cultural influences affect cognitive development in several ways, for example:

1. **The ZPD (zone of proximal development)** – Cultural influences and **experts** guide a child through the ZPD and enable the child to cope with tasks beyond their current abilities. Effective instruction supports the learner using **guided participation** and **scaffolding** (i.e. providing instructions that give hints about what to do next. In time, the learner can 'self-scaffold' (self-regulation).

**Guided participation** is related to scaffolding but emphasises the fact that at all times the learner is an active participant and is merely guided by the expert rather than being led by experts.

2. **Social and individual planes** – Learning starts as a social, shared activity, and shifts to an individual, self-regulated activity.
3. **Semiotics** – Knowledge is transmitted using semiotics (signs and symbols), such as language, and mathematical symbols. Conversations between expert and learner enable development/learning to take place. Language is first used for social and emotional functions (pre-intellectual language). At the same time, thought is conducted without language (pre-linguistic thought).

### Research evidence

**Influence of culture** – Gredler (1992) noted that the counting system in Papua New Guinea (cultural influence) limits cognitive development. They use fingers, arms, etc. to count, which limits their mathematics.

**Scaffolding** – McNaughton and Leyland (1990) observed mothers and their children solving progressively more difficult jigsaw puzzles. Mothers' help changed as the puzzles became harder (they gave progressively more explicit help) and showed their sensitivity to the ZPD. When a puzzle was below the ZPD, the mother just kept the child on the task. When a puzzle was within the ZPD, the mother gave hints.

Vygotsky emphasised how knowledge is acquired through social interaction, whereas Piaget described it as a process of self-discovery.

**ZPD** – McNaughton and Leyland (1990) re-tested the children a week later and identified the highest level of difficulty the children could achieve unaided. This was a measure of their *ability*, whereas the level achieved with their mother was a measure of their *capability*. The difference between the two sessions defined each child's ZPD.

**Self-regulation** – Wertsch *et al.* (1980) measured self-regulation by watching the time a child spent gazing at his/her mother while working on jigsaw puzzles. Less gaze represented more self-regulation. Such gazes decreased with age, suggesting increased self-regulation. In another study children were again observed as they solved puzzles; the more puzzles they did the less they gazed at their mother, showing that regulation was transferred from other to self.

Piaget and Vygotsky need not be seen as opposites. Glassman (1999) argues that in fact the two theories are remarkably similar, especially at their central core. An attempt to integrate the two approaches would be productive.

**Inner speech** – Berk (1994) observed children while they worked at school. Most of their comments either described or served to direct the child's actions, suggesting a self-regulating function. She also found that children talked to themselves more when they were faced with a difficult task, when working by themselves, or when a teacher was not available to help.

### Evaluation

- The theory has less **empirical support** than Piaget's because it is less easy to test.
- It exaggerated the importance of the **social environment**. Motivation is important too and social interaction may actually have negative effects.
- If the help of others was all that was required, the **learning of complex skills should be faster** than it is.
- It may be more relevant to **collectivist societies** because of the emphasis on social learning, whereas Piaget's theory is an individualist approach.

Piaget represents the Western, individualist approach shaped by the European society in which he lived, whereas Vygotsky's views are shaped by the collectivist, communist society in which he lived.

## Bruner's theory of cognitive development

AQA A  U3

Bruner stands somewhere between Piaget and Vygotsky in his views.

This is an **information processing approach**, concentrating on how strategies for organising information change with age. (See information processing approaches to the topic of intelligence on page 69.)

Development involves the mastery of the increasingly more complex modes of thinking – enactive to iconic to symbolic. This involves translating one mode into the next. For example, conducting an experiment (iconic mode) and then discussing the conclusions that can be drawn (symbolic mode).

Jerome S. Bruner (1915) based his theory on a general interest in thinking. He was foremost a cognitive psychologist and this is a major influence on his theory of cognitive development, which was also influenced by Vygotsky's views.

- Thought requires ways of representing the environment, which we do through action, image and word (enactive, iconic, and symbolic modes of thinking).
- Development is due in part to the maturation of biological systems.
- Development is also due in part to language, social frameworks and experience, which shape the development of thought.

### The structure of the intellect

**Categories and hierarchies** – Discovering and learning takes place by organising information into categories. Commonalities across experiences are recognised so that categories are identified. Categories are further organised into **hierarchies** – frameworks with the more general (generic) information at the top.

**Modes of thinking** – Modes of thinking are 'recurrent themes': **enactive** skills (e.g. manipulating objects, spatial awareness), **iconic** skills (visual recognition, the ability to compare and contrast) and **symbolic** skills (abstract reasoning).

**Skill acquisition** – Infants learn physical skills, such as grasping, during the enactive stage. These become automatic and act as modularised units that can be combined in different ways to build up a repertoire of new skilled behaviours and to allow attention to be freed for other things. As children grow older they also develop representational skills.

### Stages in cognitive development

Each mode of thinking is present throughout life, but each mode is dominant during particular developmental phases:

- Early years – The **enactive mode**, learning through one's own actions, such as learning to walk or play a musical instrument.
- Middle childhood – The **iconic mode**, learning to use diagrams and numbers.
- Adolescence – The **symbolic mode**, working with abstract concepts.

#### Research evidence

**Iconic and symbolic mode** – Bruner and Kenney (1966) arranged nine glasses on a 3x3 grid, in order of height and diameter. If the glasses were scrambled, all the children were able to simply replace them (reproduction task). If the left and right glasses in the bottom row were swapped, 5 year olds found it impossible to replace them all in the same manner (transposition task) because this requires use of the symbolic mode.

**Learning strategies** – Mosher (1962) looked at the strategies used by children aged 6 to 12 in the game of twenty questions, to ascertain why a car went off the road. Older children used constraint-locating questions ('was it night-time?) whereas younger children asked direct hypothesis-testing questions ('did a bird hit the window?').

**The role of tutoring** – Bruner followed Vygotsky in suggesting that expert instruction was important in stretching a child's capabilities (see evidence on previous page).

#### Evaluation

Many evaluation points related to Vygotsky's theory can be applied to Bruner's theory as both theories involve the influence of social/cultural factors.

- Bruner's theory is a **more general approach**, i.e. it applies to thinking, as well as cognitive development.
- The theory emphasises both the role of **biology** and of **experience, language and social factors**. Without language, thought is limited.

# Applications of these theories to education

AQA A ▶ U3
AQA B ▶ U3

Each theory of cognitive development has had specific implications for education, as indicated below.

## Piaget's theory

**Readiness** – Offer moderately novel stimuli when the child is ready.

**Self-discovery** and self-motivation lead to complete understanding.

**Individualised** – Children mature at different rates, therefore, learning programmes need to be individualised.

**Discovery learning** – Learning should be child-centred and active. The teacher's role is not to impart knowledge but to ask questions, thus creating disequilibrium and forcing children to make accommodations and, therefore, develop.

**Logic** is not an innate mental process, it is the outcome of cognitive development. It needs to be taught. Logic, maths and science subjects facilitate cognitive development.

**Concrete materials** should be used to teach young children (because they are in the stage of concrete operations).

**Motivation** comes from the desire for equilibration; disequilibrium is caused by cognitive conflict.

### Evaluation

- Piaget never specifically applied his theory to education. Others used it to influence **nursery and primary education** in particular, but also in Nuffield secondary science, which relies on children making their own discoveries.
- Discovery activities require **experienced teachers** who can guide students.
- Discovery learning means **less time for content learning**. Modgil *et al.* (1983) suggested that it may lead to backwardness in reading and writing in children who need more direction.
- Some research suggests that, with **practice**, children can do many things before they are 'ready'. For example, Bryant and Trebasso (1971) successfully trained young children to perform certain logical tasks before they were 'ready'). However, there is also research that shows there are limits, for example, Danner and Day (1977) found that only older adolescents could actually improve with training on abstract tasks; younger adolescents not yet in the abstract stage did not benefit.

> The notion of education includes not just teachers but extends to anyone who is expanding the knowledge and understanding of children, e.g. parents, playleaders and toy manufacturers.

> Piaget's key idea was that, if you tell children something they could have discovered for themselves, then you prevent them from ever completely understanding it because they cannot invent the schema for themselves.

> Walkerdine (1984) has argued that the move to child-centred education was not because of Piaget's theory. Educationalists just used his theories to justify the changes they wished to make. In any case the ideas are not new; the Greek philosopher Plato advocated child-centred education.

## Vygotsky's theory

**Expert intervention** (by peers or adults) is most effective when the expert is aware of the limits of the child's ZPD.

**Scaffolding** – An adult advances children's thinking by providing a framework (scaffolding) on which children can climb. Wood *et al.* (1976) found that when a learner runs into difficulty, the expert provides specific instructions. When the learner is coping well only general encouragement is needed. In time, we all learn to scaffold ourselves (self-instruction).

**Cooperative and collaborative learning** – Students work together on a common task in which each individual depends on and is accountable to each other. This social construction of knowledge then enables each individual to cope better when working on their own. Gokhale (1995) found that students who participated in collaborative learning performed significantly better on a critical-thinking test than students who studied individually.

> Vygotsky's key idea was that assistance is needed to set a learner on the road to independent behaviour.

**Peer tutoring** – Peers can be experts. Research shows that it is often the peer tutor who gains most from tutoring.

**Motivation** comes from the people around you, encouraging you through the ZPD.

**Evaluation**

- Vygotsky's approach **may not work as well in an individualist setting** where children are encouraged to be more competitive and self-reliant, and where groupwork may be less successful.
- The approach requires that teachers are **sensitive to their students' ZPD**, which may be unrealistic and, again, requires experience.
- Cooperative group work requires **careful organisation to work well**; some members of a group may be 'loafing' and not benefit.

> When evaluating any of the applications of theories of cognitive development to education, you can refer to general criticisms of the theoretical basis for the application.

## Bruner's theory

**Discovery learning** – Like Piaget's approach of the same name, this emphasises the active role of the learner, but places more emphasis on the teacher's activity than Piaget did. Teachers should take a direct role in instructing children, and identify what cognitive abilities and strategies are needed for good performance on a task, avoid overloading short-term memory, identify consistent errors, and encourage 'metacognitive' knowledge about strategies. At the same time, children must organise new information for themselves by integrating it into existing hierarchies or adapting hierarchies to fit new situations. Learning is not a matter of mastering facts but inventing the structure for the facts.

> 'Metacognition' is knowing about knowing. Learning about how to acquire knowledge is important.

**Scaffolding** – As suggested by Vygotsky, involving peers and/or adults.

**Spiral curriculum** – Successful learning is related to developing and redeveloping concepts at different ages with increasing complexity, i.e. important topics are revisited using progressively more mature modes of thinking.

**Choice of materials and activities** – Choice should match the dominant mode of thinking for a child, although a combination of concrete, pictorial then symbolic activities, will lead to more effective learning.

**Motivation** – This arises from using intrinsically interesting learning materials, rather than extrinsic rewards, such as getting good grades or emphasising the value of education.

> It is difficult to provide a truly valid assessment of any of these approaches because it is impossible to decide on a common outcome measure to assess and compare the approaches. In addition, we can't be certain that a teacher is strictly using one particular approach.

**Evaluation**

- The **spiral curriculum model has been very influential** as well as Bruner's view that learning needs to be structured.
- **Combines Piaget and Vygotsky's approach** by including the active role of the learning as well as the importance of scaffolding from teachers.

## A combined approach

The different approaches need not be mutually exclusive and can be combined usefully. For example, the CASE project (Cognitive Acceleration through Science Education) involved developing formal operations (Piaget) by giving children problems that created cognitive conflict (Piaget), but children worked together to create solutions (Vygotsky).

## Practice essays 8.1

(a) Outline and evaluate Piaget's theory of cognitive development. *(15 marks)*
(b) Outline and evaluate **one** other theory of cognitive development. *(10 marks)*

# 8.2 Development of moral understanding

*After studying this section you should be able to describe and evaluate:*

- *theories of moral understanding (Kohlberg) and/or pro-social reasoning (Eisenberg).*

**LEARNING SUMMARY**

## Kohlberg's theory of moral understanding

AQA A    U3
AQA B    U3

Piaget (1932) produced an early account of moral development, which is described on page 161. This account focused on what choices children made when given moral dilemmas. Kohlberg's interest was in *why* people made moral choices (i.e. moral reasoning).

Lawrence Kohlberg (1966) tested moral understanding by devising a set of moral dilemmas (situations with no straightforward solution), such as Heinz, and the druggist who wouldn't sell a drug to save Heinz's dying wife. The key feature of these dilemmas was that participants were asked a series of questions such as, 'Should Heinz steal the drug?', 'Why or why not?', 'Does it make a difference whether or not he loves his wife?', 'Why or why not?'.

Kohlberg tested a group of 10–16 year old boys, and used their reasoning to construct the classification scheme below.

| Level | Age | Stage |
|---|---|---|
| Level I Pre-conventional | 6–13 | 1. Deference to authority, heteronomous (basing judgment on the outcome rather than intention). |
| | | 2. Doing good to serve one's own interests, egocentric. |
| Level II Conventional | 13–16 | 3. Care for the other, interpersonal conformity, 'good boy/girl'. |
| | | 4. The primacy of social order, importance of conscience, unquestioning acceptance of authority. |
| Level III Post-conventional or principled | 16–20 | 5. Concern with individual rights, questioning the law and authority to ensure justice. |
| | | 6. Universal, ethical principles. |

**Research evidence**

A longitudinal study by Colby *et al.* (1983) followed Kohlberg's initial participants over 20 years, ending up with 58 men. They were re-tested every 3 years. By the age of 36, participants were mainly reasoning at stage 4 (65% of their responses), stage 3 still accounted for about 30%, and stage 5 was 5%.

Kohlberg (1975) predicted that people who reason at a higher level should behave in a more mature fashion. He provided support for this in a study looking at whether students would cheat on a test, given the opportunity. He found that only 15% of those in the post-conventional stage cheated, whereas 70% of those in the pre-conventional stage did.

Walker *et al.* (1987) used nine stages to allow for the fact that many children's reasoning falls between two stages, and found general agreement with Kohlberg. They found that stage 2 reasoning dominates at age 10 and stage 3 dominates at age 16. Colby and Kohlberg (1987) performed a more careful analysis of the original data and found that only 15% reached stage 5 and there was no evidence whatsoever of stage 6 judgments.

Fodor (1972) found that delinquents operate at a much lower level on the Kohlberg scales than non-delinquents, as we might expect, since delinquents are likely to have less-developed morals.

**Evaluation**

- This may be the **best available approach** and has generated much empirical interest, despite the criticisms below.
- This is a theory of **moral principles** not behaviour; moral behaviour may not be related to moral principles. For example, the classic study by Hartshorne and May (1928) found that behaviour was more governed by the probability of being caught than by any principles of morality (see page 162).
- Stages 5 and 6 may be **moral ideals**, never achieved by some people.
- Judging moral dilemmas is not the same as making **real life** *decisions*.
- **Age bias** – The dilemmas are biased towards older participants and some of the dilemmas are simply irrelevant to children. Perhaps the seemingly immature behaviour of younger children is because they don't relate to the scenarios. Eisenberg (1982) found that Kohlberg had underestimated children's moral understanding abilities.
- **Gender bias** – The classification scheme is biased towards male morality (justice) because the scenarios were **justice-oriented** and the participants were male. Kohlberg claimed that women tended to be 'less' morally developed, but it may be that they only *appeared* to be less mature because they operate a morality of care. Gilligan and Attanucci (1988) asked a group of men and women to produce accounts of their own moral dilemmas. They found that, overall, men favoured a justice orientation and women favoured a care orientation. However, Kohlberg's theory may **not be as gender biased as is claimed**; Funk (1986) used Kohlberg's dilemmas and found that women scored higher than men.
- **Culture bias** – Kohlberg claimed that the moral stages are universal. In fact, his stages reflect Western values of democracy. There are cultural differences, for example, Ma (1988) constructed a Chinese version of Kohlberg's stages, including 'Good Will' (acting in a way that complies with nature). On the other hand, there is evidence of cultural similarities. Snarey (1985) listed 27 different cross-cultural studies, which found a progression from stages 1 to 4 at about the same ages. Very few studies found any stage 5 reasoning and, where it occurred, it was likely to be in urban areas.

Carole Gilligan developed her own stage theory of moral development (see page 162). If a man's moral perspective was assessed using Gilligan's stage theory, he might appear to be morally inferior.

Gender differences may also be related to the 'tend and befriend' responses typical of women (see page 60).

## Eisenberg's theory of pro-social reasoning

AQA A    U3
AQA B    U3

Pro-social behaviours are those that aim to benefit others. Further research related to pro-social behaviour/moral development is discussed on pages 161–163.

Nancy Eisenberg broadened the idea of moral behaviour to include pro-social behaviour and emphasised role-taking skills (taking the perspective of another person) in moral development. Eisenberg created a stage theory of pro-social development.

| Level | Age range (approx.) | Brief description |
|---|---|---|
| 1 Hedonistic (self-centred) | Pre-school and early primary. | Pro-social behaviour is most likely when it will benefit self in some way. |
| 2 Needs oriented | A few pre-schoolers, mainly primary. | Sometimes considers needs of others. Not much evidence of sympathy or guilt. |
| 3 Approval oriented | Primary and some secondary. | Pro-social behaviour in return for approval and praise from others. |
| 4 Empathetic or transitional | Older primary and secondary. | Some understanding of abstract principles. Evidence of sympathy and guilt. |
| 5 Strongly internalised | Some secondary and a few primary. | Internalised principles that are important to self-respect. |

### Research evidence

Eisenberg's stage theory was based on evidence from Eisenberg *et al.* (1983, 1991). They used a different kind of moral story than Kohlberg's; for example, a moral story where a child has to decide whether to help someone when the pro-social act would be at some cost (e.g. the child sees an injured child while on their way to a birthday party – do they go to the party where they will have lots of fun, or stop and help the injured child?).

Eisenberg *et al.* (1991) found that empathy (which develops during level 4) plays an important role in producing pro-social thinking. Adolescents were more likely to help if they thought about another person's feelings of pain and anxiety.

Eisenberg suggested that pro-social development relies on a child's ability to experience **empathetic concern**; personal distress on its own does not lead to pro-social behaviour. This was supported by Caplan and Hay (1989) who found that 3–5 year olds were often very upset by another child's distress, but rarely offered to help. Hughes *et al.* (1981) found that younger children felt sad about unhappy things but only gave egocentric explanations (i.e. ones that related to the effects on themselves). Slightly older children (aged 7–9) were able to see how a situation might affect someone else, for example, if someone's dog ran away, they realised it would make the other person unhappy and that made them sad.

**Role-taking skills** are related to pro-social behaviour generally. For example, socially maladjusted girls who received training in role-taking skills became more concerned about needs of others than age mates who received no training (Chalmers and Townsend, 1990).

**Gender differences** – Feshbach (1982) found significant gender differences in empathetic responses with females being more empathetic than males. Eisenberg *et al.* (1991) found that girls aged 10–12 were more empathetic and caring but suggests this may be because girls mature earlier; by adolescence boys have caught up.

**Cross-cultural support** – Eisenberg (1986) found similar stages in other European countries, but Kibbutz-reared Israeli children showed little needs-orientation; instead they provided reasoning based on community values (as fits with being in a collectivist society).

According to Eisenberg, the ability to distinguish between personal distress and empathetic concern hinges on this ability to take the perspective of another person; perspective-taking is discussed on page 91.

### Evaluation

- Eisenberg broadened the conception of moral behaviour, **emphasising emotional factors** and focusing on pro-social reasoning rather than wrongdoing.
- Eisenberg's dilemmas are **more appropriate to younger children** than Kohlberg's dilemmas. Nevertheless, the stages of development are roughly similar to Kohlberg's stages, thus supporting both theories.
- This theory has **real world application** for teachers and parents. It can be used to enhance pro-social development by focusing on the development of empathy.
- Some evidence suggests that **empathy appears much earlier** than Eisenberg predicted. Zahn-Waxler *et al.* (1979) found that children aged 18–30 months showed concern when they saw other children in distress.
- Explanations of altruism in adults also dispute whether it is **selfish or selfless**. Like Eisenberg, Batson (1991) suggested that empathy was the key to pro-social behaviour (i.e. selfless), whereas Cialdini (1985) argued that pro-social behaviour is due to relieving one's own distress (i.e. selfish), thus contradicting Eisenberg.

## Practice essay 8.2

Discuss Kohlberg's theory of moral understanding.                    *(25 marks)*

# 8.3 Development of social cognition

After studying this section you should be able to describe and evaluate:

- the development of the child's sense of self
- the development of children's understanding of others, including Theory of Mind (Baron-Cohen) and perspective taking (Selman)
- biological explanations of social cognition, including the role of the mirror neuron system.

**LEARNING SUMMARY**

## Development of the child's sense of self

AQA A ▶ U3

The concept of **self** refers to the attitudes you have about yourself as a unique individual, separate from others.

The **mirror test** has been used to assess whether animals are capable of self-recognition (see page 75).

### Self-recognition

Lewis and Brooks-Gunn (1979) tested self-recognition by colouring infants' noses with rouge and putting them in front of a mirror (called the **mirror test**). A child who responds by touching their own nose shows self-recognition. At 9–12 months, all the children smiled at the image in the mirror, but none of the children touched their noses. By 21 months, 70% touched their noses. Lewis and Brooks-Gunn also found that, by 18 months, most children can point to a photograph of themselves.

### Gender concept

A key aspect of one's self-concept is gender. Gender identity develops around the age of 3 (see page 62) and is linked to Piaget's concept of conservation (see page 82).

### The physical versus the psychological self

Children of 3–4 years can distinguish a thinking, psychological self from their physical self. Children of this age typically describe themselves in concrete terms. However, Eder (1990) also found that they can describe how they usually behave in particular situations, which is evidence of a psychological self-concept. Selman (1980) used dilemmas to evaluate the development of private and public self. He found that by the age of 8 most children recognise the difference between their inner states and outward appearances.

**Self-esteem** is the feeling an individual has about all the components of their self-concept.

### Self-esteem

A key aspect of the self-concept is the value attached to it, i.e. self-esteem. Carl Rogers (1951) suggested that self development begins when a child distinguishes what is 'me' (the conscious concept of self) from the rest of the world. This happens as a result of interaction with the environment, and at the same time a child learns the values attached to the self concept. Rogers linked low self-esteem to lack of self-acceptance and unhealthy personal development. Vershueren *et al.* (2001) found that children aged 4–5 have a sense of self-esteem and that this was linked to their attachment history; children who were securely attached had more positive self-esteem.

**Key points from AS**

- Rogers' approach to understanding human behaviour is an example of the humanistic approach, an approach that focuses on behaviour from the point of view of the person experiencing it, see *Revise AS Unit 1.1, page 21*.

**Key points from AS**

- This research links with studies on attachment and Bowlby's view that healthy emotional development is related to secure attachment, see *Revise AS Unit 2.1, page 53*.

### Understanding of others

A sense of self is used as a reference point for understanding others, so the two are inextricably linked – the development of a sense of self is related to being able to understand others, a topic examined on the next page.

Bischof-Kohler (1991) used the mirror test to assess self-recognition. He also assessed a child's empathy when playing with an experimenter who is sad when a teddy bear's arm falls off. There was a high correlation between self-recognition and empathy regardless of age, suggesting that both develop at about the same time – around 18–20 months.

## Development of children's understanding of others

AQA A ▶ U3

### Theory of Mind (ToM)

ToM is tested using a false belief task – can other people have false beliefs? Baron-Cohen *et al.* (1985) created the **Sally–Anne test** to assess ToM. Typically, children aged 4 can cope with this task, but 3 year olds can't.

Harris (1989) argues that ToM develops from pretend play. A child first becomes aware of their own emotional state and then has to be able to use this to pretend to be someone else and share their feelings (e.g. 'My teddy bear is feeling sad'). This then enables the child to comprehend that another person may feel/think differently to what they are feeling, which happens by the age of 4.

Under the age of 4 children begin to distinguish mental states. For example, by the age of 2 they use words for emotional states, and by the age of 3 they meaningfully use words like 'thinking' (Shatz *et al.*, 1983).

The understanding of the reality-appearance distinction (see Piaget's theory, page 81) is also linked to ToM because it requires understanding that one representation is false. Flavell *et al.* (1986) found that 4 year olds could correctly identify a sponge that looked like a rock as a being a sponge, whereas 3 year olds called it a rock despite the fact that it felt like a sponge.

Simon Baron-Cohen has been especially interested in individuals who *lack* a theory of mind ('mindblindness'). For example, autistic children, even those with high intelligence, cannot cope with the **Sally–Anne task** (see left). This is linked to their difficulties with social communication and relationships, because ToM underlies these. Baron-Cohen has also suggested that women are better than men at empathising and that autism is an example of the 'extreme male brain'.

### Deception

The ability to deceive someone else depends on a theory of mind and is seen as a sign of intelligence in animals (see Machiavellian intelligence on page 75). By the age of 3, children can deceive others by hiding their own emotion. For example, Cole (1986) found that 3 year olds didn't show disappointment when receiving the worst (rather than best) present in front of others, but did show it when filmed on their own.

### Perspective taking

Selman (1980) proposed that children gain a greater understanding of themselves and others through being able to discriminate between their own perspective and those of other people, i.e. perspective-taking or role-taking; he called this **role-taking theory**. In particular, a child needs to understand the thoughts, feelings, motives and intentions.

To assess this, Selman gave children a set of interpersonal dilemmas, for example: Tom's friend Mike has lost his dog but says he doesn't want another. Tom wants to buy Mike a birthday present and sees some puppies for sale – what should he do? Selman based his stage theory on the explanations that children provided.

| | |
|---|---|
| **Stage 0** Egocentric, 3–6 years | Views based on self, e.g. 'I'd get him a puppy because I like dogs'. |
| **Stage 1** Subjective, 6–8 years | Can recognise another's perspective but assume different views are because the other person has different information, e.g. 'Mike says he doesn't want the dog, therefore, he'll be angry if Tom gives him a dog'. |
| **Stage 2** Self-reflective, 8–10 years | Can't consider both perspectives simultaneously. |

**Theory of mind** (ToM) is the ability to understand what is going on in another person's mind, to 'guess' what they are thinking or feeling. It is regarded as a feature of intelligent behaviour and is only found in some animals (see page 75).

Sally–Anne Test
- Sally puts her ball in her basket and leaves the room
- Anne moves the ball to her box.
- Sally returns. Where will Sally look for her ball?

People who have a theory of mind say that Sally will look in her basket, whereas people lacking a theory of mind say that Sally will look in Anne's box (because they cannot perceive that another person will think differently to them and they know the ball is in Anne's box).

**Key points from AS**

See Sally–Anne test illustration in *Revise AS Unit 7.3, page 167*.

On page 88 we looked at Eisenberg's theory of pro-social development. She suggested that the ability to distinguish between personal distress and empathetic concern hinges on this ability to take the perspective of another person. Perspective or role-taking marks the beginning of pro-social behaviour in children.

Altogether there are 5 stages in this model. Stage 3 is mutual role-taking (10–12 years) and stage 4 is societal role taking, taking the views of society into account.

## Biological explanations of social cognition

**Social cognition** is the study of how thinking (cognition) affects social behaviour.

### Theory of Mind Module (ToMM)

Is ToM biologically programmed? Baron-Cohen (1995) has suggested that there are innate mental structures related to ToM, in the same way that there are innate structures in the human brain for language. The ToMM develops between 18 and 48 months and enables a child to understand mental states, such as beliefs, desires and intentions.

### Shared attention mechanism (SAM)

Baron-Cohen has proposed another possible system that may be involved in mindreading. He has suggested that the SAM system develops between 9 and 18 months and allows two individuals to understand that they are attending to the same thing. The SAM system is a precursor to the development of ToM.

A **mirror neuron** is a neuron (or nerve) in the brain that is active when an animal performs a specific task, but is also active when the animal watches another animal perform the same specific task. It means that the observer's brain experiences the behaviour of another as if it were its own behaviour.

### The role of the mirror neuron system

Mirror neurons are very important in imitation, empathy and Theory of Mind.

Mirror neurons have been observed directly in primates. Rizzolatti *et al.* (1996) recorded electrical activity in single neurons in the brains of macaque monkeys. In some of the neurons of the frontal and parietal lobes they found mirror properties – the neuron would respond in the same way when the monkey saw a person pick up a piece of food as it would when the monkey picked up the food.

In humans it has not been possible to study single neurons, but brain imaging studies suggest the presence of a mirror neuron system, i.e. a network of neurons in the **frontal** and **parietal regions** of the brain that respond in the same way to the single neurons observed in monkeys (Rizzolatti and Craighero, 2004).

The importance of this neural system is that it enables the observer to share the experiences of another and, thus, to understand their actions, and more importantly, their feelings and intentions.

#### Evaluation

**Key points from AS**

Alternative explanations are presented in *Revise AS Unit 7.3, page 166.*

- One **application** of this knowledge is as a means of **explaining autism**. The suggestion is that autistic people have a dysfunction in the mirror neuron system and this impairs their empathising ability. However, there is no evidence to support this.
- A further application is the **development of psychological tests** related to biological abilities, such as Baron-Cohen's early screening test for autism, the Checklist for Autism in Toddlers (CHAT). This quick test is used at 18 months to determine whether the child is not showing behaviours, such as pointing and gaze following, which are examples of shared (or joint) attention; lack of such behaviours might suggest autistic difficulties.
- The fact that social intelligence is **present only in certain higher animals** (see page 75) suggests that there is a biological basis for such behaviour, otherwise all animals would be capable of such behaviour.

## Practice essays 8.3

(a) Explain the concept of Theory of Mind. *(4 marks)*

(b) Outline research related to the Theory of Mind. *(5 marks)*

(c) Evaluate research into the Theory of Mind. *(16 marks)*

## 1

Describe and evaluate evolutionary explanations of the function of sleep. *(25 marks)*

See pages 9–11 for a breakdown of the marking criteria used to mark this question.

The question requests more than one evolutionary approach. This answer contains two – one from Meddis and one from Webb, plus a general evolutionary discussion. If the candidate had only presented one explanation, full marks would not be available (partial performance penalties would apply where a maximum of about 2/3 of the marks would be available).

The description is accurate and well structured and material has been selected wisely. These are the criteria for the top band of AO1. However, there is one other AO1 criteria –substantial balance of depth and breadth; both explanations could have been a little sharper/more detailed for the top band. So **8 out of 9 AO1 marks**.

The commentary (AO2) is all in the second half of the answer, starting from the fourth paragraph. The candidate has used restoration theory as a means of evaluation and managed to avoid the 'AO2 description trap' where you end up giving a load of description instead of using the material as commentary.

The AO2 has been used effectively and shows coherent elaboration and a focused line of argument. However, it is not highly effective or thorough and there is only some evidence of issues/debates or approaches. Therefore, it is closer to the top of band 2 = **12 out of 16 AO2 marks**.

**The total mark is 19 out of 25 marks.**

The basis of the evolutionary approach is that the reason why all animals sleep (and it is a fact that all animals sleep) is because sleep serves some adaptive function. The notion of adaptiveness comes from the theory of evolution. The idea is that any behaviour that has continued in an animal's gene pool is because it must have been naturally selected because it, in some way, has helped promote the survival and reproduction of an animal possessing that characteristic.

So sleep is likely to serve some adaptive function. Meddis proposed that the function is a protective one. When an animal does not have to be out and about finding food, then it would be adaptive for them to be quiet and hidden. At the same time an animal that is likely to be preyed upon would be better off sleeping very little, whereas predators can afford to sleep a lot because they are not in much danger.

Another evolutionary explanation was suggested by Webb. This is the hibernation theory. This theory suggests that sleep is adaptive because when an animal is asleep it is not using up energy. For most animals finding food is their biggest problem so there is a vicious cycle: the more active the animal is, the more food has to be found; the more food finding, the more energy that is used. When an animal hibernates or sleeps this reduces the amount of food that is needed and would increase survival.

Evolutionary theory can be used to explain why different animals sleep in different ways. For example, one species of dolphin sleeps one hemisphere at a time possibly in order to surface regularly and breathe. Observations of the animal world support Meddis' theory. Predator species, such as cats, sleep a lot more than prey species such as gazelles. Herbivores have to spend a lot of time finding food and will sleep little. The cow is not preyed upon and sleeps only a little. The point is that the evolutionary argument can be used to explain almost any sleep pattern!

Certainly some aspects of sleeping are adaptive, however, it may not be the main function of sleep. The alternative theory is the restoration theory, which proposes that all animals sleep because certain functions take place during sleep, which help the animal restore itself physiologically and psychologically. Of course this in itself may be adaptive. Physiological and psychological restoration can take place when an animal is relaxing, so why then is it necessary to become unconscious during sleep? In terms of protection one would think it is more adaptive for animals not to lose consciousness. Perhaps the reason is that for good restoration to take place the brain has really got to go off-line. So this suggests that restoration theory may be more correct than the evolutionary approach.

One of the key criticisms made, in relation to evolutionary theories of sleep, is that many of them suggest that animals sleep in order to waste time (Empson called them 'waste of time' theories). Whereas the restoration view is that sleep is not wasting time but offers the opportunity for key functions to take place.

Another criticism that is made is that evolutionary theories may not be suitable for explaining human sleep. Sleep may have been adaptive during the environment of evolutionary adaptation (EEA) but this hasn't been true for a long time and one wonders why humans haven't evolved different patterns of sleep if evolution was all there was to patterns of sleep. We haven't got predators and don't need to waste time so we should be sleeping less.

In general, evolutionary approaches have been criticised for lacking research evidence to support the 'just so' stories, however, this may not be justified.

See pages 9–11 for a breakdown of the marking criteria used to mark this question.

**2**

(a) Outline **one** theory of cognitive development. *(9 marks)*

(b) Assess the research evidence that has been used to support this theory.

*(16 marks)*

(a) This answer contains a sound description of Piaget's theory, perhaps too much detail of the ages and stages and no mention of other key features of the theory (such as disequilibrium and schema). But, answers are marked positively so marks are not deducted for concepts that may be missing as long as a good range of material has been included, as here. **9 out of 9 AO1 marks.**

(a) Piaget's theory is the best known and most comprehensive theory of cognitive development. It has been called an 'ages and stages' theory because Piaget identified the stages that an infant and child pass through as they develop cognitively. The key point about these stages is that they represent differences in biological maturation. As the child gets older they are capable of progressively different kinds of thinking rather than just having an increase in their general knowledge (a quantitative change). A child moves from one stage to another when their mind is mature enough. The first stage is sensori-motor, when the infant is learning to co-ordinate what he sees/hears with what his body is doing. The infant repeats actions (circular reactions) in order to establish these sensori-motor links.

At the end of the first year the child starts to use language and this is the beginning of the second stage, the pre-operational stage. 'Operations' are mental rules of logic. In this second stage the child cannot cope with internally consistent logic. They have their own form of logic but it wouldn't be any use in mathematics. They are 'fooled' by the appearance of things and mistake that for reality. This explains why they find the conservation task difficult.

The third stage is the stage of concrete operations (age about 7) where the child can now cope with conservation and with logical operations – but only if they are presented in a concrete form rather than abstract. The child's problem-solving abilities also tend to be rather random. The game called 'Mastermind' is one way to demonstrate this because younger children can't deduce the solution using logical steps.

At the age of 11 children move into the formal operational stage, when they are capable of abstract and systematic (scientific) thought. It may not be a universally-achievable stage.

(b) The most obvious point is that this answer is rather thin on AO2 – there should be significantly more AO2 than AO1 given the mark division. The commentary that has been provided shows sound analysis/ coherent elaboration – the student is able to expand each critical point and present relevant evidence and explain the implications. These are criteria for the top band. Quality of written communication (QWC) is also excellent. On the down side, the answer does not provide a thorough commentary and also lacks mention of issues/debates and approaches. It therefore clearly belongs in Band 2 and would receive **11 out of 16 AO2 marks.**

(b) Piaget's methods largely involved naturalistic observation of his own children. He may have been biased in making observations. He also used semi-structured interviews. These are good for eliciting unexpected information because there are no preset directions to take. However, the way an interviewer asks a question may bias a child's response.

In the area of object permanence, Piaget claimed that infants were only aware of this after the age of 8 months. However, a study by Bower showed that younger infants were surprised when a screen was lifted and an object was not there. This suggests that Piaget underestimated the age that infants could achieve this cognitive step, thus, challenging Piaget's evidence.

Piaget's research on conservation has been especially challenged. One suggestion has been the fact that he used two questions, which may have confused younger participants who thought that if there is a second question, there perhaps is a second answer. Therefore, they changed their answer in the second condition. Older children were less confused, which is why they appear to do better on the conservation task. Research by Samuel and Bryant supports this, showing that younger children are more capable than Piaget suggested – however, there are still age differences.

Piaget's theory claimed to be a biological and, therefore, universal theory, of behaviour yet some of this research may not generalise to other cultures, though its usefulness in education suggests that it does have a place there.

**The total mark is 20 out of 25 marks.**

# Schizophrenia

## 9.1 Classification and diagnosis of schizophrenia

**After studying this section you should be able to describe and evaluate:**

*Note that AQA A students only need to study **one** mental disorder, i.e. they only need to study chapter 9 or 10 or 11 or 12.*

- *clinical characteristics of schizophrenia*
- *issues surrounding the classification and diagnosis of schizophrenia, including reliability and validity.*

**LEARNING SUMMARY**

### Clinical characteristics of schizophrenia

AQA A  U4
AQA B  U3

The term **psychotic** refers to disorders where the patient has lost touch with reality.

Schizophrenia is one of the most chronic and disabling of the major mental illnesses affecting thought processes. A sufferer is unable to separate reality from unreal experiences, such as hallucinations. Some patients may only have one **psychotic** episode, and others may have many episodes during a lifetime, but lead relatively normal lives during interim periods.

In order for a diagnosis of schizophrenia to be made, two or more of the symptoms listed below must be present for more than one month, along with reduced social functioning. The symptoms are divided into **positive** and **negative** symptoms, though not all symptoms fit this pattern. Positive symptoms are an excess or distortion of normal functions and negative symptoms are a diminution or loss of normal functions.

**Schizophrenia** means literally 'split-mind', but it is wrongly confused with multiple personality disorder (or dissociative identity disorder). Schizophrenia refers to a group of psychoses, which are not enduring disorders of the whole personality.

- **Thought disturbance** (positive symptoms), such as thought insertion (e.g. thoughts controlled by aliens), hallucinations (e.g. hearing voices) and delusions (e.g. of grandeur).
- **Language impairments** (positive symptoms) are also characteristic. Patients may repeat sounds (echolalia) or use invented words (neologisms).
- **Inappropriate of affect/volition** (positive symptoms), such as smiling when told bad news.
- **Blunted and flat affect/volition** (negative symptoms), such as showing little emotion, reduced motivation and interest, and difficulty planning actions.
- **Psychomotor disturbances**, such as catatonia (immobility, bizarre statues), stereotypy (e.g. rocking) and frenetic activity (e.g. strange grimaces).

#### Types I and II

Schizophrenia occurs in about 1% of the population, though there is a wide difference between rural and urban environments; different research has shown prevalence rates of between 0.33% and 15%.

A distinction is made between Type I schizophrenia, which is dominated by positive symptoms, and Type II schizophrenia, which features negative symptoms and has a poorer prognosis (i.e. a less favourable outcome).

#### Subtypes

DSM-IV identifies five main subtypes:

**Paranoid type** – positive symptoms; awareness and language are relatively unimpaired.

**Disorganised type** – disorganised speech and behaviour, vivid hallucinations, flat emotion, and inappropriate affect; the most severe form, onset in early adulthood.

Schizophrenia may be better characterised as a range of disorders with different causes, rather than one single disorder.

**Catatonic type** – apathy and psychomotor disturbances.

**Undifferentiated type** – psychotic symptoms are present, but the criteria for paranoid, disorganised, or catatonic types have not been met.

**Residual type** – where positive symptoms are present at a low intensity only.

## Issues surrounding the classification and diagnosis of schizophrenia

AQA A ▸ U4

Mental disorders are classified using **DSM** or **ICD**. The DSM (*Diagnostic and Statistical Manual of Mental Disorders*) is a list of typical symptoms for mental disorders, which is used to aid diagnosis of mental illness. DSM is used in America, whereas **ICD** (*International Classification of Diseases*) is used in Europe and the UK.

Studies often report a kappa statistic rather than a simple percent agreement; the kappa statistic (κ) is better because it takes into account the agreement occurring by chance.

It is important to remember that diagnosis of physical illness is not 100% reliable. However, physical illnesses have a (usually known) physical cause and, therefore, diagnoses of physical illnesses have the potential for greater reliability and validity.

### Reliability

#### General issues

Reliability concerns consistency of measurements. In relation to classification and diagnosis, this can be established in two ways:

- **Inter-rater reliability** – Whether two or more clinicians make the same diagnosis when independently assessing a patient. Some of this error may be due to the fact that the same patient may give different information to different clinicians, but some studies provide written material to control for this.
- **Test-retest reliability** – Whether the same clinician gives the same diagnosis when presented with the same information on separate occasions.

Obviously, a diagnosis is meaningless if it is not consistent. Current versions of DSM and ICD are regarded as being considerably more reliable than earlier versions. For example, Beck *et al.* (1962) found 54% agreement between four experienced clinicians when interviewing 153 patients. Söderberg *et al.* (2005) reported +.81 reliability with the most recent form of DSM (DSM-IV-TR).

DSM is claimed to have higher reliability than ICD because of the degree of specificity in the symptoms identified for each category. Nilsson *et al.* (2000) reported an inter-rater reliability of +.60 (or 60%) between clinicians using ICD.

#### Reliability of diagnoses of schizophrenia

There is evidence both for and against the reliability of a diagnosis of schizophrenia.

**Pro** – The diagnosis of schizophrenia has relatively high reliability (e.g. +.81 reported for schizophrenia whereas +.63 for anxiety disorders).

**Anti** – Read *et al.* (2004) reported that test-retest reliability was as low as +.37 and also described a 1970 study where 194 British and 134 American psychiatrists were asked to provide a diagnosis on the basis of a case description. 69% of the Americans diagnosed schizophrenia whilst only 2% of the British did so. They claim that there is no definitive evidence to suggest that the reliability of the diagnosis has improved since that date.

#### Evaluation

- Despite the rather low reliability of classification schemes, they are claimed to be useful because they are **better than nothing**. They enable research to be conducted linking syndromes to treatments and are better than just making a stab in the dark as to what treatment is likely to be most appropriate.
- Classification systems are **always being improved** and with increased understanding of mental disorders, the reliability should improve.

### Validity

#### General issues

Validity concerns the extent to which a diagnosis represents something real. There are a number of approaches to establishing validity:

- **Reliability** – An unreliable diagnosis cannot, by definition, be valid.
- **Predictive validity** – If a diagnosis results in a successful treatment then the diagnosis must have been valid. Heather (1976) claimed that the same diagnosis had a 50 : 50 chance of leading to the same or a different treatment, which suggests that diagnoses lack validity.
- **Aetiological validity** – The cause of the disorder should be the same for all patients in that category.

- **Descriptive validity** – Patients in different diagnostic categories should differ from each other. Descriptive validity is reduced by **comorbidity**. Where comorbidity occurs it suggests that the 'illnesses' are not separate categories and thus not valid.
- **Cultural bias** – Western classification systems are culturally biased. The symptoms of a disorder are often culture-specific and, therefore, members of other cultural groups may be identified as ill when they exhibit behaviours that are normal within their own culture (e.g. hearing voices).

**Comorbidity** refers to the diagnosis of two or more conditions at the same time.

A classic study by David Rosenhan (1973) demonstrated the poor validity of psychiatric diagnosis. He arranged for 8 'normal' people to be examined by admitting doctors in psychiatric hospitals. The 'pseudopatients' were instructed to behave normally, except for reporting that they heard a voice. All except one was admitted as schizophrenic, and later released (between 2 and 52 days later) as schizophrenics in remission (this is a rare diagnosis which might suggest recognition of unusual circumstances) It would seem that the context mattered more than the symptoms, though it might be a case of a **Type II error** – the psychiatrists preferred to call a healthy person sick rather than a sick person healthy.

The lack of agreement between psychiatrists demonstrates low reliability.

What would happen if the hospital knew some patients were pseudopatients? Rosenhan described his study to the staff at one psychiatric hospital and told them to expect one or more pseudopatients over the next three months. In that time 193 patients were admitted and all staff were asked to rate the likelihood of whether they were 'real'. In fact, all patients were genuine but more than 20% were judged as pseudopatients by one member of staff and 10% were judged so by two members of staff.

### Validity of diagnoses of schizophrenia

**Culture bias** – Cochrane (1977) found that more people of African-Caribbean origins were diagnosed as schizophrenic in the UK than whites (possibly 7 times as many). This may be because the disease has a genetic origin, but diagnosis rates for African-Caribbeans are not as high elsewhere in the world. It may be because members of minority ethnic groups in Britain have more stressful lives.

### Evaluation

The **idiographic approach** is explained on page 185.

- The fact that diagnoses can be unreliable and inaccurate (invalid) suggests that they **should not be used**. However, the same is at least partly true of medical diagnosis generally, yet we wouldn't suggest abandoning that. There are alternatives, e.g. using a more **idiographic** approach that doesn't require classification (which is *nomothetic*), but emphasises listening and analysing each patient's problems.
- A major issue with psychiatric diagnoses is that they result in **labelling**, for example a person becomes a 'schizophrenic' rather than a person with schizophrenia, and this label tends to stick even when the disorder has disappeared. This problem with labelling is less true for physical diagnoses and, therefore, an invalid psychiatric diagnosis has more serious and lifelong implications. For this reason many critics would prefer to avoid the use of such labels. Another alternative is to use a system that focuses on the behaviours only.

## Practice essays 9.1

(a) Outline the clinical characteristics of schizophrenia, with reference to examples. *(9 marks)*

(b) To what extent are diagnoses of schizophrenia reliable and/or valid? *(16 marks)*

# 9.2 Explanations of schizophrenia

*After studying this section you should be able to describe and evaluate:*

- *biological explanations of schizophrenia, for example, genetics and biochemistry*
- *psychological explanations of schizophrenia, for example, behavioural, cognitive, psychodynamic and socio-cultural.*

LEARNING SUMMARY

## Biological explanations of schizophrenia

AQA A  U4
AQA B  U3

There is strong evidence that a predisposition for schizophrenia is inherited, and then life experiences trigger the condition (the **diathesis-stress model**, see page 54).

Gene mapping involves comparing the genetic material from families who have schizophrenia with samples from families without schizophrenia to identify common factors.

The abbreviation MZ stands for monozygotic (identical) and DZ for dizygotic (non-identical or fraternal).

### Genetic explanations

Individuals may inherit a gene or genes that cause their schizophrenia. Research suggests that it is not likely to be one gene (see gene mapping studies) and that such genes predispose individuals to develop the disorder, rather than being a certainty (identical MZ twins don't show 100% concordance).

### Research evidence

**Gene mapping** – Sherrington *et al.* (1988) found evidence for a cluster of genes on chromosome 5, which might make an individual susceptible to schizophrenia. Subsequent studies have found a range of potential candidates on chromosomes 5, 6, 8, 9, 10, 11, 13, 18, 19 and 22 (Kendler *et al.*, 2000). Hahn *et al.* (2006) produced evidence that linked the gene associated with **neuregulin** with a predisposition for schizophrenia.

**Twin studies** – Gottesman (1991) summarised about 40 studies, concluding that the concordance rate is about 48% for MZ twins but only 17% for DZ twins, indicating some environmental influence but a larger genetic component.

**Adoption studies** – Tienari (1991) reported on the Finnish adoption study, following 155 adopted children whose natural mothers were schizophrenic. In adulthood 10.3% of those with schizophrenic mothers had developed schizophrenia compared to only 1.1% of those without schizophrenic mothers.

**Family studies** – Kendler *et al.* (1985) found that first-degree relatives of schizophrenics are 18 times more likely to be similarly diagnosed. In the Copenhagen high-risk study, Parnas *et al.* (1993) followed 207 children (aged 10–18 at the start) who had schizophrenic mothers. At a 27-year follow-up 16% had been diagnosed as schizophrenic compared with 2% in a low-risk group.

### Evaluation

- High concordance rates in MZ twins may be because they are **treated more similarly** than DZ twins (Loehlin and Nichols, 1976).
- Family similarities can also be explained by **shared environmental influences**.
- Genetic factors are involved but are **not solely responsible**. Less than 50% of children where one parent was schizophrenic develop the disorder (Fish *et al.*, 1992). The **diathesis-stress model** can be used to explain this. However, Rabkin (1980) found that schizophrenics do not report significantly more stressful episodes during the months preceding the initial onset of the disorder.

If schizophrenia is genetic then the genes may cause neuroanatomical and/or biochemical differences.

Known organic disorders, such as brain tumours, lead to psychotic states, which suggests an organic basis for schizophrenia.

### Neuroanatomical explanations

Research has linked schizophrenia, particularly Type II, to abnormalities in brain structure. For example, Torrey (2002) found enlarged ventricles (the brain cavities that hold cerebrospinal fluid). This may be the result of having less developed parts of the brain. Kim *et al.* (2000) found evidence of smaller frontal lobes and abnormal blood flow to certain areas.

Post-mortem examinations of some schizophrenics show that their brains are 6% lighter and have fewer neurons in the cerebral cortex than 'normal' brains.

## Biochemical explanations

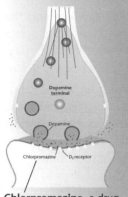

Diagram showing dopamine activity and D2 receptors on the receiving neuron.

**Chlorpromazine**, a drug that blocks symptoms of schizophrenia, occupies the dopamine site on the $D_2$ receptor, preventing receptor activation by dopamine.

The **dopamine hypothesis** (Snyder, 1976) proposes that schizophrenics have abnormally high levels of dopamine. This may be due to the fact that schizophrenics have abnormally high numbers of D2 receptors on receiving neurons, leading to more dopamine binding and more neurons firing. The original hypothesis was based on evidence that the drugs used to alleviate schizophrenic symptoms (**neuroleptics**) block dopamine synapses and the release of dopamine. In addition, the side-effects of neuroleptic drugs are similar to the symptoms of Parkinson's disease, a condition associated with low levels of dopamine, which is improved through the use of L-dopa (Grilly, 2002). Finally, evidence also comes from post-mortem examinations of schizophrenics, which show abnormally high levels of dopamine.

**Revised dopamine hypothesis** – The original dopamine hypothesis was revised by Davis *et al.* (1991) because it was recognised that dopamine (DA) was high in some patients, but not others. Also, a new drug, clozapine, is more effective in reducing schizophrenic symptoms, but blocks dopamine activity less. Therefore, the revised hypothesis suggests that:

- DA high in mesolimbic dopamine system (associated with positive symptoms) → <u>hyper</u>dopaminergia
- DA low in mesocortical dopamine system (and associated with negative symptoms) → <u>hypo</u>dopaminergia

The **glutamate hypothesis** (Olney and Farber, 1995) suggests that it is not dopamine that is the key, but it is implicated because of its role in glutamate production. DA receptors inhibit glutamate release and glutamate may be more closely related to root cause.

### Evaluation

- Neurological differences may be a **cause or effect**.
- Neurological differences may be genetic or could arise from birth complications, i.e. **nurture rather than nature**. Harrison (1995) found that at least some schizophrenics may have experienced brain damage from anoxia (lack of oxygen) at birth. Torrey (1996) suggests a viral cause, which would explain why more schizophrenics were born in late winter.
- Neuroleptic drugs block dopamine fairly rapidly, yet they are **slow to reduce** the symptoms of schizophrenia.
- Healy (2000) suggests that **drug companies** have inappropriately promoted the dopamine hypothesis because it makes money for them.

## Evolutionary explanations

**Group splitting hypothesis** – Stevens and Price (1996) suggest that some schizophrenic traits (e.g. bizarre beliefs, delusions) serve an adaptive function under certain conditions, such as when social groups become too big and they are more at risk from predation and have more difficulty with food; a 'crazy' individual may act as a leader and enable one subgroup to split off from a main group.

**Origin of language theory** – Crow (2000) proposes that schizophrenia is due to a disruption of language mechanisms. This is supported by the fact that schizophrenics often believe they are hearing voices and/or may use strange language (e.g. word salads). Language is normally highly adaptive but it might be that sometimes the brain malfunctions, giving rise to abnormal linguistic functions. Schizophrenia is the price that humans pay for language.

**Key points from AS**

- You can read about neurotransmission in more detail in *Revise AS Unit 5.3, page 112*.

**Key points from AS**

- General criticisms of the biological approach to explaining abnormality can be found in *Revise AS Unit 7.1, page 151*.

It is important to remember that evolutionary explanations for mental disorders are based on the assumption that such disorders are inherited, or at least a predisposition for the disorder is inherited.

The evolutionary approach can be criticised for being determinist and not accounting for individual and cultural differences.

## Psychological explanations of schizophrenia

### Behavioural explanations

**Labelling theory** (Scheff, 1966) – Schizophrenia results from learning that escape to an inner world is rewarding. Individuals who have been labelled as schizophrenic then continue to act in ways that conform to the label. Bizarre behaviours are rewarded with attention and sympathy; this is known as secondary gain.

**Operant conditioning** – Some psychologists (e.g. Liberman, 1982) suggest that some children may receive abnormal reinforcements for social behaviours when they are young so they 'learn' to behave in bizarre ways to inappropriate stimuli. Subsequently, people avoid or respond strangely to the child's bizarre behaviour, which is further reinforcing and leads eventually to a psychotic state.

### Evaluation

- The success of token economies (see page 103) with schizophrenia offers modest support for explanations based on operant conditioning.

### Cognitive explanations

Many symptoms of schizophrenia relate to cognitive malfunction (e.g. hallucinations, disordered thinking), which suggests a cognitive basis for the abnormality. These malfunctions may be due to physiological abnormalities, for example, hallucinations may be produced by brain abnormalities and are, therefore, 'real'. However, other people are not likely to believe someone who reports hallucinations and, therefore, a sufferer may be labelled 'mad' and may also start to feel they are persecuted.

### Evaluation

- Research has found evidence of **real hallucinations and other sensory problems** in schizophrenics (Elkins and Cromwell, 1994), which supports this explanation.

### Psychodynamic explanations

Freud (1924) proposed that two psychological processes were involved in the development of schizophrenia:

1. **Regression to a pre-ego state** – A harsh emotional environment (such as a cold, unloving family) leads a person to regress to an infantile state (a pre-ego state) where they may talk (neologisms) and behave like a baby.
2. **Efforts to re-establish ego control** – The effect of regression is for the ego to try to re-take control, which results in other typical schizophrenic symptoms such as auditory hallucinations.

### Evaluation

- There has been **little empirical support** for psychodynamic explanations.
- Family relations **may be an effect**. Oltmanns *et al.* (1999) found that parents of schizophrenics did behave differently from parents of other kinds of mental patient. Studies of schizophrenogenic families usually occur after the onset of the disease and, therefore, the dynamics have probably been altered by the stresses of having an ill son/daughter.

See page 72 for an explanation of operant conditioning.

**Key points from AS**

- General evaluations of the behaviourist approach to explaining abnormality can be found in *Revise AS Unit 7.1, page 153*.

Cognitive explanations are focused on maladaptive ways of thinking.

**Key points from AS**

- General evaluations of the cognitive approach to explaining abnormality can be found in *Revise AS Unit 7.1, page 154*.

**Regression** is a form of ego-defence where the ego deals with anxiety by regressing to an earlier state in life that was stress-free.

**Key points from AS**

- Bettelheim (1967) proposed that cold parenting could explain autism (the 'refrigerator mother'), see *Revise AS Unit 7.3, page 166*.

**Key points from AS**

- General evaluations of the psychodynamic approach to explaining abnormality can be found in *Revise AS Unit 7.1, page 153*.

## Socio-cultural explanations

**Double-bind theory** – Bateson *et al.* (1956) proposed that schizophrenia is a learned response to mutually-exclusive demands being made on a child and also conflicting messages. Prolonged exposure results in a child developing their own, internally consistent construction of reality. R.D. Laing (1959) regarded schizophrenia as a sane response to a disordered environment.

**Expressed emotion (EE)** – Another family factor that has been implicated in schizophrenia is expressed emotion – the extent to which a family communicates in a critical, hostile and over-emotional way. In fact, EE has been found to be particularly significant as a variable that prevents recovery; schizophrenics in high EE families have been found to be less likely to recover. For example, Vaughn and Leff (1976) found 51% relapse in schizophrenics returning to high EE homes, compared with 13% relapse for those returning to low EE homes.

**Social causation hypothesis** – Members of lower social classes have more stressful lives, and this makes them more vulnerable to schizophrenia. However, it may be that developing schizophrenia leads to reduced social status (**social drift hypothesis**). Turner and Wagonfeld (1967) found that the fathers of schizophrenics tended to belong to the lower social classes.

### Evaluation

- The genetic evidence shows that any account **must include biological factors**.
- Family abnormalities may be a **reasonable response** to a child with brain damage.
- If the family is at fault, **all children should develop the disorder**. This suggests that only vulnerable individuals are affected, or those who are made scapegoats.
- The importance of EE is supported by an adoption study, which showed that children whose natural mothers had schizophrenia were more likely to develop the disorder than their 'normal' adoptive siblings. However, this difference only emerged when the adopted family was rated as disturbed (Tienari *et al.*, 1994). This shows an **interaction between genetic vulnerability and environmental stressors** (the diathesis-stress model).
- Environmental factors may be more important in understanding the **course rather than the cause** of schizophrenia.

**Socio-cultural explanations** explain schizophrenia in terms of social and cultural factors, such as the sufferers' immediate family or their wider social circle.

Some of the other psychological explanations can also be seen as socio-cultural – such as *labelling theory* (labels provided by members of society) and *schizophrenogenic families* (the influence of others in your social group).

## Practice essay 9.2

Discuss biological explanations of schizophrenia. *(25 marks)*

# 9.3 Treatments for schizophrenia

After studying this section you should be able to describe and evaluate:

- *biological therapies for schizophrenia, including their evaluation in terms of appropriateness and effectiveness*
- *psychological therapies for schizophrenia, for example, behavioural, psychodynamic and cognitive-behavioural, including their evaluation in terms of appropriateness and effectiveness.*

LEARNING SUMMARY

## Biological therapies for schizophrenia

AQA A    U4
AQA B    U3

The term **psychotic** refers to a person who lacks contact with reality. Schizophrenia is a psychotic disorder.

### Key points from AS

- For a diagram of a neuron synapse (the gap between two neurons) see *Revise AS Unit 5.3, page 112.*

**Placebos** are substances that have no pharmacological effects but the person taking them thinks they are the real thing. This means you can separate the psychological from the physical effects of being given a drug treatment.

### Key points from AS

- General criticisms of drug therapies are given in *Revise AS Unit 7.2, page 156.*

### Key points from AS

- ECT is described in *Revise AS Unit 7.2, page 157.*

### Chemotherapy: drugs

**Anti-psychotic drugs** are used to treat psychotic illnesses, such as schizophrenia.

- **Typical anti-psychotics**, for example, *chlorpromazine*, are used to treat the positive symptoms of schizophrenia, such as hallucinations. They bind to dopamine receptors at the end of neurons and, thus, block dopamine action, reducing the positive symptoms.
- **Atypical anti-psychotics**, such as *clozapine*, treat negative symptoms of schizophrenia (such as reduced emotional expression) as well as positive symptoms. They act on the serotonin system as well as the dopamine system by temporarily occupying receptor sites and then allowing normal transmission. This may explain why side effects are less severe than when typical anti-psychotics are used.

### Appropriateness and effectiveness

- Conventional anti-psychotics have a range of serious **side effects**, such as **extrapyramidal effects** – where patients develop movement disorders (e.g. muscle tremors) typical of patients with Parkinson's disease.
- There are serious side effects with the newer atypical anti-psychotics, for example, clozapine is linked with **agranulocytosis**, a potentially life-threatening drop in the number of white blood cells.
- Davis *et al.* (1989) looked at over 100 studies comparing anti-psychotic drugs with placebo treatment and found that the **drugs came out as more effective** in the vast majority of the studies. Overall, more than 70% of patients treated with conventional anti-psychotics were much improved after 6 weeks, compared with fewer than 25% of patients treated with a placebo only.
- Studies **comparing conventional anti-psychotics with the newer anti-psychotics** suggest that the former can be just as effective. For example, the CATIE study (2005), involving 1400 patients, found that the conventional anti-psychotic drug, *perphenazine*, was just as effective as the newer (and more expensive) atypical drugs, and no more likely to cause side-effects.

### ECT

### Appropriateness and effectiveness

- Tharyan and Adams (2005) report that ECT **remains a common treatment** option for people with schizophrenia. They reviewed 26 studies (about 800 patients) and concluded that courses of ECT resulted, in the short term, in better overall improvement in schizophrenics than the use of a placebo (sham treatment).
- However, drug therapies had greater success than ECT alone; anti-psychotic **drugs plus ECT produced the best outcomes.**

# Psychological therapies for schizophrenia

AQA A ▶ U4
AQA B ▶ U3

A **secondary reinforcer** is one that has become reinforcing through association with things that are primary needs.

### Key points from AS

• General criticisms of psychological therapies are given in *Revise AS Unit 7.1, pages 158–160*.

Your evaluation of treatments can include information about the reliability and validity of the diagnoses. If the original diagnosis lacks reliability/validity then the treatment may not be effective.

### Key points from AS

• Psychoanalysis and CBT are described and evaluated in *Revise AS Unit 7.1, page 158 and 160 respectively.*

Psychotherapies such as psychoanalysis and CBT are only suitable for mental illnesses where some insight is retained, so they may not be especially suitable for schizophrenia.

The problem with a review of a number of studies (**meta-analysis**) is that they average a variety of results and are likely to produce rather inconclusive results.

There have been a number of well-publicised cases where a schizophrenic patient being cared for in the community has committed a murder. Usually, this is because the patient has stopped taken his/her medications.

## Behavioural therapy: token economy (TE)

Institutionalised patients are given tokens when they engage in pre-defined correct/socially desirable behaviours. The tokens can be exchanged for food or privileges. They act as **secondary reinforcers**, whereas food and privileges are **primary reinforcers** (reinforcing in their own right). This system enables patients to cope better when living independently and may focus particularly on negative symptoms, such as poor motivation and social withdrawal.

### Appropriateness and effectiveness

• Allyon and Azrin (1968) used TE to control the behaviour of 45 chronic schizophrenics who had been institutionalised for an average of 16 years. They were given tokens for making their beds or combing their hair. The number of **chores the patients performed each day increased** from about 5 to over 40.
• The drawback to this therapy is that it often fails to transfer to life outside the institution. McMonagle and Sultana (2000) reviewed several studies and found **low support for maintenance of behaviours beyond the treatment** programme. However, Woods *et al.* (1984) found fundamental long-term effects.
• The effectiveness of tokens **may be due to other factors**, such as being positively reinforcing for the nursing staff, who feel they are making positive gains and, therefore, are stimulated to persist. They also help to structure the situation and ensure consistent rewards.

## Psychodynamic therapy: psychoanalysis

Spotnitz (1969) pioneered the use of psychoanalysis with schizophrenic patients. He believed that treatment needed to focus on redirecting aggression outwards rather than being inward-focused self-hate, which was at the root of serious mental disorders like schizophrenia. Spotnitz is credited with founding modern psychoanalysis.

## Cognitive-behavioural therapy (CBT)

CBT is a recommended treatment for people with schizophrenia (Cochrane Review, 2006). This approach helps to link the person's feelings and patterns of thinking that underpin distress.

### Appropriateness and effectiveness

• Sensky *et al.* (2000) compared CBT with a 'non-specific befriending control intervention'. **CBT was effective** in treating negative and positive symptoms that were resistant to standard anti-psychotic drugs, with a sustained effect over 9 months later.
• However, Jones *et al.* (2004) reviewed 30 studies of CBT and found fairly **minimal evidence of effectiveness** when treating schizophrenia.

### The role of community care

The advent of drug therapies has meant many mental patients can be cared for in the community where they receive a mixture of care from mental health teams as well as structured psychotherapy (e.g. CBT).

## Practice essays 9.3

(a) Outline the clinical characteristics of schizophrenia.  *(5 marks)*
(b) Describe and evaluate **one** behavioural therapy for schizophrenia.  *(10 marks)*
(c) Describe and evaluate **one** psychodynamic therapy for schizophrenia.  *(10 marks)*

# Chapter 10

# Depression

## 10.1 Classification and diagnosis of depression

**After studying this section you should be able to describe and evaluate:**

*Note that AQA A students only need to study* **one** *mental disorder, i.e. they only need to study chapter 9 or 10 or 11 or 12.*

- *clinical characteristics of depression*
- *issues surrounding the classification and diagnosis of depression, including reliability and validity.*

LEARNING SUMMARY

### Clinical characteristics of depression

AQA A    U4
AQA B    U3

There are two forms of depression: unipolar (also called major depression), and bipolar or manic-depression. AQA A students do not need to study both but can read about bipolar disorder on page 164.

About 10% of men and 20% of women become clinically depressed at some time in their lives.

Depression is a disorder of mood or affect. It may exist on its own or may be just one aspect of a more involved disorder. The clinical characteristics are listed below, organised into four main groups:

- **Emotional:** sadness, feelings of guilt, thoughts of suicide.
- **Motivational:** loss of interest and energy, shift in energy level (becoming lethargic or more agitated).
- **Cognitive:** difficulty concentrating and slowed thinking.
- **Somatic:** loss of, or increase in, appetite and weight; sleep disturbance (insomnia or oversleeping).

DSM-IV (see page 96) requires that the diagnosis of a major depressive episode requires that five of the above clinical characteristics occur nearly every day for a minimum of two weeks. In addition, a patient should either show a depressed mood or loss of interest and pleasure. The symptoms must also cause clinically significant distress or impairment in general functioning, nor be better accounted for by bereavement, i.e. the loss of a loved one. It may be useful to distinguish between **endogenous** depression (e.g. related to hormone changes or biochemical factors) and **reactive** depression (triggered by external events).

### Issues surrounding the classification and diagnosis of depression

General issues related to reliability and validity of classification and diagnosis are discussed on pages 96–97.

#### Reliability

**Inter-rater agreement** – Brown *et al.* (2001) found reasonable inter-rater agreement in assessments made of about 350 patients, in terms of their anxiety and mood disorders, using DSM-IV.

**Test-retest reliability** – Moca *et al.* (2007) found high inter-rater reliability (.877) and test-retest reliability (.776) though these figures were lower than for schizophrenia.

There are times when we all feel depressed. The symptoms of clinical depression are similar to 'normal' depression, but more intense and long-lasting.

#### Validity

**Descriptive validity** – Zigler and Phillips (1961) found that the symptoms of depression were just as likely to be found in someone diagnosed with bipolar disorder as in someone labelled 'neurotic', and in 25% of those termed schizophrenic. This suggests that a diagnosis of depression conveys little information about a patient.

### Practice essays 10.1

(a) Outline the clinical characteristics of depression, with reference to examples.

*(9 marks)*

(b) To what extent are diagnoses of depression reliable and/or valid?   *(16 marks)*

# 10.2 Explanations of depression

*After studying this section you should be able to describe and evaluate:*

- *biological explanations of depression, for example, genetics, biochemistry*
- *psychological explanations of depression, for example, behavioural, cognitive, psychodynamic and socio-cultural.*

**LEARNING SUMMARY**

## Biological explanations of depression

AQA A  U4
AQA B  U3

> There is strong evidence that depression is related to biological factors, though not as strong as the evidence for schizophrenia (see pages 98–99).

### Genetic explanations

Individuals may inherit a gene or genes that cause their depression. Research suggests that it is not likely to be one gene (see gene mapping studies) and that such genes predispose individuals to develop the disorder, rather than being a certainty (identical MZ twins don't show 100% concordance).

### Research evidence

> **Gene mapping** involves comparing the genetic material from families who have depression with samples from families who don't have depression in order to identify common factors.

**Gene mapping** – Caspi *et al.* (2005) have found a link between abnormalities in the **5-HTT gene** and depression. 5-HTT is linked to the production of serotonin (see biochemical explanations below), so this research links genetic and biochemical explanations.

**Twin studies** – Kendler and Prescott (1999) studied nearly 4,000 pairs of US twins and found 39% heritability for depression. This study found no gender differences, whereas Bierut *et al.* (1999) found a stronger genetic component in female twins' depression.

> There is stronger evidence of genetic factors in bipolar disorder (see page 165)

**Adoption studies** – Wender *et al.* (1986) found that biological relatives of adopted depressives were about eight times more likely than adoptive relatives to have had major depression themselves. Wender *et al.* (1986) also found that adopted children were eight times more likely to develop depression if their biological parents had suffered from clinical depression.

### Evaluation

> If depression is genetic then the genes may cause neuroanatomical and/or biochemical differences.

- The research indicates **more environmental than genetic** influence.
- The 5-HTT gene has also been linked to a number of other disorders, such as autism, so it is **not a specific vulnerability factor** for depression – though of course depression does underlie a whole range of mental disorders.

### Biochemical explanations: neurotransmitters

The **permissive amine theory** of mood disorder (Kety, 1975) suggests that depression is caused by a deficiency of **noradrenaline**. Noradrenaline is controlled by serotonin and dopamine. When levels of the latter are low, noradrenaline may fluctuate wildly, leading to depression. The theory refers to 'amine' because noradrenaline, serotonin and dopamine are all neurotransmitters of the monoamine group. In 'normal' circumstances these neurotransmitters are involved in arousal and mood, so it makes sense that they are involved in mood disorders.

> The **diathesis-stress model** suggests that people inherit a vulnerability (diathesis) to develop depression, but it only occurs when triggered by life experiences (stressors).

The importance of **serotonin** is supported by the fact that one of the most successful anti-depressants (SSRIs) increases levels of serotonin (see page 109), and usually reduces the symptoms of depression. Other anti-depressants also increase levels of noradrenaline.

The effect of **dopamine** is also supported by the effectiveness of some anti-depressants – SSRIs also increase levels of dopamine. However, this effect may be slower than the effects for serotonin, which could explain why SSRIs do not have an immediate effect on depression (Zhou *et al.*, 2005).

### Research evidence

Teuting *et al.* (1981) analysed the urine of depressed and normal people and found lower levels of products associated with noradrenaline in the depressed people.

Mann *et al.* (1996) found impaired serotonin production in people with depression.

### Evaluation

- It is hard to know whether neurotransmitter changes are a **cause or effect** of depression.
- The effects of anti-depressants **are not the same** for everyone, which suggests that the causes are not likely to be the same.
- Anti-depressants raise neurotransmitter levels immediately, yet it may take weeks before there are psychological effects. In addition, the fact that there are also placebo effects (see page 102) suggests that biochemical explanations **do not provide a complete account of depression**.
- Anti-depressants are also used to treat other conditions (such as anorexia), which suggests that neurotransmitter dysfunction is not specific to major depression.

Hormonal causes of depression may explain why more women than men suffer from depression.

## Biochemical explanations: hormones

Some forms of depression, are linked to hormonal changes, for example, endogenous disorders such as **post-partum depression** (PPD) and **pre-menstrual syndrome** (PMS), and reactive disorders such as **seasonal affective disorder** (triggered by changing day length, causing changes in melatonin levels, see page 16).

### Research evidence

Abramowitz *et al.* (1982) found that 41% of women who were admitted to psychiatric hospital entered on or within a day of the start of their menstrual period.

About 20% of women report moderate depression in the first weeks after giving birth, however, Cooper (1988) found that a similar number of non-pregnant women reported feelings of depression.

**Cortisol** tends to be elevated in depressed patients. Carroll *et al.* (1980) showed that dexamethasone does not suppress cortisol in 50% of depressed individuals, whereas it does in normal individuals. This may be because levels of cortisol are so high in depressives they can't be suppressed.

PPD may be due to 'normal' hormonal cycles, or may be a reactive rather than an endogenous disorder – caused by lack of emotional support, low self-esteem and unrealistic ideas about motherhood.

### Key points from AS

- General criticisms of the biological approach to explaining abnormality can be found in *Revise AS Unit 7.1, page 151.*

### Key points from AS

- The hormone **cortisol** is produced when an individual is stressed or anxious – see *Revise AS Unit 5.1, page 98.*

### Evaluation

- Hormonal changes could be an **effect rather than a cause**.
- Hormonal changes may act as a **predisposing factor**; depression occurs when there are other stressors, as in PPD (the **diathesis-stress model**, see page 54).

## Evolutionary explanations

**Rank theory** – Nesse and Williams (1995) suggest that depression is an adaptive response to losing rank, because it prevents further injury from re-engaging in combat. Conflicts are common in any social group and depression helps the individual to accept losing and settle for an inferior role. In time, depression became associated with other kinds of loss, such as loss of a loved one. 'Clinical depression' is a pathological outcome of an adaptive emotional mechanism.

**Genome lag** – Nesse and Williams (1995) suggest that depression may occur increasingly more because we are not adapted to live in urban situations. In addition, there are high commercial and achievement pressures in modern life, which are stressful. These can lead to depression because of our inability to cope with such aspects of modern life, things that we are not adapted for.

It's important to remember that evolutionary explanations for mental disorders are based on the assumption that such disorders are inherited, or at least a predisposition for the disorder is inherited.

The evolutionary approach can be criticised for being determinist and not accounting for individual and cultural differences.

## Psychological explanations of depression

AQA A   U4
AQA B   U3

**Key points from AS**

• General evaluations of the behaviourist approach to explaining abnormality can be found in *Revise AS Unit 7.1, page 153*.

### Behavioural explanations

**Learned helplessness** – Seligman (1974) suggested that if an animal finds that its responses are ineffective, then it learns that there is no point in responding and, thereafter, behaves passively, which is a form of conditioning. This explanation was further developed by Abramson *et al.* (see below).

**Reinforcement** – Lewinsohn (1974) suggested that depressed people do very little and are socially withdrawn. This results in a lack of reinforcement and so they become trapped in a cycle of social withdrawal, perpetuating depression. Socially unskilled individuals are more likely to be socially withdrawn and this explains why they may be more prone to depression (see next page on socio-cultural explanations).

#### Research evidence

Hiroto and Seligman (1974) showed that college students who were exposed to uncontrollable aversive events (learned helplessness) were more likely to later fail on cognitive tasks.

Jacobson *et al.* (1996) found that reinforcement could be used to successfully treat depression (see page 110).

Cognitive explanations focus on the way a person *thinks* about their life; it is this style of thinking that creates depression.

**Key points from AS**

• **Attribution theory** is discussed in *Revise AS Unit 6.3, page 139*.

**Attribution** is the process of explaining causes of behaviour. We do not observe traits, we observe behaviours and infer personal attributes.

Beck's model has also been used to explain bipolar disorder, see page 166.

### Cognitive explanations

**Attributional style** – Abramson *et al.* (1978) applied the concept of learned helplessness to mental disorder, suggesting that depressed individuals have an attributional style where they tend to attribute failure to themselves (internal) rather than to external factors. Such individuals see these attributions as unchanging (stable) and as global, rather than specific. Abramson *et al.* (1989) extended their theory of attributional style into a broader **hopelessness theory**. Negative attributional style does not necessarily result in depression, for example, a person may just avoid traumatic experiences. But in cases where a person has a negative attributional style *and* believes that bad things are likely to happen (i.e. is hopeless), then depression is likely.

**The cognitive triad** – Beck (1967) suggested that depressed individuals hold negative thoughts about three things:

• **Themselves** – they regard themselves as helpless, worthless, and inadequate.
• **The world** – it is seen to contain obstacles that cannot be handled.
• **The future** – one's worthlessness prevents any improvements.

Such negative cognitions are self-defeating and lead to depression.

#### Research evidence

Seligman (1974) found that students who made stable, global attributions stayed depressed for longer after exams. However, Ford and Neale (1985) found that depressed students didn't underestimate their sense of control, contrary to the predictions of the theory.

Support for Beck comes from Bates *et al.* (1999), who found that depressed participants who were given negative automatic thought-like statements became more and more depressed.

#### Evaluation

• The success of **cognitive-behavioural therapies** in treating depression offers support for cognitive explanations (see page 110).
• The fact that there is a link between negative thoughts and depression does not mean that the former **caused** the latter.

**Key points from AS**

• General evaluations of the cognitive approach to explaining abnormality can be found in *Revise AS Unit 7.1, page 154*.

## Psychodynamic explanations

Freud suggested that loss in early life leads to depression later (he called it 'melancholia'). Repressed anger towards the lost person is directed inwards towards the self, reducing self-esteem. If loss is experienced later in adult life, this leads a person to re-experience early loss.

**Key points from AS**

• Bowlby's views on separation are discussed in *Revise AS Unit 3.1, page 53*.

Bowlby (1973) suggested that separation from a primary caregiver in early childhood may increase susceptibility to depression later.

### Research evidence

Bifulco *et al.* (1992) studied 249 women who, under the age of 17, had experienced maternal loss either through separation (for more than a year) or death. These women were twice as likely to suffer from depressive or anxiety disorders as adults, and this was particularly true where death occurred before the age of 6.

**Key points from AS**

• General evaluations of the psychodynamic approach to explaining abnormality can be found in *Revise AS Unit 7.1, page 153*.

Barnes and Prosen (1985) found that men whose fathers had died during their childhood scored higher on a depression scale than 'normal' men.

Spitz (1945) used the term **anaclitic depression** to describe the severe and progressive depression found in institutionalised infants, resulting from a loss of attachments.

### Evaluation

• The evidence is **inconsistent**, for example, Paykel (1981) reviewed studies and found that half weren't supportive of early loss as an explanation.

## Socio-cultural explanations

**Socio-cultural explanations** explain depression in terms of social and cultural factors, such as the sufferers' immediate family or their wider social circle.

**Life events** have been associated with depression, acting as stressors. Ohrenwend *et al.* (1986) found that depressed patients typically experienced higher levels of negative life events than normal in the year before a depressive episode.

**Social networks** – People with little social support are more likely to become depressed and also remain depressed. This is also related to having social skills; some people lack interpersonal skills and, therefore, find it difficult to maintain friendships, which makes it more likely that they will become depressed.

The **life events** approach fits the **diathesis-stress model** where an individual has a vulnerability to depression, which is triggered by stressful life events.

### Research evidence

Kendler *et al.* (1995) found that the highest levels of depression were in women who were exposed to recent negative life events (such as an assault or serious marital problems) *and* were most genetically at risk for depression (i.e. the identical twin of a woman diagnosed with depression). This supports the **diathesis-stress model**.

Davila *et al.* (1995) found that adolescents with poor interpersonal problem-solving skills were more likely to become depressed, which supports the view that such characteristics are a cause of depression.

Brown and Harris (1978) studied depressed women in London and found that key factors were long-term relationship difficulties and being at home looking after children, i.e. life events and social factors.

### Evaluation

• Poor social skills/reduced social circle could be a **cause or effect** of depression. Even if it is a cause, the resulting effect would be a downward spiral.

## Practice essay 10.2

Discuss biological explanations of depression.  *(25 marks)*

# 10.3 Treatments for depression

**After studying this section you should be able to describe and evaluate:**

- biological therapies for depression, including their evaluation in terms of appropriateness and effectiveness
- psychological therapies for depression, for example, behavioural, psychodynamic and cognitive-behavioural, including their evaluation in terms of appropriateness and effectiveness.

**LEARNING SUMMARY**

## Biological therapies for depression

AQA A   U4
AQA B   U3

### Chemotherapy: drugs

**Anti-depressant drugs** (stimulants), such as Prozac, promote activity of noradrenaline and serotonin, which leads to increased arousal but can be affected by rebound (depression after initial euphoria).

- **Tricyclics** increase activity of noradrenaline and serotonin by blocking their re-uptake. When a neuron fires, the neurotransmitters are released into the synapse; they are then re-absorbed by the neuron, preventing further action. By blocking re-uptake the neurotransmitter levels are increased.
- **SSRIs (selective serotonin re-uptake inhibitors)** block mainly serotonin.
- **Selective noradrenaline re-uptake inhibitors** are also now available.

### Appropriateness and effectiveness

- The fact that effectiveness **varies considerably between individuals** detracts from its power as a therapy. For example, Spiegel (1989) found that only 65% of depressed patients improved using tricyclics.
- Anti-depressants have been found to be **more effective than placebos**. For example, Furukawa *et al.* (2003) reviewed 35 studies comparing low dosage tricyclics with **placebos**, and found a significant beneficial effect for tricyclics.
- However, **placebo effects** are significant, which suggests that some of the effects of anti-depressants are psychological rather than biological.
- Anti-depressants have been linked to **suicidal and homicidal behaviour**, leading to several high-profile court cases against drug companies.

### Electroconvulsive therapy (ECT)

#### Appropriateness and effectiveness

- ECT appears to be **successful for cases of severe depression**. Janicak *et al.* (1985) found that 80% of all severely depressed patients respond well to ECT, compared with 64% recovery when given drug therapy.
- However, Sackheim *et al.* (2001) found that 84% of patients **relapsed within 6 months**. Even when ECT is used in conjunction with anti-depressants, the relapse rate was relatively high (39%).

### Light therapy

Light therapy is used for treating seasonal affective disorder (SAD). It uses very bright, full-spectrum lights, often at a particular time of day. It is often used in addition to drug therapy.

#### Appropriateness and effectiveness

- Tuunainen *et al.* (2004) reviewed a number of studies, which showed that high quality light therapy had a significant effect on SAD as compared to drugs.

### Key points from AS

- For a diagram of a neuron synapse (the gap between two neurons) see *Revise AS Unit 5.3, page 112.*

### Key points from AS

- General criticisms of drug therapies are given in *Revise AS Unit 7.2, page 156.*

**Placebos** are substances that have no pharmacological effects but the person taking them thinks they are the real thing. This means you can separate the psychological from the physical effects of being given a drug treatment.

### Key points from AS

- ECT is described in *Revise AS Unit 7.2, page 157.*

On average, chronically depressed patients recover spontaneously after about three months. About 10% of patients remain depressed. Drug therapies have proved useful.

## Psychological therapies for depression

AQA A ▶ U4
AQA B ▶ U3

### Behavioural therapy

**Behavioural action (BA)** – Jacobson *et al.* (1996) based a therapy on the behavioural view that reinforcement was the key; if you teach patients to elicit higher rates of reinforcement, their depression will lift (as Lewinsohn had suggested, see page 107). Jacobsen *et al.* claimed that cognitive methods are inefficient, whereas BA just focuses on the consequences of behaviour.

**Social skills training** – Patients are taught better social skills through reward and modelling.

#### Appropriateness and effectiveness

- Gortner *et al.* (1998) compared CBT and BA and found no significant differences even 24 months after treatment, i.e. the simpler method was just as efficient. However, in both treatment groups the level of success was 50% after treatment and 25% after two years.

### Psychodynamic therapy

According to the psychodynamic view, depression has its origins in childhood. Therefore, unless these roots are explored and dealt with, the symptoms will reappear. Therefore, psychoanalysis is the only effective cure. **Short-term psychodynamic psychotherapies (STPP)** have been developed to make this process quicker.

#### Appropriateness and effectiveness

- The success of other therapies for treating depression suggests that it is **not always necessary to have insight** into the causes of the disorder.
- Henken *et al.* (2007) found that **family therapy** is an effective intervention in treating people of any age with depression.

### Cognitive-behavioural therapy (CBT)

Beck (1976) used his concept of the cognitive triad to propose a treatment for depression; the therapist identifies the patient's self-defeating assumptions and substitutes more adaptive ones.

**Rational-emotional behaviour therapy (REBT)** – Ellis (1962) developed his own therapy, which also focused on changing irrational beliefs. Ellis suggested an ABC model: (A) Activating event leads to (B) Beliefs about the activating event, which leads to (C) Consequences. A therapist is directive and aggressive and challenges beliefs through **disputing**, e.g. asking the patient to justify the logic of the beliefs (logical disputing) or to consider the evidence for irrational beliefs (empirical disputing).

#### Appropriateness and effectiveness

- CBT can be **combined with drug therapy** to increase effectiveness. Keller *et al.* (2000) found a 73% response rate for combined therapy compared to 48% for one therapy alone.
- CBT is a **relatively short form** of psychotherapy, taking about 16 weeks, and the strategies can be applied to future situations.

---

**Key points from AS**

- General criticisms of psychological therapies are given in *Revise AS Unit 7.1, pages 158–160.*

Your evaluation of treatments can include information about the reliability and validity of the diagnoses. If the original diagnosis lacks reliability/validity then the treatment may not be effective.

**Key points from AS**

- Psychoanalysis and CBT are described and evaluated in *Revise AS Unit 7.1, pages 158 and 160 respectively.*

Cognitive explanations focus on thinking; cognitive-behavioural treatments are a combination of cognitive and behavioural approaches.

The American Psychiatric Association (2000) rated CBT as one of the best approaches to treating depression.

---

## Practice essays 10.3

(a) Outline the clinical characteristics of depression.    *(5 marks)*
(b) Describe **one** behavioural therapy for depression.    *(10 marks)*
(c) Describe and evaluate **one** psychodynamic therapy for depression. *(10 marks)*

# Chapter 11
# Anxiety disorder – phobias

## 11.1 Classification and diagnosis of phobic disorders

*After studying this section you should be able to describe and evaluate:*

*Note that AQA A students only need to study **one** mental disorder, i.e. they only need to study chapter 9 or 10 or 11 or 12.*

- *clinical characteristics of phobic disorders*
- *issues surrounding the classification and diagnosis of phobic disorders, including reliability and validity.*

## Clinical characteristics of phobic disorders

AQA A ▶ 114

About 50% of all clinically-diagnosed phobics are suffering from agoraphobia with panic disorder. However, many people do not seek treatment, which may disguise the frequency of specific and social phobias. The BBC website on phobias suggests a rate of about 1 in 10 people for simple phobias and about 2–3 in 100 for social phobias and agoraphobia.

All categories of phobias are twice as common in women as men.

Specific phobias generally have little impact on overall quality of life.

A phobic disorder involves extreme, persistent, and irrational fear, which is coupled with a lack of control and is strongly out of proportion with possible danger. DSM-IV (see page 96) includes various phobias within the category of anxiety disorders:

**Agoraphobia** (with or without panic disorders) is the fear of open spaces. When it is accompanied by panic disorder, the panic disorder usually starts first; fear of having another attack makes the individual feel insecure about being in public.

**Social phobias** are a fear of, for example, talking or eating in public; extreme concern about your own behaviour and the reactions of others.

**Specific or simple phobias** are fears of specific things, such as zoophobias (fear of animals), fear of natural environments (e.g. water, heights, the dark), fear of blood or injury, and fear of dangerous situations (e.g. being trapped).

The common diagnostic characteristics of phobias are as follows:

- Exposure to the feared stimulus nearly always produces a high level of anxiety.
- The anxiety experienced is out of proportion to the actual situation.
- The sufferer is aware of the extremity of their reaction.
- The feared situations are either avoided or responded to with great anxiety.
- Significant interference with life, or marked distress.

## Issues surrounding the classification and diagnosis of phobic disorders

General issues related to reliability and validity of classification and diagnosis are discussed on pages 96–97.

Fear and anxiety are adaptive responses. A fear becomes a phobia when it interferes with normal functioning.

### Reliability

**Inter-rater reliability** – Skre *et al.* (1991) found high inter-rater reliability for social phobias – a kappa statistic of +.72 for three raters assessing 54 interviews.

**Test–retest reliability** – Kendler *et al.* (1999) assessed the patients on separate occasions, 8 years apart, concluding that single personal interviews lack reliability.

### Validity

Descriptive validity is poor, for example, Eysenck (1997) reported that up to two-thirds of patients with an anxiety disorder have also been diagnosed with one or more additional anxiety disorders.

## Practice essays 11.1

(a) Outline the clinical characteristics of phobic disorders, with reference to examples.

*(9 marks)*

(b) To what extent are diagnoses of phobic disorders reliable and/or valid?

*(16 marks)*

# 11.2 Explanations of phobic disorders

*After studying this section you should be able to describe and evaluate:*

- *biological explanations of phobic disorders, for example, genetics and biochemistry*
- *psychological explanations of phobic disorders, for example, behavioural, cognitive, psychodynamic and socio-cultural.*

LEARNING SUMMARY

## Biological explanations of phobic disorders

AQA A   U4

**Gene mapping** involves comparing the genetic material from families who have phobic disorders with samples from families without such disorders to identify common factors.

### Genetic explanations

Individuals may inherit a gene or genes that cause their phobic disorder. Research suggests that it is not likely to be one gene (see gene mapping studies) and that such genes predispose individuals to develop the disorder, rather than being a certainty (identical MZ twins do not show 100% concordance).

#### Research evidence

**Gene mapping** – There is some evidence of a link between anxiety disorders and a gene related to serotonin (Lesch *et al.* (1996)).

**Twin studies** – Torgersen (1983) found 31% concordance for panic disorder with agoraphobia in MZ twins versus zero concordance in DZ twins, although none of them shared the same phobias. However, Kendler *et al.* (1992) found a lower concordance rate between MZ twins for agoraphobia than in DZ twins.

**Family studies** – Solyom *et al.* (1974) found that 45% of phobic patients studied had a family history of the disorder compared with 17% of 'normal' controls. Ost (1989), in a study on blood phobics, found that 64% had at least one close relative who also suffered from blood phobia.

#### Evaluation

If there is a genetic predisposition for phobic disorders, this does not mean they will inevitably develop. The **diathesis-stress model** suggests that such conditions only occur when triggered by life experiences (stressors).

- Individuals who are related may acquire phobias through **imitation** rather than genetic inheritance.
- Kendler *et al.* (1992) concluded that specific **phobias have a small genetic component** whereas agoraphobia appears to be more related to genetic vulnerability. They provided heritability estimates for different phobias of 67% for agoraphobia, 59% for blood/injury, 51% for social, and 47% for animal phobias.
- Phobias may involve genetic factors but require additional exposure to negative environmental influences (the **diathesis-stress model**).
- The evidence for a genetic basis for phobic disorders is **poor in relation to other disorders, such as schizophrenia** (see page 98).

If phobic disorders are genetic then the genes may cause neuroanatomical and/or biochemical differences.

### Biochemical explanations

**GABA** – People who develop phobias tend to have higher levels of physiological arousal than normal, which means they are especially sensitive to their environment. This may be related to a dysfunction of GABA, which is normally produced to reduce anxiety levels. GABA reduces activity in the nervous system by slowing down transmission between nerve cells and, thus, makes a person feel calmer.

**Key points from AS**

- Both GABA and BZs are discussed in *Revise AS Unit 5.2, page 109.*

**Biogenic amines** – Another explanation is that neurotransmitters in the amine group (**noradrenalin, serotonin** and **dopamine**) may play a role in phobias. Van der Wee *et al.* (2008) found evidence that dopamine and serotonin levels may be abnormal in people with social phobias.

**Key points from AS**

• General criticisms of the biological approach to explaining abnormality can be found in *Revise AS Unit 7.1, page 151*.

### Evaluation

• The **success of chemotherapies** suggests that GABA and/or biogenic amines may be involved in phobic disorders (see page 116).
• However, it is likely that the success of chemotherapies is due to the fact that they reduce the anxiety component of the phobia and, therefore, enable a sufferer to cope. They **do not target the actual disorder**, which suggests that biochemical factors are not *causes* of phobic disorders.

## Evolutionary explanations: biological preparedness

It is important to remember that evolutionary explanations for mental disorders are based on the assumption that such disorders are inherited, or at least a predisposition for the disorder is inherited.

Seligman (1971) described the concept of **biological preparedness**: that animals have an innate predisposition to develop certain 'ancient' fears because this would be an adaptive behaviour – enhancing their survival and thus reproductive success. In particular, animals would be biologically predisposed to acquire certain conditioned responses more easily than others, e.g. a fear of snakes or heights (see also page 74). It would be advantageous to have a predisposition to *learn* fears rather than inheriting a fixed fear of certain classes of object.

Note that this explanation suggests that phobias have to be learned; it is the predisposition for such learning that is inherited.

The evolutionary approach can be criticised for being **determinist** and not accounting for individual and cultural differences.

### Research evidence

Garcia and Koelling (1966) demonstrated that rats had a predisposition to learn quickly to avoid substances that made them feel sick.

Bennett-Levy and Marteau (1984) found that fear was highly correlated with certain aspects of an animal's appearance – the more the animal's appearance was different to human form, the more the animal was feared. This suggests some innate preparedness.

Mineka *et al.* (1984) found that rhesus monkeys developed a fear of snakes if they saw another monkey showing fear to a snake – social learning. However, fears were not learned so rapidly if the monkey was seen behaving fearfully towards a flower. This supports the view that ancient fears are learned more readily.

DeSilva (1988) found that 88 phobic patients studied in Sri Lanka tended to exhibit fears that were biologically-based, demonstrating the universal (and, thus, innate) nature of such fears.

### Evaluation

Genome lag could explain why innate fears tend not to relate to modern dangers – this is the concept that it takes time for our genes to evolve and better fit the current environment.

• This explains why people are **less likely to develop fears of modern day items** that are dangerous – such as electricity or cars. The reason is we are only biologically prepared to develop 'ancient' fears.
• This explanation can't account for **fears of harmless situations** or things, such as slugs. Though a further explanation may explain this – animals have evolved fears to things that are disgusting, which might also be adaptive.

## Psychological explanations of phobic disorders

AQA A    U4

### Behavioural explanations

Classical and operant conditioning are explained on page 72.

**Classical conditioning** – Watson and Rayner (1920) conditioned 'Little Albert' to fear white furry objects by pairing a loud noise with a white furry object. It is likely that most phobias are learned through the association of trauma with some neutral stimulus. In addition, the fact that phobics avoid their feared situation means the response is never extinguished.

**Operant conditioning** – Mowrer (1947) proposed that the first stage involves classical conditioning followed by operant conditioning (**two-process theory**), because avoidance of the phobic stimulus reduces fear and is, therefore, reinforcing.

**Social learning theory** – Fears may be learned through imitation. Bandura and Rosenthal (1966) arranged for participants to watch someone else ostensibly receiving a painful electric shock every time a buzzer sounded. Later, the participants showed a fear response when they heard the buzzer. The experiment by Mineka *et al.* (see previous page) also demonstrated imitation.

### Evaluation

**Key points from AS**

• General evaluations of the behaviourist approach to explaining abnormality can be found in *Revise AS Unit 7.1, page 153.*

• Learning explanations can be **combined with biological ones** – either in terms of genetic vulnerability (diathesis-stress model) or biological preparedness (we acquire ancient and adaptive fears more readily, see previous page).
• **Not everyone who is exposed to conditioning develops phobias.** For example, DiNardo *et al.* (1988) found that as many people without dog phobias as with reported negative experiences with dogs. However, many people do attribute their phobias to a specific incident (Sue *et al.*, 1994).
• **Stimulus generalisation** (see page 73) could be used to explain how a negative experience with one object has transferred to a fear of something else.
• The **success of behavioural therapies** in treating phobias supports their value as explanations (see page 116).

### Cognitive explanations

Cognitive explanations are focused on maladaptive ways of thinking.

Phobias may be the result of irrational thoughts. For example, the sensation of crowding in a lift may develop into a cognition that lifts are associated with suffocation. This then turns into a fear of lifts, which may be generalised to other situations. So, it is the persons' irrational thoughts in response to an initial fearful situation that trigger off a phobia. Beck *et al.* (1985) suggested that people with phobias are most concerned with their fear of fear rather than fear of actual objects.

### Research evidence

Eysenck (1997) reports research on biological challenges (e.g. breathing a mixture of carbon dioxide and oxygen). This often provokes a panic attack in patients suffering from panic disorder with agoraphobia, but rarely in normal controls. Panic-attack patients may differ in the way they *interpret* their bodily symptoms.

Williams *et al.* (1997) studied patients with agoraphobia and found that they were more concerned with their feelings of anxiety rather than their actual safety, which indicates that it is the patients' thoughts that are the problem.

### Evaluation

**Key points from AS**

• General evaluations of the cognitive approach to explaining abnormality can be found in *Revise AS Unit 7.1, page 154.*

• This approach can explain why **some people are more susceptible** than others to phobias – because of the tendency to think in irrational ways.
• The **success of cognitive-behavioural therapies** in treating phobias supports their value as explanations (see page 117).

## Psychodynamic explanations

Freud (1909) suggested that phobias arise as an ego defence for dealing with repressed anxieties. The anxiety is displaced onto the phobic object (another person or object), which symbolises the initial conflict. If the conflict is resolved the phobia will disappear.

Bowlby (1973) suggested that agoraphobia might be linked to a fear of losing someone important. He suggested that the origins of phobias lie in early separation anxiety and overprotective parents.

### Research evidence

Freud (1909) used the case study of 'Little Hans' to support his explanation of phobias. Hans developed a fear of horses and this was explained as a representation of the boy's unconscious fear of his father, because the horses' bridle represented his father's moustache. Hans' fear specifically was of being bitten by white horses, which was linked to an occasion when he heard a child being told not to touch a white horse because it might bite. Hans was actually scared that his mother would leave him because he asked his mother to touch his penis but she told him off for this. Therefore, not touching something was associated with the white horse. Finally, Hans was further fearful of horses pulling laden carts because the horse might fall over and die. This was linked to his fears related to pregnancy (like a laden cart) and his secret wish that his younger sister would die, a wish that made him feel guilty.

Gerslman *et al.* (1990) suggested, on the basis of a literature review, that phobics (especially social phobics and agoraphobics) had lower than normal parental affection and more parental control or over-protection. This might increase their levels of anxiety.

### Evaluation

- Hans might have developed his fear through **classical conditioning**.
- A case study of one child is **not reliable evidence**.
- In addition, the case study and interviews with Little Hans were recorded by his father so the data may have been affected by **leading questions and subjective interpretations**.
- Such data is **correlational** and doesn't demonstrate a causal link.

## Socio-cultural explanations

Cultural attitudes might be linked to incidence of phobias. For example, Whiting (1966) considered the prevalence of phobias in other cultures and concluded that they were more common in societies that had stricter upbringings. This might also be related to psychodynamic explanations as stricter upbringings might lead to greater repression.

### Research evidence

Cultural influences – Kirmayer (1991) reports a social phobia that is common in Japan but not elsewhere – *taijin kyofusho* is the fear of offending or harming others through one's own awkward social behaviour.

Social influences – Kleiner and Marshall (1987) report that 84% of agoraphobics had experienced family problems in the months before they had their first panic attack. This further supports the diathesis-stress model.

### Key points from AS

- Bowlby's views on separation are discussed in *Revise AS Unit 3.1, page 53*.

### Key points from AS

- General evaluations of the psychodynamic approach to explaining abnormality can be found in *Revise AS Unit 7.1, page 153*.

**Socio-cultural explanations** explain phobic disorders in terms of social and cultural factors such as the sufferers' immediate family or their wider social circle.

## Practice essay 11.2

Discuss biological explanations of phobic disorders. *(25 marks)*

# 11.3 Treatments for phobic disorders

After studying this section you should be able to describe and evaluate:

- biological therapies for phobic disorders, including their evaluation in terms of appropriateness and effectiveness
- psychological therapies for phobic disorders, for example, behavioural, psychodynamic and cognitive-behavioural therapies, including their evaluation in terms of appropriateness and effectiveness.

LEARNING SUMMARY

## Biological therapies for phobic disorders

AQA A    U4

**Key points from AS**

- Anxiolytic drugs were reviewed in studies of stress for AS level, see *Revise AS Unit 5.2, page 109*.

**Key points from AS**

- General criticisms of drug therapies are given in *Revise AS Unit 7.2, page 156*.

Your evaluation of treatments can include information about the reliability and validity of the diagnoses. If the original diagnosis lacks reliability/validity then the treatment may not be effective.

### Chemotherapy: drugs

- **Anxiolytic drugs** are drugs that reduce anxiety, and may be used to treat phobias to reduce the accompanying anxiety. For example, **benzodiazepines** (BZs e.g. *Valium* and *Librium*) enhance the effect of the neurotransmitter **GABA**, and also reduce **serotonin** activity. The common side-effects of BZs are sleepiness and dependence.
- **Anti-depressants** are also used to treat phobias. For example, **SSRIs** (selective serotonin re-uptake indicators, see page 109) are used, which reduce levels of serotonin. **MAIOs** (monoamine oxidase inhibitor) are also used. These are an older class of anti-depressants, which increase serotonin and noradrenaline.

### Evaluation in terms of appropriateness and effectiveness

- Drugs deal effectively with the symptoms of anxiety, for example, Kelly *et al.* found an **88% improvement after one year** of phobic patients being treated with anti-depressants.
- Phobias tend to be treated with psychological rather than biological techniques. However, drugs are **useful in reducing the anxiety** so a person is better able to benefit from psychotherapy. For example, Urukawa *et al.* (2007) reviewed 23 studies and found that combined therapies (anti-depressants and CBT) were more effective in the treatment of panic disorder with or without agoraphobia than either treatment alone.

## Psychological therapies for phobic disorders

AQA A    U4

**Key points from AS**

- General criticisms of psychological therapies are given in *Revise AS Unit 7.1, pages 158–160*.

**Key points from AS**

- SD was described and evaluated as part of your AS course, see *Revise AS Unit 7.2, pages 159*.

ERP (exposure with response prevention) was developed for obsessive compulsive disorder, but is also used with phobias. See page 124.

### Behavioural therapy: Systematic de-sensitisation (SD)

SD is mainly used in the treatment of phobias (rather than other forms of mental disorder). It was devised by Wolpe (1958) and is a process in which a patient learns to pair the feared thing with relaxation rather than anxiety.

The basic steps are (1) teaching relaxation, (2) developing a de-sensitisation hierarchy, (3) visualising fearful scenes and (4) progressing through the hierarchy. The whole process typically takes 3–4 weeks but can be completed more quickly.

This is an example of classical conditioning because the patient is learning to associate the progressively more fearful stimulus with relaxation. It is characterised as **'counter-conditioning'** because the patient is replacing previously learned associations – between object and fear – with a new CS and CR (object and relaxation). **Reciprocal inhibition** also takes place because relaxation and fear are incompatible responses.

SD may involve simply imagining the feared stimulus (**covert desensitisation**) or may involve dealing with the feared object (**in vivo desensitisation**). An alternative is to skip the hierarchy and the relaxation and just experience being with the feared stimulus. This is called **flooding**.

### Evaluation in terms of appropriateness and effectiveness

- McGrath *et al.* (1990) found that 75% of patients with phobias recover after a course of SD. However, **people may recover spontaneously** from phobias so the recovery rate would be almost as good with no treatment.
- **In vivo desensitisation tends to be more effective** than covert desensitisation.
- Marks (1973) suggests that SD works just because of exposure to the feared stimulus. Therefore, the success of SD **may have nothing to do with relaxation**.
- Klein *et al.* (1983) compared SD with supportive psychotherapy for patients with a social phobia (agoraphobia) or with a specific phobia. They found no difference in effectiveness (those receiving supportive psychotherapy had also done well), suggesting that the 'active ingredient' in SD or CBT may simply be the generation of **hopeful expectancies that their phobia can be overcome**.
- There are **ethical objections** to flooding and even some forms of SD, which may be quite traumatic.

*Key points from AS*

- Psychoanalysis and CBT are described and evaluated in *Revise AS Unit 7.1, pages 158 and 160 respectively.*

## Psychodynamic therapy

The aim of psychoanalytic treatments is to uncover the repressed conflicts that are expressed as phobias, analyse what they mean to the patient, and substitute more realistic understandings of childhood events.

### Evaluation in terms of appropriateness and effectiveness

- The case study of Little Hans (see page 115) suggests that **phobias can be 'cured' by dealing with the underlying issues**.
- Knijnik *et al.* (2004) found that a variation of psychoanalysis (**psychodynamic group treatment, or PGT**) was superior to a placebo control group in a 12–week randomised trial.

## Cognitive-behavioural therapy (CBT)

**REBT** has been used with phobias, see page 110.

**CBGT** (cognitive-behavioural group therapy is CBT within a group setting) – Individuals with phobias follow a programme similar to systematic desensitisation (SD) but engage with group members who provide a safe and supportive environment. Each group member works through their hierarchy of fears, learning to relax through each stage. There is also a cognitive element to CBGT where patients are encouraged to replace the irrational beliefs they hold that lead to anxiety with more realistic and rational beliefs. During the simulation scenarios, group members challenge each other's irrational beliefs, giving the individual the opportunity for cognitive restructuring.

### Evaluation in terms of appropriateness and effectiveness

- Beck *et al.* (1994) found CBT to be **more effective than supportive therapy, relaxation and drugs** in the treatment of panic disorder and agoraphobia.
- The **long-term effects** of CBT have also been shown to be superior to other techniques (Clark *et al.*, 1994).

## Practice essays 11.3

(a) Outline the clinical characteristics of phobic disorders. *(5 marks)*

(b) Describe **one** behavioural therapy for phobic disorders. *(10 marks)*

(c) Describe and evaluate **one** psychodynamic therapy for phobic disorders. *(10 marks)*

# Anxiety disorder – OCD

## 12.1 Classification and diagnosis of obsessive compulsive disorder

*After studying this section you should be able to describe and evaluate:*

*Note that AQA A students only need to study **one** mental disorder, i.e. they only need to study chapter 9 or 10 or 11 or 12.*

- *clinical characteristics of obsessive compulsive disorder*
- *issues surrounding the classification and diagnosis of obsessive compulsive disorder, including reliability and validity.*

### Clinical characteristics of obsessive compulsive disorder (OCD)

AQA A ▶ U4

In the general population, the prevalence of OCD is 1 to 2%, twice that of schizophrenia or panic disorder.

OCD is considered to be an anxiety disorder, and, therefore, shares some similarities with phobias. Namely, both are associated with high levels of anxiety.

The essential features of OCD are:

- Recurrent obsessions or compulsions present for at least two weeks:
  - **Obsessions** are persistent ideas, thoughts, impulses or images that are classed as inappropriate or forbidden, and which cause intense anxiety.
  - **Compulsions** develop as a means of controlling the obsessional thoughts. These compulsions are repetitive behaviours or thoughts, such as repeated hand-washing. Most OCD patients recognise that their compulsions are unreasonable but cannot control them. This creates further anxiety.
- The obsessions/compulsions are severe enough to be time consuming (i.e. they take more than one hour a day) or cause marked distress or significant impairment.
- The person recognises that the obsessions or compulsions are excessive.
- The obsessions/compulsions are not related to drug abuse or medication.

### Issues surrounding the classification and diagnosis of OCD

General issues related to reliability and validity of classification and diagnosis are discussed on pages 96–97.

Tourette's syndrome is characterised by tics – sudden involuntary movements or vocalisations (such as swear words) that are repeated. These tics occur in spasms and may appear many times a day or only occasionally throughout a year. Individuals have some control over the tics but usually feel a compulsion to produce them. If the person tries to hold back the tics, this eventually leads to a strong outburst.

#### Reliability

**Inter-rater reliability** is reasonably high, for example, Williams *et al.* (1992) reported a kappa score of .59 (see page 96 for an explanation of a kappa score).

**Test–retest reliability** – Mannuza *et al.* (1989) reported a kappa score of .91 for a diagnosis of OCD using DSM-III-R (see page 96 for an explanation), based on two independent administrations of a structured interview.

#### Validity

**Descriptive validity** – Brown and Barlow (1992) reported high comorbidity (see page 97 for an explanation) with 50% of patients who were diagnosed with OCD also receiving a diagnosis of an additional mood or anxiety disorder. Baer *et al.* (1990) found that 50% of OCD patients also met the criteria for at least one personality disorder. There is also evidence of an overlap with **Tourette's syndrome**. Leckman and Chittenden (1990) found that between 36% and 52% of patients with Tourette's also meet the criteria for OCD. All of this suggests that OCD is not a separate category but perhaps better categorised as OCD spectrum disorders.

### Practice essay 12.1

(a) Outline the clinical characteristics of obsessive compulsive disorder, with reference to examples.

*(9 marks)*

(b) To what extent are diagnoses of obsessive compulsive disorder reliable and/or valid?

*(16 marks)*

# 12.2 Explanations of obsessive compulsive disorder

*After studying this section you should be able to describe and evaluate:*

- *biological explanations of obsessive compulsive disorder, for example, genetics and biochemistry*
- *psychological explanations of obsessive compulsive disorder, for example, behavioural, cognitive, psychodynamic and socio-cultural.*

## Biological explanations of obsessive compulsive disorder

AQA A     U4

### Genetic explanations

Individuals may inherit a gene or genes that cause their phobic disorder. Research suggests that it is not likely to be one gene (see gene mapping studies) and that such genes predispose individuals to develop the disorder rather than being a certainty (identical MZ twins do not show 100% concordance).

#### Research evidence

**Gene mapping** – Karayiorgou *et al.* (1997) found evidence that a gene related to production of **COMT** was more common in OCD sufferers. This enzyme terminates the action of **dopamine** and **noradrenaline**. Dickel *et al.* (2006) found evidence that a **glutamate** transporter gene called **SLC1A1** might be related to OCD (glutamate production is linked to dopamine – see page 99). Both of these possibilities link to biochemical explanations (see below).

**Twin studies** – Billett *et al.* (1998) reviewed 14 twin studies which found that MZ twins were on average twice more likely to both develop OCD than DZ twins. Rasmussen and Tsuang (1986) reported concordance rates of 53–87% for OCD.

**Family studies** – Nestadt *et al.* (2000) found that people with a relative who had OCD were five times more likely to develop OCD at some time in their lives than members of the general population.

> **Gene mapping** involves comparing the genetic material from families who have OCD with samples from families who don't have the disorder in order to identify common factors.

#### Evaluation

- The evidence for a genetic basis for OCD is **stronger than for other mental illnesses** such as depression. However, the same genes may be related to other disorders (e.g. Tourette's) and this would explain the comorbidity of such conditions.
- When relatives experience OCD the **actual symptoms may differ**, i.e. they are not obsessed by the same things. It is the predisposition to respond to situations in a certain way rather than the obsessions themselves that are inherited.

> The **diathesis-stress model** suggests that people inherit a vulnerability (diathesis) to develop depression, but it only occurs when triggered by life experiences (stressors).

### Biochemical explanations

OCD has been linked to low levels of the neurotransmitter **serotonin** and high levels of **dopamine**.

#### Research evidence

Jenicke (1992) reported that anti-depressants which reduced serotonin levels also reduced the symptoms of OCD, whereas anti-depressants which had a less dramatic effect on serotonin levels did not affect OCD. Some research suggests that 'classic' OCD is related to serotonin, whereas tic-related OCD is related to dopamine abnormalities (tic-related types include Tourette's syndrome and also nail-biting and trichotillamania – pulling out hair) (Van Ameringen *et al.*, 2001). Goodman *et al.*, (1992) found that drugs blocking dopamine were effective in treating OCD symptoms in patients who did not respond to SSRIs.

> If OCD is genetic then the genes may cause neuroanatomical and/or biochemical differences.

### Evaluation

- One problem with biochemical explanations is that it is not clear whether abnormalities are a **cause or effect**.
- The **success of drug therapies** supports the role of biochemical factors, for example SSRIs (which increase serotonin levels) have been shown to be effective (see page 123).
- The fact that a large number of OCD patients do not respond to anti-depressants that affect serotonin suggests that **other factors are involved**.
- The fact that anti-psychotics (which affect dopamine levels) can reduce the severity of OCD symptoms points to the involvement of **dopamine as well as serotonin**.

## Neuroanatomical explanations

Brain scans indicate differences between OCD patients and normal individuals, in particular the pathway linking the **frontal lobe** (associated with thinking and decision making) to the **basal ganglia** (involved in planning and executing movements). There is also a link between the **orbitofrontal cortex** (OFC, in the frontal lobe) and the **caudate nucleus** (in the basal ganglia).

### Research evidence

Baxter *et al.* (1987) used PET scans and found increased glucose metabolic rates in the left orbital gyrus of the frontal lobe in OCD patients, which became normal after patients received drug treatment or behaviour therapy.

Tailarach *et al.* (1973) found that electrical stimulation of parts of the frontal lobe induced stereotypic motions characteristic of OCD compulsions.

Murphy *et al.* (1997) investigated a link between the onset of OCD in childhood and Sydenham's chorea, a disorder associated with streptococcal infections. It may be that the immune response reacts with tissues in the basal ganglia, causing movement disorders and OCD symptoms. Infection-induced OCD has been successfully treated with drugs.

> There are also links between neuroanatomy, biochemistry and the outcome of gene mapping studies (see previous page).

### Evaluation

- The role of key areas of the brain is further supported by the **effectiveness of psychosurgery** (see page 123).
- There are **links between this neuroanatomical explanation and the biochemical explanation** of OCD because low levels of serotonin cause the OFC and caudate nucleus to function poorly, and dopamine activity is associated with the basal ganglia. However, brain abnormalities may be a cause or an effect of the abnormal neurotransmitters.

> **Key points from AS**
>
> - General criticisms of the biological approach to explaining abnormality can be found in *Revise AS Unit 7.1, page 151*.

## Evolutionary explanations

**The adaptive nature of compulsions** – It may be that some aspects of OCD behaviour are adaptive and, therefore, humans are predisposed to develop the disorder. For example, ritualistic behaviours often concern hygiene (e.g. repeated hand-washing) and may be adaptive insofar as extra vigilance over cleanliness might promote survival. Polimeni *et al.* (2003) further suggest that other compulsive behaviours – checking, counting, hoarding and requiring precision would all be beneficial to cultures focused on hunting and gathering (as in the **EEA**, see page 20) and would, therefore, be potentially adaptive.

**Harm-avoidance strategies** – Abed and de Pauw (1998) suggest that OCD is an extreme form of our evolved capacity to represent future scenarios and imagine the consequences of our own thoughts and actions in order to deal with risk situations before they happen.

> One should remember that evolutionary explanations for mental disorders are based on the assumption that such disorders are inherited, or at least a predisposition for the disorder is inherited.

> The evolutionary approach can be criticised for being determinist and not accounting for individual and cultural differences.

## Psychological explanations of obsessive compulsive disorder

AQA A    U4

### Behavioural explanations

**Mowrer's two-process theory** – This can be used to explain OCD (it is also used to explain phobias, see page 114):

Classical and operant conditioning are explained on page 72.

- **Classical conditioning** – Some thoughts become associated with an event that creates anxiety and then they take on the associated properties of the event. For example, a mother looks at her baby and thinks 'I could smother this child'; such thoughts create intense anxiety and, in the future, just looking at the child creates intense anxiety.
- **Operant conditioning** – Distress and compulsive behaviours are maintained because the person learns to avoid the anxiety by escaping (e.g. going to wash their hands).

You can read about Skinner and his pigeons on page 72.

**Superstition hypothesis** – Skinner (1948) suggested that the chance association of a behaviour with a reinforcer can produce a link between body movements (routines) and superstitious behaviour. The pigeons he used in his experiments sometimes learned unique sequences of body movement because they just happened to be performing them when they were given food.

### Research evidence

Carr (1974) demonstrated that compulsive behaviours can reduce anxiety; patients performed their compulsive rituals when activity in the autonomic nervous system (ANS) was high. Arousal of the ANS was reduced after performing the rituals.

### Evaluation

**Key points from AS**

- General evaluations of the behaviourist approach to explaining abnormality can be found in *Revise AS Unit 7.1, page 153.*

- OCD patients are **not always able to identify a traumatic event** that may have triggered the disorder, and several obsessions can be present within one individual or obsessions can change without the occurrence of new traumas.
- The behavioural explanation has led to a successful therapy for OCD patients called **exposure and prevention therapy** (ERP), see page 124.
- The behaviourist approach cannot explain the development of **intrusive thoughts**, which are typical of OCD.

### Cognitive explanations

Cognitive explanations are focused on maladaptive ways of thinking.

OCD patients suffer from impaired information-processing (i.e. faulty thinking). People often have unwanted or intrusive thoughts (such as being infected by germs or harming someone), which are usually easily dismissed. However, for some people they cannot be ignored. Such people think in terms of rigidly defined categories or believe they should have total control, which are examples of maladaptive or faulty thinking. The thoughts create self-blame, depression and anxiety. Neutralising thoughts or acts reduce the obsessive thoughts and these become compulsive, because each time they are performed they reduce the unwanted thoughts. This makes them harder and harder to resist.

### Evaluation

**Key points from AS**

- General evaluations of the cognitive approach to explaining abnormality can be found in *Revise AS Unit 7.1, page 154.*

- There is some evidence that OCD patients do have **more intrusive thoughts than normal** people (Clark, 1992).
- There is no evidence to show that faulty thinking is the **cause rather than a consequence** of OCD symptoms.
- Some people have genetically-determined personality characteristics, which may predispose them to developing OCD, **linking cognitive explanations to genetic explanations** (Rachman and Hodges, 1987).

## Psychodynamic explanations

**Obsessive behaviour** is linked to fixations in the anal stage of development. Freud suggested that children who experience conflicts during the anal phase of development (18 months to 3 years) may develop anal personality traits, i.e. characteristics related to 'control', such as orderliness, stubbornness, as well as an interest in collecting, possessing, and retaining objects. OCD may be an exaggeration of this personality type.

**Unacceptable impulses dealt with by ego defences** – Freud (1949) proposed that OCD develops when the id produces unacceptable impulses, which create anxiety for the ego and thus are dealt with by ego defences. The three most common ego defences for OCD are:

- **Isolation** – The ego isolates itself from the unacceptable impulses, but occasionally they intrude as obsessional thoughts.
- **Undoing** takes over when obsessional thoughts intrude. The ego deals with the anxiety by producing compulsive acts that symbolically undo the unacceptable impulses originating from the id. For example, compulsive hand-washing is a symbolical undoing.
- **Reaction formation** – Behaviours are performed that are opposite to the unacceptable impulses as a means of reducing anxiety, for example, being exceptionally kind when experiencing very aggressive impulses.

**Feelings of inferiority** – Adler (1931) produced a different psychodynamic explanation for OCD, which suggests that OCD develops because of feelings of inferiority or incompetence. Obsessions such as excessive cleansing allow the individual to develop mastery in some areas of life. Therefore, the treatment derived from this approach focuses on building confidence.

### Evaluation

- There is no evidence that people with **obsessive personality style** are any more likely to develop OCD (Peterson, 1992).
- Psychoanalysis (the therapy related to Freud's psychodynamic theory) may actually have a **negative effect** on OCD recovery, which does not support the Freudian explanation.

## Socio-cultural explanations

Cultural factors play a significant role in OCD, but only in terms of the symptoms expressed rather than the core features of the disorder. Palanti (2008) compared prevalence rates across different national groups and found surprising consistency. Palanti also found that the symptoms take on the characteristics of the patient's culture, for example there was a correlation between compulsive washing and religious rituals among Egyptian Muslims. Fontenelle *et al.* (2004) found that aggressive and religious obsessions were typical of Brazilian and Middle Eastern samples.

### Evaluation

Socio-cultural evidence emphasises the role of biological factors in the understanding of OCD because it seems to be **unaffected by different cultural practices**.

---

Obsessive behaviours are common within 'normal' personalities and children often engage in behaviours that are obsessive-compulsive, such as avoiding the cracks in the pavement.

**Key points from AS**

- General evaluations of the psychodynamic approach to explaining abnormality can be found in *Revise AS Unit 7.1, page 153*.

**Socio-cultural explanations** explain schizophrenia in terms of social and cultural factors such as the sufferers' immediate family or their wider social circle.

---

## Practice essay 12.2

Discuss biological explanations of obsessive compulsive disorder. *(25 marks)*

# 12.3 Treatments for obsessive compulsive disorder

*After studying this section you should be able to describe and evaluate:*

- *biological therapies for obsessive compulsive disorder, including their evaluation in terms of appropriateness and effectiveness*
- *psychological therapies for obsessive compulsive disorder, for example, behavioural, psychodynamic and cognitive-behavioural, including their evaluation in terms of appropriateness and effectiveness.*

LEARNING SUMMARY

## Biological therapies for obsessive compulsive disorder

AQA A    U4

**Key points from AS**

- General criticisms of drug therapies are given in *Revise AS Unit 7.2, page 156.*

Placebos are substances that have no pharmacological effects but the person taking them thinks they are the real thing. This means you can separate the psychological from the physical effects of being given a drug treatment.

The reason for conducting a **cingulotomy** is that the one suspected cause of OCD is abnormalities in the brain, focused on the OFC and the caudate nucleus, which communicate via the cingulate gyrus.

### Chemotherapy: drugs

**Anti-depressant drugs** that promote the activity of serotonin, such as **SSRIs** (selective serotonin re-uptake inhibitors) are used to treat OCD. (See more on anti-depressants on page 109.)

**Anxiolytic drugs** are drugs that reduce anxiety, and may be used to treat OCD. (See further details on page 116.)

**Anti-psychotic drugs** reduce levels of dopamine and have also been found to be effective with OCD patients. (See further details on page 102.)

### Evaluation in terms of appropriateness and effectiveness

- SSRIs have been **shown to be effective**. For example, Soomro *et al.* (2008) reviewed 13 studies and found that people receiving SSRIs were twice as likely as those receiving a placebo to experience a reduction in clinical symptoms.
- Drug treatments **do not cure OCD** – Maina *et al.* (2001) report that patients relapse within a few weeks if their medication is stopped.

### Psychosurgery

Psychosurgery involves either the removal of sections of the brain, or lesions (cuts) are made so that areas of the brain become 'functionally' removed. In extreme cases this method is used to treat OCD patients i.e. where the patient is incapacitated by the disorder. A **bilateral cingulotomy** is performed where the **cingulate gyrus** is functionally removed. Stereotactic devices and precise brain scanning techniques are used to locate the exact area of the brain to be altered.

### Evaluation in terms of appropriateness and effectiveness

- It is an irreversible operation and even with refined modern techniques there may be **highly undesirable side effects**. In the 1950s and 60s some amygdalotomies resulted in patients who were confused, lacking in motivation, and unable to work (Eysenck and Eysenck, 1989).
- Cosgrove *et al.* (1996) report **successful treatment** of patients with depressive or anxiety disorders using cingulotomies. These patients had not benefited from all other available therapies. In contrast, Dougerty *et al.* (2002) studied 44 OCD patients who had been unresponsive to other treatments. Only 32% improved after a cingulomtomy and a further 14% were slightly improved. The reported side effects included memory deficits and incontinence as well as one case of seizures.
- It may be that psychosurgery simply **reduces motivation** and this explains the apparent reduction in symptoms (Sachdev and Hay, 1995).

## Psychological therapies for obsessive compulsive disorder

AQA A  U4

**Key points from AS**

• General criticisms of psychological therapies are given in *Revise AS Unit 7.1, pages 158–160*.

Your evaluation of treatments can include information about the reliability and validity of the diagnoses. If the original diagnosis lacks reliability/validity then the treatment may not be effective.

### Behavioural therapy

**Systematic desensitisation (SD)** can be used to treat OCD (see page 116). A patient is exposed to an object that normally triggers their obsession and is trained to relax until the anxiety subsides.

**Exposure and response prevention (ERP)** was developed specifically for OCD. Patients are also exposed to situations that would normally trigger their obsessions but are prevented from producing their usual obsessive response. This is usually done as a form of homework where, for example, a patient with a cleanliness obsession is told that they must not clean the house for a week. This permits the patient to realise that obsessions which previously caused anxiety no longer produce this response, i.e. ERP permits re-learning to take place. OCD develops through reinforcements, but avoidance of anxiety-producing situations then prevents re-learning.

### Evaluation in terms of appropriateness and effectiveness

• **Success rates are fairly high,** for example, Albucher *et al.* (1998) reported that 60–90% of OCD patients improve considerably using ERP.
• In addition, **relapse is much less of a problem** than for drug therapies; it is a lasting form of treatment.
• The therapy may produce quite **high levels of anxiety,** which may be traumatic and some patients may not persist. For that reason ERP is often combined with drug therapies.

### Psychodynamic therapy

Psychoanalysis was the treatment of choice for OCD for many decades until the arrival of more modern psychotherapies. It is a suitable form of treatment for OCD because patients have some insight into their disorder.

### Evaluation in terms of appropriateness and effectiveness

• Insight alone may **not be enough to 'cure' OCD,** given that the evidence suggests a strong biological component.

**Key points from AS**

• Psychoanalysis and CBT are described and evaluated in *Revise AS Unit 7.2, pages 158 and 160*.

### Cognitive-behavioural therapy (CBT)

Cognitive therapies focus more on changing obsessional *thoughts* whereas behavioural therapies focus on changing compulsive *behaviour*. One example of cognitive therapy is **habituation training** where patients are asked to revisit their obsessional thoughts over and over in order to reduce the fear they create. Some psychologists classify ERP as a form of cognitive therapy because it involves 'exposure', which may include exposure to frightening thoughts as well as to compulsive behaviours.

### Evaluation in terms of appropriateness and effectiveness

• Gava *et al.* (2007) compared cognitive and/or behavioural treatments with control groups and found **symptom reduction from all psychotherapies** reviewed.

## Practice essays 12.3

(a) Outline the clinical characteristics of obsessive compulsive disorder. *(5 marks)*

(b) Describe **one** behavioural therapy for obsessive compulsive disorder. *(10 marks)*

(c) Describe and evaluate **one** psychodynamic therapy for obsessive compulsive disorder. *(10 marks)*

# Chapter 13

# Media psychology

## 13.1 Media influence on social behaviour

After studying this section you should be able to describe and evaluate:

- explanations of media influences on pro- and anti-social behaviour
- the effects of video games and computers on young people.

**LEARNING SUMMARY**

### Explanations of media influences on pro- and anti-social behaviour

AQA A ▶ U4

The term '**media**' refers to any medium of communication – television, films and video most obviously but also books, magazines, plays, songs and so on.

It is easy to confuse **disinhibition** and **desensitisation** – one is concerned with changed social norms, the other is concerned with reduced emotional sensitivity.

Many programmes use **counter-stereotypes** (such as a black female doctor) to try to alter our stereotypical views. However, the deliberate manipulation of stereotypes, for good or bad, is ethically questionable because it presumes that certain stereotypes are preferable.

**Imitation** – We learn to behave in a pro- or anti-social manner from observational learning and vicarious reinforcement (**social learning theory**). This is especially likely if the observer identifies with the characters. Bandura *et al.*'s research (see page 40) shows that children imitate specific acts and also shows that general levels of aggression increase.

**Disinhibition effect** – Normally we are inhibited about behaving in certain ways. The media present social norms, which may change our view of what behaviours are common and acceptable.

**Desensitisation** – Exposure to violence may desensitise us so that we tolerate it more easily in real life. Drabman and Thomas (1975) showed young children a film which was either non-violent but exciting, or violent. The participants were then asked to monitor the behaviour of two younger children via a TV link. When the confederates started hitting each other, the children who had been exposed to the violent film were slower to call for help.

**Cognitive priming** – Cues in the media may later trigger pro- or anti-social thoughts and feelings. Josephson (1987) showed a violent TV programme involving a walkie-talkie to one group of boys, while another group watched a programme about motocross. Later, during a game of hockey, the most violent boys were those who were given instructions via a walkie-talkie *and* had watched the violent film.

**Stereotypes** – All media need to communicate a great deal of information in a relatively short time, so they use standard cultural stereotypes such as foreigners playing 'baddies', overweight people being depicted as 'jolly', and wolves as being big and bad. Such stereotypes may or may not reflect reality, and may be positive or negative. Gunter (1986) found that people who watch a lot of television hold more stereotyped beliefs, suggesting that the use of stereotypes on television does have an influence. Alternatively, people (e.g. children) who have a more simplistic cognitive style may prefer to watch more television.

**Displacement effect** – A media bias would be less harmful if it was sufficiently counterbalanced by experience of the real world. However, people who spend a lot of time watching television or reading books have less time for real interactions. Gerbner and Gross (1976) found that people who watch a lot of television rate the outside world as being more dangerous than it actually is (**deviance amplification**).

**Stimulation hypothesis** – Television is an ideal medium to present educational information, and is a resource much used by schools. *Sesame Street* provides preschool children with carefully considered material to promote emotional, social and intellectual development. The value of television and all media is related to what you actually watch, read or listen to.

#### Evaluation

- There are **individual differences**. For example, people who are more aggressive may watch anti-social programmes and/or are more influenced by them.

## The effects of video games and computers on young people

AQA A ▸ U4

Video games often include scenes of violent behaviour and have adult sexual content. For example, in *Grand Theft Auto* players have to murder police officers or plot against other racial groups (inciting racial hatred). One US court case involved a murderer's claims that he was inspired to shoot 3 police officers because of the game. We read about many criminals who blame violent behaviour on video games, but that doesn't mean it is the true cause.

The difference between video gaming and other media effects is that in the former the player is given a more active role and is often rewarded for committing crimes, thus, such behaviour might be expected to be repeated in everyday life.

The topic of 'computers' is a broad one and can encompass, for example, video gaming (above), educational programmes and content (strong pro-social value) and the use of email and the internet.

The effects of **deindividuation** (which can be pro-social as well as anti-social) are discussed on page 41.

### Video games

Satcher (1999) reported on a survey of research by the US government. Research suggests that media violence is linked to aggressive behaviour but that the impact is relatively small compared to other factors, such as home background.

Freedman (2002) reviewed 200 relevant studies and concluded that there was little evidence of a causal link between gaming and violent behaviour.

Grossman (1995) argues that video games are 'murder simulators' and result in training children to use weapons. In addition, such games desensitise children to the act of murder. Grossman points to the fact that the US army uses similar techniques to train shooting responses in their soldiers.

Anderson (2000) testified to the US senate that research has shown consistent effects: increased aggressive behaviour, thoughts and feelings; increased physiological arousal; and decreased pro-social behaviour. Bushman and Anderson (2001) found that boys are more easily influenced than girls. However, there is evidence that individuals who are more prone to be aggressive are more likely to play video games.

Most studies focus on the effects of video games on violence, but it may also affect sexual behaviour and racial prejudice. Yao *et al.* (2006) found that sexually explicit video games prime thinking related to sex, encourage men to think of women as sex objects and increase the likelihood of inappropriate sexual behaviour. Dill and Thill (2007) found that video games portray both genders in a highly stereotyped fashion. Dill *et al.* (2008) found that men exposed to sex-typed video games were more tolerant of sexual harassment. Burgess *et al.* (2007) reported examples of racial stereotypes in video games and linked this to racist thinking.

### Computers

A main concern with internet usage (**computer mediated communication** or **CMC**) is the formation of relationships over the internet. There are several issues:

- **Deception** – People can take on a false persona and this may allow them to target vulnerable individuals.
- **Deindividuation** leads to disinhibition – People can behave in ways that are atypical of them because their behaviour is usually governed more by social norms. This may increase anti-social behaviour. However, the **SIDE model** (social identity model of deindividuation) suggests that loss of personal identity is replaced by social identity, which means stronger social relationships are developed in such circumstances.
- **Lack of face-to-face (F2F) contact** means there are reduced cues leading to conversations in a social vacuum (Culnan and Markus, 1987). However, people have always formed relationships in non-F2F situations, such as penpals writing letters to each other.

On the other hand, internet relationships are good for people who are shy or who live in rural areas, who lack time and/or have physical handicaps. Young (1999) described the ACE model of CMC as Anonymity, Convenience and Escape.

## Practice essays 13.1

(a) Describe **one** study related to the effects of video games on young people and evaluate the research methods used.            *(10 marks)*

(b) Discuss explanations of media influences on pro- and anti-social behaviour.            *(15 marks)*

# 13.2 Persuasion, attitude and change

*After studying this section you should be able to describe and evaluate:*

- *persuasion and attitude change, including Hovland-Yale and Elaboration Likelihood models*
- *the influence of attitudes on decision making, including roles of cognitive consistency/dissonance and self-perception*
- *explanations for the effectiveness of television in persuasion.*

**LEARNING SUMMARY**

## Persuasion and attitude change

AQA A ▸ U4

An **attitude** is a liking or disliking of an object based on cognitions about the object. It leads to a readiness to behave in a certain way.

The Hovland-Yale model is sometimes called the Yale Model of Communication after Yale University in the US, where the early research was conducted.

### Key points from AS

- The topic of attitudes is considered in *Revise AS Unit 6.3, page 142.*

People resist attitude change because attitudes are a key element of one's personality. Attitudes can be changed through experience (learning), persuasion or brainwashing. Persuasive communications aim to induce a person to adopt a particular set of values and are commonly used, for example, in advertising and politics.

### Hovland-Yale model

Hovland *et al.* (1953) identified key features to consider in relation to persuasive messages:

- The communicator or **source**, e.g. expertise, trustworthiness, likeability, status.
- The communication or **message**, e.g. order of arguments, form of conclusion.
- The **audience**, e.g. initial position, intelligence, self-esteem, personality.

They also identified four distinct steps in the persuasion process: attention, comprehension, acceptance and retention.

Zimbardo *et al.* (1977) used the model to generate suggestions for producing persuasive messages:

- The **source** of the message should be credible.
- The **argument** should be one-sided unless the audience is not sympathetic to the message, in which case a two sided message is best.
- **Conclusions** should be stated rather than being left to the individual to work out.
- The **message** should be short, clear and direct. It should be vivid and not full of technical terms.
- The person should **actively** participate in receiving the message if possible.

The Hovland-Yale model has generated a vast amount of research, for example:

**Source** – Kiesler and Kiesler (1969) found that popular and attractive communicators were most effective. Miller *et al.* (1976) found that people who speak rapidly are more persuasive, possibly because it makes it sound as if they are more confident and knowledgeable.

**Message** – Hovland *et al.* (1949) found that when the audience is hostile, it is more effective to present both sides of an argument. Arkes *et al.* (1991) found that repeated messages were more persuasive.

**Audience** – Janis (1954) found that people who had low self-esteem were more easily persuaded. Allyn and Festinger (1961) found that people were more easily persuaded if they were distracted, rather than paying full attention.

### Evaluation

- The model is **descriptive rather than explanatory**, in contrast with the Elaboration Likelihood model on the next page.

## Elaboration Likelihood model (ELM)

Petty and Cacioppo (1986) presented a model to explain *how* people process persuasive messages (rather than describing the characteristics of persuasive messages, as in the Hovland-Yale model). Petty and Cacioppo suggested there are two alternatives:

1. The **central route** – Arguments are attended to carefully and elaborated by the message recipient. This route is likely to be followed for important messages only because it requires considerable cognitive effort. In such cases it is important for the message to be strong because persuasion will depend on the quality of the arguments.

2. The **peripheral route** – Only superficial cues are processed by the message recipient and, therefore, successful persuasion will be related to surface persuasion cues; the logic of the arguments is likely to be irrelevant. This is called 'peripheral' because people are affected by factors that are peripheral to the message itself.

The ELM can be tested by varying (1) the strength/elaboration of message arguments and (2) the presence of peripheral cues (such as status or likeableness of source).

The factors that affect the decision over which route to take are **motivation** and **ability to process the message** (e.g. lack of distraction). As these factors increase the central route then becomes more likely.

**Motivation** may be a function of personal relevance, accountability or a person's 'need for cognition' (i.e. enjoyment of thinking). Petty *et al.* (1981) assessed students' responses to arguments about whether an exam should be introduced for final year students. The message was either personally relevant (students were told their college was seriously considering this option) or not personally relevant, and the arguments given were persuasive or not. Petty *et al.* found that the strong (elaborated) arguments were most effective when the students were personally motivated but when the students were not personally motivated the status of the speaker (a peripheral cue) mattered more than the strength of the arguments.

**Ability to process the message** – Petty *et al.* (1976) varied the level of distraction and the quality of the argument. Participants in the high distraction condition agreed less with the message than those in the low distraction condition when the arguments were strong. But, when the arguments were weak, distraction had the opposite effect. This shows that distraction leads to the peripheral route.

### Evaluation

- The model predicts that **attitude change will be greater if the central route is followed**, which is supported by a study by Chaiken (1980). Participants listened to arguments and were then contacted 10 days later; they were more likely to have maintained their new attitude if their attitude change had occurred via the central route (argument had had personal relevance and strong logic).
- The model **lacks predictive power** because it is difficult to predict the effect of certain variables in different contexts (Eagly and Chaiken, 1993).
- Petty *et al.* (2002) have **continued** to **adapt the model** to deal with such criticisms. They have attempted to specify the role of variables in different contexts, for example, source expertise is one such variable. This may in fact act as a biasing factor in conditions of high elaboration or may act as a peripheral cue in conditions of low elaboration.
- An alternative model by Chaiken (1980) (the **heuristic-systematic model**) uses two modes of processing. In this model messages which are listened to carefully are systematically processed (e.g. an analytic approach), otherwise heuristics (mental shortcuts) are used (e.g. judgments based on stereotypes). This model produces a wider range of predictions which are also more specific.

## The influence of attitudes on decision making

AQA A ▶ U4

There is some debate about the extent to which attitudes are related to behaviour – if people change their attitudes, does their behaviour change as well? For example, you might convince someone that smoking is bad for their health but they continue smoking nevertheless.

### Key points from AS

- The relationship between attitudes and behaviour is discussed in *Revise AS Unit 6.3, page 142*

### Key points from AS

- **Self-perception theory** is related to attribution theory covered in *Revise AS Unit 6.3, page 139* which is a theory to explain how people construct explanations of their own behaviour. We do not observe traits, we observe behaviour and infer personal traits. We use this to infer the traits of other people and also for ourselves.

The link between self-perception theory and decision-making is that we discover our own attitudes through observing our behaviour, and these attitudes influence decisions.

### The role of cognitive consistency/dissonance

Festinger (1957) outlined the **theory of cognitive dissonance** – a general theory of what motivates human thought and behaviour, which is supported by a wealth of research. Cognitive dissonance occurs when a person holds two or more inconsistent views (or cognitions) and this creates a drive to create consistency.

Festinger and Carlsmith (1959) conducted an experiment where students were engaged to perform a very boring task (turning pegs on a board). Participants were paid $1 or $20. Afterwards they were asked to tell other participants what the job was like. Those paid least rated the task as more interesting – presumably because they experienced dissonance (boring task, no money so no reason to do it) and unconsciously had to rate the task as more interesting in order to reduce their dissonance.

Gibbons *et al.* (1997) found that smokers who gave up smoking after going to an anti-smoking clinic but who then restarted also had then lowered their perception of the danger of non-smoking – presumably in order to reduce their dissonance due to the decision to start smoking.

Brehm (1956) demonstrated **post-decisional dissonance**. Women were asked to rate various household items and then given their top two. They were asked to rate all the items again and Brehm found that ratings for their top two went up and other ratings went down – the women had altered their attitudes towards the items so they were more consistent with their choices, reducing any dissonant feelings that might have arisen from making the wrong choice.

### The role of self-perception – self-perception theory

Bem (1972) suggested that when people are uncertain about their attitudes they infer what their attitudes are by observing their own behaviour. **Self-perception theory** may explain the results of dissonance experiments. Self-perception theory predicts that if a person is induced to perform a task for high rewards then task performance is attributed to factors outside the individual (i.e. 'I am doing it to get the reward') and the motivation to perform well is reduced. If the proposed reward is low then a person produces internal attributions (e.g. 'I am doing this because I like the task'), which results in higher motivation. In other words, if a person believes that their behaviour is caused by something external they assume it does not reflect their internal feelings. This is called the **overjustification effect**.

One outcome is that external rewards destroy internal motivations, as demonstrated by Lepper *et al.* (1973) in an experiment where nursery children were asked to draw some nice pictures. Some were told they would get a reward if their pictures were good. At the end all the children did actually receive a reward. When the children were observed a few days later, those children who had been promised a reward spent half as much time drawing as the other children, suggesting that their internal motivation had been destroyed by the expectation of external rewards.

### Integrating dissonance and self-perception theories

Sherif and Sherif (1967) proposed **social judgment theory** – when making a decision, people have a **latitude of acceptance** and a **latitude of rejection**. A latitude of acceptance means that they will accept decisions that are around the same level, for example, if you decide that 30mph is a reasonable speed to drive in a built-up area then you would probably also accept 25mph and 35mph as reasonable speeds as well. A latitude of rejection means that you would be clear that driving at 15mph is too slow and 45mph is way too fast. Self-perception theory best accounts for decisions within the latitude of acceptance, whereas dissonance theory accounts for decisions within the latitude of rejection.

## Explanations for the effectiveness of television in persuasion

AQA A    U3
AQA B    U3

The models of attitude change examined on pages 127 and 128 can be used to explain the effectiveness of television in persuasion.

The 'topic of television' includes advertisements that are both commercial and non-commercial (such as anti-smoking campaigns), programmes with political content that may change your views, and programmes related to health issues, etc.

### Hovland-Yale model

This model predicts that there are three factors that can account for the effectiveness (or not) of television:

- **Source** – TV often relies on expert sources who are attractive and have good verbal skills. Familiarity also increases their persuasiveness because we identify with them.
- **Message** – The medium is important so TV generally has greater influence than radio or magazines because it is more immediate and accessible. However, if the message is complex then written material may be better because people can go back over the arguments. Chaiken and Eagly (1983) found that when the message was easy to comprehend attitude change was greatest for video presentations, whereas difficult messages led to greatest attitude change when the message was written.
- **Audience** – Research shows that women are more persuadable than men, although this may only apply to male-oriented topics. When the topic is female-oriented men are more persuadable (Sistrunk and McDavid, 1971).

The effectiveness of television in persuasion can also be related to social learning theory – figures on TV act as role models. In fact all of the explanations on page 125 for the pro- and anti-social effects of the media could be made relevant to the discussion on this page.

### Elaboration Likelihood Model (ELM)

Persuasion is more likely to be effective if the listener is addressed via the central route. This can be achieved by making the message personally relevant, by presenting strong arguments, trying to make people scrutinise and think about your arguments, and by trying to avoid distractions.

### Emotional influences

None of this may matter if you don't have people's attention. One way to do this is to start by emotionally involving the viewer, such as using fear or sentimentality. Emotion has an interesting effect on persuasion.

**Good mood** – When people are in a good mood they are less keen to have their mood spoiled and, therefore, more likely to take the peripheral route. Bless *et al.* (1990) demonstrated this, asking students to write about happy or sad events in their lives and then listening to speeches about college fees where the argument was either strong and well-reasoned or not. People in a sad mood (after writing about sad events) showed attitude change with the strong arguments only, people in a happy mood showed no attitude change in either condition.

**Fear** – Too much fear reduces persuasion; people become defensive and don't think rationally. However, Leventhal *et al.* (1967) found that showing people an anti-smoking film that scared them but then giving them a pamphlet to show them how to give up smoking (i.e. reduce their fear) was more effective than a film or pamphlet on its own.

### Mediating factors

The effect of TV advertising/programmes can be moderated in children by active parental involvement. Huesmann and Bachrach (1988) reviewed research and concluded that TV has less influence on attitudes towards aggression than parental attitudes.

## Practice essays 13.2

(a) Describe what research shows us about the Hovland-Yale model of attitude change. *(5 marks)*

(b) Describe and evaluate the influence of attitudes on decision-making. *(20 marks)*

# 13.3 The psychology of 'celebrity'

*After studying this section you should be able to describe and evaluate:*

- *the attraction of 'celebrity', including social psychological and evolutionary explanations*
- *research into intense fandom, for example, celebrity worship, stalking.*

**LEARNING SUMMARY**

## The attraction of 'celebrity'

AQA A    U4

A **celebrity** is a famous, widely-recognised person who commands a high degree of public and media attention. It has been said that they are well known for being well known.

It is crucial that any discussions you have on this topic are firmly rooted in psychology rather than being idle banter!

The modern phenomenon of celebrity is linked to the media as they (magazines, TV, films) create fame. You couldn't have celebrity without the media. However the value of celebrity is linked to **gossip** – it is gossip on a global scale. Gossip is casual conversation about the personal affairs of other people.

The basis of evolutionary explanations is described on page 20. In a nutshell, we inherit certain mental modules because at some time in the past these enabled people to solve critical problems that were important for survival and reproduction. Thus, the behaviours are genetically based and adaptive – at least adaptive to that past environment (the EEA or environment of evolutionary adaptedness).

### Social psychological explanations

**Social learning theory (SLT)** – Celebrities act as role models because we identify with them. They are also a source of vicarious reinforcement. SLT is explained on page 40.

**Social construction theory** – Celebrity is a social construction of the media, such as magazines and fan clubs on the internet. Social construction theory (or social constructionism) proposes that all of the phenomena around us (such as scientific knowledge, understanding gender roles, etc.) are constructed and maintained through social interactions; all knowledge is related to the social/cultural context. The media create the attractiveness of celebrity in order to serve their own ends (greater sales).

**Social identity theory (SIT)** (see page 63) – Membership of fan clubs and shared admiration for certain celebrities contributes to our social identity. The attraction of celebrity is that it is a means to define your social group and, therefore, yourself.

**Group cohesion** – Celebrities provide a common topic to talk about that helps build up social networks. It is safer to gossip about celebrities than about the people you know.

**Leadership** – Groups of people search for leaders, and celebrities may fulfill that function.

### Evolutionary explanations

**Gossip** – One explanation of the evolution of language is that it allows a mechanism for gossip, so animals can pass on information about their social group. Dunbar *et al.* (1997) suggest people spend about 2/3 of their conversation time on social topics.

**Successful reproduction** – Gossiping is related to reproduction because the focus is on spreading information about who is successful in the mating game. This explains why so much celebrity gossip today is related to who is pregnant and who is getting together with whom or separating from whom. We gossip about relationships, especially those involving the alpha males or females (i.e. those individuals in a community to whom the others follow and defer). This approach also explains why celebrity interest is so concerned with beauty – because physical attractiveness is important for sexual selection and relationships.

**Gender difference** – The evolutionary approach can also explain why women are more interested in gossip and celebrity than men. Celebrity interest allows women to identify socially desirable men and compare notes on which men are better than others, to aid their own selection. When gossiping about other women they are considering the competition and learning how to copy alpha females.

**Leadership** – Humans are social animals and, therefore, any behaviour that enhances group dynamics is likely to be selected. One such adaptive behaviour is leadership; interest in celebrities is an offshoot of interest in and allegiance to a leader.

## Research into intense fandom

> A **fan** is someone who has an intense liking for another person, a group of people or thing. A group of fans are a fanbase or fandom.

### Celebrity worship

Maltby *et al.* (2003) developed a celebrity worship scale and gathered data from over 1,700 British people aged between 14 and 16. They categorised the responses into three dimensions, each typical of particular kinds of fans:

* **Entertainment-social** – attraction to celebrity because of entertainment value.
* **Intense-personal** – feelings of obsession towards celebrity.
* **Borderline-pathological** – uncontrolled behaviours and fantasies.

Low levels of fan worship (entertainment-social) are not related to any pathological behaviours (such as depression). Maltby *et al.* (2004) found that intense worship was related to higher levels of depression, anxiety, stress and illness.

Celebrity worship has elements of obsessive love. Moore (2006) believes that rejection is the trigger for obsessive love. Treatment may involve cognitive therapy where the individual's irrational thoughts are challenged.

> **Key points from AS**
>
> * **Cognitive therapy** is discussed in *Revise AS Unit 7.2, page 160*.

Hodgkinson (1991) suggests that there are several factors that contribute to obsessive love, such as having too much spare time (boredom), feeling vulnerable and lacking self-confidence, and perceiving oneself as a failure. All of this leads to needing an outlet for such anxieties and to seek an individual with the attributes one is seeking for oneself. In addition, a person's own feelings of unworthiness and insignificance are confirmed by the love that is sought, such as being 'in love' with someone famous.

### Stalking

> **Stalking** refers to the obsessive following or observing of another person. Most cases of stalking do not escalate to the levels of reports that appear in the media.

**Motivation** – Mullen *et al.* (1999) studied reports of stalking and developed five categories that explain the reasons for stalking: intimacy seekers (those who wished to establish a close relationship with someone); rejected stalkers (those who had been rejected by the person they stalked); resentful (those who wished to punish someone who had wronged them); incompetent suitors (those who used this as a means to get a date) and sexually-motivated stalkers (which was solely male stalkers).

**Gender** – Purcell *et al.* (2002) studied 40 female stalkers and 150 male stalkers. The males reported more history of criminal offences and substance abuse. Females and males differed in terms of their motivation for stalking. The female stalkers generally were looking for intimacy and they usually stalked someone they knew, often someone who worked in a 'caring' profession (such as a nurse or teacher). Males showed a broader range of reasons for stalking.

**Psychological profile** – Kienlan *et al.* (1997) examined the case histories of 25 stalkers. One third had a diagnosed psychotic mental disorder (i.e. lack of contact with reality). The personality profile of the non-psychotic stalkers included traits such as anger, hostility, obsession, dependency and jealousy. The non-psychotic stalkers made more violent threats and carried out these threats. No single profile of the 'stalker personality' emerged.

> The term **'psychotic'** refers to individuals who are suffering from a mental disorder, which involves detachment from reality, such as schizophrenia.

**Effect on victim** – Pathe and Mullen (1997) asked 100 victims of stalking to complete a questionnaire. The effects reported were increased anxiety, intrusive recollections, plans to move house and/or leave job, and suicidal thoughts. These symptoms are similar to those related to post-traumatic stress disorder (PTSD).

## Practice essays 13.3

(a) Outline social psychological explanations of the attraction of 'celebrity'.

*(5 marks)*

(b) Discuss research into intense fandom. Include research evidence in your answer.

*(20 marks)*

# Chapter 14

# The psychology of addictive behaviour

## 14.1 Models of addictive behaviour

*After studying this section you should be able to describe and evaluate:*

On pages 170–172 further research on substance use and abuse is covered, as required by AQA specification B

- *biological, cognitive and learning models of addiction, including explanations for initiation, maintenance and relapse*
- *explanations for specific addictions, including smoking and gambling.*

**LEARNING SUMMARY**

### Biological models of addiction

AQA A   U3
AQA B   U3

**Addiction** occurs when the body relies on a substance for normal functioning. If the substance is removed, withdrawal symptoms may occur. There are physical (e.g. drugs) and psychological addictions (e.g. gambling), both of which draw on physical and psychological explanations.

When you are feeling depressed, dopamine levels are low. Increased dopamine (released when experiencing a reward) affects the reward centres of the brain and this is reinforcing (i.e. it encourages the behaviour to be repeated).

Any model of addiction should explain three aspects of addiction: initiation, maintenance and relapse. In the case of the biological model initiation can be explained by inheriting a genetic vulnerability (which would be triggered by life stressors), maintenance can be explained by activation of dopamine, which is reinforcing. Relapse may also be linked to dopamine, but is probably better explained by psychological factors.

**Key points from AS**

- General evaluations of the biological approach are relevant here. See, for example, *Revise AS Unit 7.1, page 151.*

**Hereditary factors** – Alcohol dependence is four times more likely in children whose parents are alcoholic (Sarafino, 1990). This is true even when the children have been adopted and it is their natural parents who are alcoholics.

Gene mapping studies (see page 98) have identified possible candidate genes. Blum *et al.* (1990) found an association between the **DRD2** (D2 dopamine receptor) gene and alcoholism; the gene leads to fewer dopamine receptors in the reward centre of the brain and, therefore, a person is more receptive to experiencing rewards. Subsequent research has found this gene to frequently be present in drug abusers, smokers, and other addictive, compulsive or impulsive disorders.

**Physiological factors** – The genetic explanation is linked to production of the neurotransmitter **dopamine**, which is a major component in the brain's reward pathways, i.e. it provides feelings of pleasure (a 'high') and is associated with reinforcement, encouraging an individual to repeat actions that led to its release. People with addictions may have higher than normal sensitivity to dopamine and/or low dopamine levels. Therefore, any increase is especially rewarding. Certain drugs have a direct effect on dopamine. For example, cocaine and amphetamines increase dopamine levels (cocaine prevents re-uptake, whereas amphetamine enhances dopamine release).

**The addictive personality** – Genetic explanations are also linked to the concept of the 'addictive personality'. Common factors have been identified, such as obsessiveness, impulsive behaviour, difficulty delaying gratification, disposition towards sensation-seeking and a general tolerance for deviance (Lang, 1983). Some of these traits have been linked to biological causes, for example, obsessive personality may be inherited and linked to low levels of serotonin (see obsessive-compulsive disorder on page 119).

**Evaluation**

- There is debate over the **role of the DRD2** gene. For example, Gelertner *et al.* (1993) concluded from a research review that no significant association between the DRD2 gene and alcoholism had been proven. A recent study (Riley, 2007) found that a neighbouring gene **ANKK1** might be a more likely candidate.
- Biological evidence is often based on **research with non-human animals** and may not be applicable to human behaviour.
- The biological model is linked to the **disease model** – which suggests that addiction is a disease state and, therefore, can be treated like a disease by giving appropriate drugs. Szasz (1974) suggests that the disease model is entirely inappropriate for addiction, which is linked to psychological factors.
- Addiction is such a personal experience that biological explanations are **unlikely to be very helpful**. In any case, genes cannot be the only explanation because not everyone with such genes becomes addicted. Therefore, psychological explanations are equally important.

## Psychological models of addiction

AQA A    U4
AQA B    U3

Psychological explanations are more relevant to psychological addictions, although they also apply to physical addictions such as alcoholism and drug dependency.

### Key points from AS

- Attribution theory, as an explanation of addiction, is explained in *Revise AS Unit 6.3, page 139*. It is an example of the cognitive approach to explaining addiction.

Biological explanations may be most relevant to the initiation of addiction. However, psychological factors may be more important in maintenance and relapse.

Classical and operant conditioning are explained on page 72.

Explanations based on the role of rewards link to biological explanations for addiction. The initial experience may be psychological (feeling a sense of reward or escape from negative feelings), which produces dopamine and activates the reward centre in the brain. This then leads to the maintenance of the addiction because of reinforcement.

See 'vulnerability for addiction' on page 136 – many of these factors can also be given as explanations of addiction.

### Cognitive models of addiction

Cognitive explanations focus on the role of maladaptive cognitive processes. One example of this is the fact that addicts typically minimise the negative effects of their behaviour, focusing on the positive effects. This serves to maintain their addiction.

Another example is impaired decision-making abilities. Bechara and Damasio (2002) reported that a significant number of addicts selected options in an experiment that provided a higher immediate reward, even when they knew this strategy would be unprofitable in the long run. This behaviour resembles that of people who have experienced brain damage in their frontal cortex.

In addition, research using brain scanning techniques (e.g. Grant *et al.*, 1996) has shown heightened activity during craving in the areas of the frontal cortex that regulate decision-making, linking biology to cognitive explanations.

### Psychodynamic model of addiction

The psychodynamic view is that addicts have dependency problems. In early childhood their needs for nurturance were not met and, therefore, in later life, they are not fully independent. This leaves them vulnerable to developing dependence relationships.

### Learning models of addiction

**Classical conditioning** – Abusers come to associate drug use with certain situations and emotions. Those situations may then produce the euphoria of the drug-induced state. Meyer *et al.* (1995) found that just the sight of a hypodermic needle produced a sense of comfort for drug abusers.

**Operant conditioning** – This suggests that any behaviour that is rewarded will increase. Drug users experience a reduction of tension (negative reinforcement) and euphoria (positive reinforcement), which are both rewarding, increasing the likelihood that they will try the drug again. These rewards may also encourage them to use higher doses in order to increase the rewarding effects.

Once this stimulus–response link has been learned it may be resistant to unlearning because the user is afraid to experience life without the drug and, therefore, does not discover that they can cope without their addiction – a self-reinforcing cycle.

Evidence supports the negative reinforcement explanation. For example, Marlatt *et al.* (1975) found that participants drank more alcoholic drinks if they had taken part in a stressful taste task than an unstressful one.

**Social learning theory** – Addiction tends to run in families, which may be due to modelling and vicarious reinforcement rather than biological factors. In fact, research has shown that gambling often begins at home (Wynne *et al.*, 1996).

#### Evaluation

- Addiction patterns vary according to **social and cultural practices**. This supports the relevance of learning models.
- The **success and importance of psychological therapies** in treating addiction points to the role of cognitive factors at least in maintenance and relapse. Physical therapies rarely work on their own (see page 138).
- **Psychological models of addiction** are supported by the fact that not all addicts experience withdrawal symptoms, and also that biological factors cannot explain psychological addictions nor can they even explain physical addictions entirely.

# Explanations for specific addictions

AQA A ▶ U4
AQA B ▶ U3

The statistics show that smoking is clearly very damaging to people's health. So why do people continue to smoke?

In 2004 25% of people in the UK aged 16 and over were smokers. Amongst the under-16s it is often girls who smoke more than boys.

The physiological effects of nicotine are discussed on page 171.

## Smoking tobacco and nicotine

**Social learning theory** – The main reason why people start to smoke is probably imitation of desirable role models and peers. McKennell and Bynner (1969) found that smoking is associated with being attractive and tough. Therefore, pressure is put on the media to reduce examples of people smoking in films and on TV, and advertising of cigarettes is banned. The NHS 'stop smoking' website has stories of people who gave up to act as alternative role models.

**Physical addiction** – Addiction to smoking is explained in terms of nicotine, a substance that influences dopamine production and the reward centre in the brain. For that reason one of the ways to stop smoking is to replace the nicotine (i.e. with chewing gum, patches, nasal sprays). However, many people stop smoking without nicotine replacement or without experiencing any withdrawal symptoms. This supports the role of social and cognitive factors in smoking addiction.

Townsend *et al.* (1994) documented a negative correlation between the number of cigarettes smoked and the price of cigarettes, suggesting that people can stop if the immediate costs become too high. This further suggests that smoking addiction is not solely due to a physical addiction.

**Social norms** – Further support comes from the fact that the percentage of men who smoked used to be more than women, presumably because of social norms. However, today there is almost no gender difference, which is related to changing social norms about gender.

## Gambling

About 1% of the adult population in Britain are problem gamblers. In 2005 the National Lottery collected £4.9 million. Gambling is claimed to be the fastest growing addiction in the US.

**Cognitive distortions** – In a study of fruit machine gambling Griffiths (1994) found that regular fruit machine gamblers (RGs), compared to non-regular users, were significantly more likely to use irrational verbalisations (e.g. 'I lost because I wasn't concentrating'). RGs also showed more evidence of flexible attributions (e.g. blaming failure on external factors and crediting success to their own skill). Anholt *et al.* (2003) found similar patterns of obsessive-compulsive thinking in OCD patients and compulsive gamblers, supporting the view that both groups have similar cognitive dysfunctions.

**Personality** – Loxton *et al.* (2008) found that problem gamblers were more impulsive, reward-driven and more sensitive to punishment than non-gamblers. Their reward-orientation and sensitivity to punishment would mean that success at gambling produced a stronger positive effect than in most people and that might be why they are more likely to continue gambling.

### Key points from AS

- Making internal and external attributions is related to **locus of control** which is discussed on page 144 and also in *Revise AS Unit 6.2, page 135.*

**Emotional factors** – Gamblers Anonymous claims that the three key characteristics of a gambler are an inability to accept reality, emotional insecurity and immaturity. Gambling provides emotional comfort and permits the gambler to feel powerful. Wood and Griffiths (2007) interviewed 50 gamblers about the role gambling played in their lives. For most, the prime motive for gambling was as a means to escape and put them in a better mood. It enabled them to avoid their problems and 'fill the void'.

**Biological factors** may be significant as well. Zack and Poulos (2007) found that dopamine enhances the rewarding effects of gambling.

## Practice essays 14.1

(a) Outline and evaluate the cognitive model as an explanation of initiation and maintenance of gambling behaviour. *(10 marks)*

(b) Discuss the problem of relapse in relation to addiction. Include research evidence in your answer. *(15 marks)*

# 14.2 Factors affecting addictive behaviour

After studying this section you should be able to describe and evaluate:

The role of the media in addictive behaviour can be explained in a similar way to explanations of pro- and anti-social behaviour (see page 125).

- *vulnerability to addiction including self-esteem, attributions for addiction and social context of addiction*
- *the role of the media in addictive behaviour.*

## Vulnerability to addiction

AQA A    U4
AQA B    U3

Various factors have been linked to addiction and act as vulnerability factors, i.e. factors that make someone vulnerable to becoming addicted:

- **Low self-esteem** has been found in problem gamblers (Gupta and Derevensky, 1998), and in adolescents addicted to mobile phone use (Leung, 2007). Low self-esteem is likely to create dependency needs and lead to addiction in order to satisfy these needs.
- **Higher rates of depression** are related to low self-esteem. Addiction is a means of escaping reality (Gupta and Derevensky, 1998).
- **Greater risk takers** and sensation seekers (Zuckerman, 1996).

The explanations suggested for addictive behaviour on the previous pages can also be considered as factors that create a vulnerability to addictive behaviour – the initiation and maintenance of addictive behaviour as well as the problems with relapse.

### Attributions for addiction

How do addicts explain their own addiction (i.e. provide an attribution)? **Attribution theory** is about how we explain the causes of our own and other people's behaviour. The **fundamental attribution error** suggests that people prefer to explain their own behaviour using situational attributions whereas they tend to explain other people's behaviour using dispositional explanations. This explanation may account for relapse behaviour in addicts. For example, Seneviratne and Saunders (2000) found that alcoholics were more likely to believe their relapse was due to situational factors whereas they believed that relapse in others was due to dispositional factors (such as low will power). This would hamper their ability to deal effectively with relapse because they view it as being outside their own control.

### Key points from AS

- **Attribution theory** is discussed in *Revise AS Unit 6.3, page 139.*

**Attribution** is the process of explaining causes of behaviour. We do not observe traits, we observe behaviours and infer personal attributes.

Support for attribution theory as a factor in addiction comes from Robins *et al.* (1974) who found that US serviceman who were regular opium users when fighting in Vietnam found it easy to stop when returning to the US. The explanation is that they associated their addiction with external (environmental) cues, but once these were left behind they could give up. This explanation is supported by the fact that when people are successfully treated for addictions in a clinic they fail to transfer this to the outside world because they have attributed their behaviour (giving up) to the clinical setting.

### Social context of addiction

Explanations and vulnerabilities to addiction are important indicators of what treatments might be effective. The treatment of addiction is considered on page 138 onwards.

**Peer influences** – Many addictions, such as smoking or alcohol, are a means of conforming to group norms and, therefore, being accepted by the group. Addiction may determine one's immediate circle of friends. For example, adolescent gamblers tend to make new friends through their gambling, so that old friendships are lost (Derevensky, 1999).

**Poor environmental conditions** – Tension and poverty are linked with drug addiction.

## Practice essays 14.2

(a) Outline **two** explanations of vulnerability to addiction (for example, self-esteem, social context).                    *(10 marks)*

(b) Discuss the role of the media in addictive behaviour.                    *(15 marks)*

# 14.3 Reducing addictive behaviour

After studying this section you should be able to describe and evaluate:

- *models of prevention, including theory of reasoned action and theory of planned behaviour*
- *types of intervention, including biological, psychological, public health interventions and legislation, and their effectiveness.*

## Models of prevention

AQA A ▶ U4
AQA B ▶ U3

Attitudes are discussed on page 127.

The TRA and TPB models are used generally with health behaviours (such as encouraging safe sex) and also used to understand attitudes generally (such as effective advertising strategies).

See also Prochaska's spiral model of behavioural change on page 172, another model of prevention.

### Theory of reasoned action (TRA)

Ajzen and Fishbein (1980) developed a theory to explain how beliefs are linked to intentions about how to behave. They suggested that a behavioural intention is determined by (1) perceived facts and their personal consequences and (2) social norms. For example, smoking behaviour might be determined by (1) 'smoking causes cancer' (a fact) and (2) 'my parents smoke' (a social norm). This leads to (3) the intention 'I won't be so foolish' and finally (4) to a behaviour such as refusing a cigarette.

#### Evaluation

- This model enabled **clear predictions** about behaviour to be made, and generated useful research.
- However, there are various problems such as the model assumes there is a **direct link between thoughts and behaviour**, however, the evidence doesn't support this (e.g. DeFleur and Westie, 158).
- The model is also **limited to the effect of attitudes and social norms** on behaviour and assumes that **people behave rationally**, whereas this is not always true.

### Theory of planned behaviour (TPB)

Ajzen (1988) modified the TRA model to produce the TPB model. This model includes the influence of perceived control, i.e. behavioural change depends on a third factor – your belief about whether you have control over a particular behaviour. Perceived control is affected by past experience and current obstacles. Perceived control may act on behavioural intention or may act directly on behaviour, and can, therefore, explain why intention is not always linked to behaviour.

A diagram of the theory of planned behaviour.

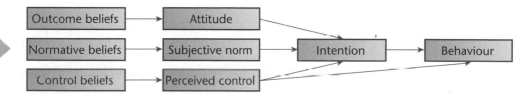

#### Evaluation

- This model still assumes that behaviours are **conscious, reasoned and planned**.
- TPB is **supported by** Oh and Hsu (2001) who sent questionnaires to about 400 gamblers living in the US state of Iowa, asking them about past gambling behaviour, attitudes, social norms, perceived behavioural control (i.e. budgetary affordability, self-controllability, perceived gambling skills, time availability), and behavioural intentions. Two months later they sent out a further questionnaire and found significant positive links between attitudes and behavioural intentions and behaviour, as the model predicts.

## Types of intervention

AQA A ▸ U4
AQA B ▸ U3

### Biological interventions

**Detoxification programmes** require medical supervision. One approach is to reduce the substance gradually. Alternatively, an addict may be required to quit in one go. Either way drugs may be used to reduce side effects, such as the use of anti-anxiety drugs to reduce anxiety.

**Drug maintenance therapy** – Substitute drugs are given, such as nicotine gum for smoking or giving **methadone** as a pharmacological substitute for heroin. Addicts become addicted to methadone but it can be taken by mouth and, therefore, the dangers of dirty needles are avoided. Methadone also doesn't have the same euphoric effects. The effectiveness may be due to several factors: the lack of euphoria may break the addiction cycle, and contextual dependency is lessened because methadone is oral and given by doctors.

**Antagonist drugs** are drugs that block or change the effects of the addictive drug. For example, the drug **antabuse** is given to alcoholics; if they drink anything alcoholic they almost immediately feel nauseous and develop a throbbing headache and other signs similar to a hangover.

**Dopamine agonists** such as L-dopa. One possible treatment for people who inherit a lack of D2 receptors is to be given drugs to stimulate these receptors. Such treatment may also benefit withdrawal symptoms because the effect of addiction can be to increase dopamine levels, which leads to a reduction in the number of dopamine receptors. The result is that when addictions are reduced there is less dopamine in the brain encouraging a person to renew their addiction in order to increase dopamine. Dopamine agonists do that for them.

#### Effectiveness

- Callahan (1980) found methadone therapy was successful as long as addicts were **prevented from continuing with other substance abuses**.
- Detoxification programmes tend to have a **high drop-out rate**, especially when not accompanied by some form of psychotherapy. This is likely to do with the fact that they are not pleasant and require considerable willpower.
- **Dopamine advice is contradictory**. For example, one study found that use of dopamine agonists for the treatment of Parkinson's disease actually led to pathological gambling rather than reduced it (Barclay and Vega, 2005) and Soares *et al.* (2003) found no benefit for cocaine addicts of using dopamine to reduce their symptoms during withdrawal.
- Biological treatments are not effective with psychological addictions, except where there is **comorbidity**, such as where a problem gambler is also suffering from severe depression. Use of anti-depressants may treat the depression and, therefore, remove one of the vulnerability factors for gambling.
- Biological interventions **assume that addiction is purely biological**. The fact that psychological factors are also important means that biologically-oriented treatment programmes must include psychological components in order to be successful. Amato *et al.* (2004) found that methadone treatment programmes had significantly improved success when used in combination with psychosocial interventions.

### Psychological interventions

**Aversion therapy** – Negative affect is paired with the abused substance to recondition the patient. For example, the patient might be made to smoke a lot of cigarettes which makes them feel sick, then cigarette smoking is associated with nausea instead of being associated with pleasure. The success of **antabuse** (above) may be explained as a form of aversion therapy.

There are two important criteria for assessing the effectiveness of any therapy for addiction:
(1) To what extent will addicts persist with the treatment? (If it is unpleasant they are likely to quit before completing treatment.)
(2) To what extent does the therapy prevent relapse?

**Comorbidity** refers to the diagnosis of two or more conditions at the same time.

**Key points from AS**
- Aversion therapy is described in *Revise AS Unit 7.3, page 168*. It is based on the principles of classical conditioning.

CM is similar to **token economy**, see page 103.

**Contingency management (CM)** uses principles of **operant conditioning**; addicts are given rewards each time they produce drug-free urine samples. The rewards might be vouchers to be exchanged for clothing or food, or for patients being treated in a rehabilitation programme they might get extra time using the internet. Higgins *et al.* (1994) found that 75% of cocaine addicts using CM plus psychotherapy completed an outpatient treatment programme, compared to only 40% who received the psychotherapy only.

**Key points from AS**

• CBT is described in *Revise AS Unit 7.2, page 160.*

**Cognitive-behavioural treatment (CBT)** – Many programmes use CBT techniques, for example, self-help groups target the way a person thinks about their addiction. Specific CBT programmes include **behavioural self-control training** where patients are asked to keep a record of where and when they drink, smoke, gamble, etc. so they can become aware of when they are at risk. They are also taught coping strategies such as relaxation techniques to use when resisting temptation, assertiveness skills and also practical ideas such as sipping rather than gulping a drink.

Changing addictive behaviour requires a major shift in attitudes for the individual. In fact, they almost have to re-invent themselves – change friends, change habits and find new ways to gain pleasure.

**Self-help groups**, such as Alcoholics Anonymous (AA), provide social support and an opportunity to make a public statement of intention. This is important in attitude change (see theory of planned behaviour on page 137). They also provide successful role models, vicarious reinforcement and a social identity that empowers individuals.

**Self-management strategies** – This refers to methods without the benefit of formal treatment where individuals may employ a variety of the above techniques such as rewarding their behaviour or designing their own coping strategies. Such strategies may be carried out under professional guidance or with the use of self-help books.

### Effectiveness

• Glasgow *et al.* (1985) found that people stop smoking by using **oral substitutes,** or rewards for quitting and punishments for backsliding.
• Ferri *et al.* (2006) reviewed research on the effectiveness of the **12-step AA programme** and did not find any greater success than other programmes. However, they acknowledged the problems in such research – the studies cover a variety of different programmes and individuals so it is difficult to draw firm conclusions. Self-help techniques are also difficult to assess because of the anonymity.
• According to the US Surgeon General, 95% of smokers **quit on their own** (self-management).

### Public health interventions and legislation

**Legislation and policing** – Outlawing drugs may prevent some usage but it means that the sources are not regulated, thus, allowing poor quality substances, spread of diseases like Aids and association with crime. Anti-smoking bans may reduce cues to smoking in certain situations but actually may provide new cues, e.g. smoking areas outside pubs.

### Health promotion campaigns

**Key points from AS**

• Social inoculation is similar to stress inoculation training (SIT), which was part of your AS studies. See *Revise AS Unit 5.2, page 107.*

**Social inoculation** – McGuire (1964) suggested that you can prepare people to resist temptation by giving them a set of strong counterarguments ('inoculation defence'), in the same way that inoculations provide us with antibodies. You can also provide them with 'supportive defence', which is strengthening the arguments they already hold.

**Use of fear-arousing appeals** – The use of fear may increase the persuasiveness of a message, for example, anti-smoking campaigns that show a picture of a diseased lung. See discussion of such appeals on page 130.

**Identifying and targeting 'risk' groups** – The New Zealand Government has recently launched a campaign to reduce problem gambling (Perese *et al.*, 2005). The primary target is raising general public awareness of the problem, but the secondary target is focus on high-risk groups such as young males (aged 18–24), who are unemployed or have low incomes. They are targeted because they have a high risk of gambling problems.

### Effectiveness

- Health promotion campaigns **based on models of behaviour change** (such as the theory of planned behaviour) are more likely to be successful, though it is important that such models are related to cultural factors.
- The anti-smoking ban in the UK resulted in an 11% drop in cigarette sales during the first month of the ban in England (BBC, 2007). However, in the US stringent bans have **not resulted in continuing decreases in smoking**. 'Hardcore' smokers may become more defiant in the face of such bans; the same applies to all attempts to legislate against activities that are harmful.
- McAlister *et al.* (1980) found that a **local health promotion campaign** (anti-smoking) used in a high school reduced the likelihood of smoking by half.
- Jackson *et al.* (2002) evaluated an **anti-gambling campaign** in Australia and found a dramatic increase in helpline calls and 71% awareness of the campaign.
- Campaigns may be more effective if they **target 'risk' groups**.
- It is difficult to assess the effectiveness of any programme because **different measures can be used**, such as reduction among high-risk groups or changed attitudes in the general population.

## Practice essays 14.3

(a) Assess the theory of reasoned action as a means of reducing addictive behaviour. *(5 marks)*

(b) Discuss types of intervention that can be used to reduce addictive behaviour. *(20 marks)*

# Chapter 15

# Anomalistic psychology

## 15.1 Theoretical and methodological issues in the study of anomalous experience

*After studying this section you should be able to describe and evaluate:*

- *issues of pseudoscience and scientific fraud*
- *controversies relating to Ganzfeld studies of ESP and studies of psychokinesis.*

LEARNING SUMMARY

### Pseudoscience and scientific fraud

AQA A    U4

The phrase **'anomalous experience'** refers to strange experiences that, as yet, have no proven explanation. It includes, but is not restricted to, paranormal phenomena.

**Paranormal** (or psi-phenomena) are those activities which cannot be explained using known laws and principles. 'Psi' is the hypothetical force underlying such phenomena.

The studies on the right show that scientific fraud occurs both in the pseudosciences and mainstream psychology.

Surveys indicate that about 60% of adults believe in paranormal phenomena, with more women than men being believers.

The term **'pseudoscience'** refers to practices that may look like they are evidence-based or claim to be scientific, but they are not. Scientific subjects use the scientific method, which is outlined on page 149. Pseudosciences (such as astrology or spiritualism) frequently rely on vague claims that cannot be tested (falsified). The importance of evidence-based research is that without it we can be easily fooled into believing fraudulent claims.

Some examples of scientific fraud:

- **Sir Cyril Burt and IQ testing** – Burt (1966) published data to support his original research on intelligence using data from twins. Both studies showed a high correlation in IQ scores for identical twins, supporting the role of genetic factors. However, Kamin (1974) accused Burt of inventing the data because the statistics in the two studies were too similar. Later, Gillie (1976) discovered that the research assistants Burt claimed to work with didn't exist. This claim was challenged but the conclusion appears to be that Burt was astonishingly dishonest (Mackintosh, 1995).
- **Soal and Bateman** used Zener cards to test ESP. These cards have 5 symbols repeated on 25 cards. The experimenter looks at each card and the participant reports what they think the experimenter is seeing. Soal and Bateman (1954) produced highly significant results with a man called Basil Shackleton. However, Marwick (1978) reanalysed Soal and Bateman's data and found some numbers had been added (fraud). When these were removed, the results were at chance level. Other researchers failed to replicate the original work by Rhine (1934), which had produced significant findings. Rhine suggested this was due to negative experimenter effects because other investigators were goats (non-believers).
- **Ganzfeld research** (see next page). Blackmore (1987) reported her observations of one Ganzfeld trial where the researcher (Sargent) had altered the procedures in such a way to reduce objectivity. For example, Sargent pushed one letter towards the subject when asking the subject to make his choice. Sargent rebutted the criticisms but stopped working in parapsychology after this.

The benefits of studying pseudoscience are to increase one's understanding of the importance of proof and disproof. This has been demonstrated in a study that looked at the effect of a course on pseudoscience on students' belief in the paranormal (Morier and Keeports, 2006). The course, called 'Science and pseudoscience', explored legitimate methods of scientific inquiry and compared them to the faulty, and often fraudulent, methods of the pseudosciences. Students doing an alternative course on 'psychology and law' were used as a control. At the beginning of term all the students completed the *Belief in the Paranormal Scale* and they again completed this at the end of term. The students in the 'Science and Pseudoscience' class demonstrated a substantially reduced belief in the paranormal relative to the control class.

## Controversies relating to Ganzfeld studies of ESP

**Ganzfeld** is the German for 'total field'.

The Ganzfeld technique was developed by Honorton (1974) as a method to test ESP. A receiver is placed in total isolation and to ensure full sensory isolation ping-pong ball halves are taped over their eyes and white noise is played through headphones. The sender is also isolated and concentrates on a picture randomly selected from four other pictures. The receiver tries to identify the image. Honorton (1985) analysed 28 studies using the Ganzfeld technique and found that 38% of the time participants were able to identify the correct picture. A chance level would be 25% correct guesses (1 in 4).

**ESP (extrasensory perception)** includes telepathy, clairvoyance and precognition – perceptions occurring outside any known sensory system.

Hyman (1985) criticised the Ganzfeld work saying the experimental procedures were not rigorous enough and there were problems with the statistical analysis. When he reanalysed the same 28 studies he found that less than half of them had significant results, which might be because some experimenters are sheep (i.e. believers in paranormal phenomenon) and others are goats (i.e. non-believers). Believers might produce **demand characteristics** so that they found what they aimed to find. Honorton (1985) also did a meta-analysis and came up with different results to Hyman, supporting his original conclusions.

**Demand characteristics** occur in experimental research. Participants look for *cues* about what is expected of them. This means they are receptive to certain features of the experiment, such as leading questions. These features of the experiment almost *demand* a particular response from participants.

Honorton *et al.* (1990) designed a fully automated project (auto Ganzfeld) to deal with the criticisms, producing a 34% hit rate, which was statistically significant. Hyman continued to doubt these findings, claiming that they could only be believed if replicated by an independent investigator. Milton and Wiseman (1999) conducted a meta-analysis of studies carried out by independent researchers and found no psi-effect. This was criticised for including all studies, including those with slightly different methods. When Bem *et al.* (2001) analysed just those studies using the strict Ganzfeld procedure a significant result was found.

Honorton's automated trials were conducted under rigorous conditions where the receiver was in a sound-proof steel room. However, Wiseman claimed that this was not true for all trials.

### Conclusions

- The findings **match up to the beliefs of the researcher**, i.e. those who do believe in ESP seem to find significant results, whereas those who are skeptical produce non-significant results.
- Hyman (1995) claims that a **theory needs to be put forward** explaining how such psi phenomena could occur. Until then, the results will be meaningless.

## Controversies relating to studies of psychokinesis (PK)

**Psychokinesis** refers to situations where one person influences a physical event without direct intervention.

**Macro-PK** is cases of PK that have a large effect, such as being able to move objects or bend spoons. Weil (1974) was at first convinced by Uri Geller's ability to bend spoons until James Randi, a magician, demonstrated the same feats and showed Weil how they were done. Weil concluded that what we perceive is not the same as what is real; our beliefs alter what we perceive. Randi takes the view that psychic feats, such as spoon-bending, merely serve to increase our understanding of fraud.

**Micro-PK** involves small effects on probabilistic systems like dice throwing.

J.B. Rhine was one of the key figures in early research on the paranormal.

Rhine (1947) used a dice-throwing machine to try to demonstrate the power of the mind over random events. As the machine 'rolled' each die the participants had to try to influence the outcome. Rhine found significantly more 'hits' (the predicted outcome matched the actual outcome) than would be expected by chance. A review of nearly 150 dice-throwing studies by Radin and Ferrarui (1991) showed a weak but significant effect, overcoming criticisms that success was due to selective reporting or methodological flaws.

Schmidt (1970) devised the equivalent of an electronic coin-tossing task. He asked participants to watch a circle of nine lamps. Whenever a lamp lit up, they had to try to make it move either clockwise or anti-clockwise by thinking about the direction they wished it to move in. The lamps used a strontium-90 radioactive source emitting particles at random intervals so that movement was caused by microscopic changes. Some participants appeared to be able to influence the subatomic processes.

Schmidt (1976) was also successful with another task, where a radioactive source generated random numbers that were converted into clicks on an audio-tape. Participants were able to influence the clicks, for example, making them mainly strong or weak, even when the tapes had been made some time in advance.

More recently, Stevens (1999) invited people accessing a web page to try to influence the path of laser beams. The path of the beam was altered significantly more often than in a control condition when there was no attempt to change its course.

### Conclusions

- There is a large list of **successful PK studies**. However, attempts to replicate this research by skeptics have not been successful.
- **Magicians** who claim no special powers can often demonstrate psychic abilities, suggesting that other processes are at work.
- The results may be explained in terms of **participant and experimenter bias**. People who volunteer to be participants are likely to be believers and the same is true of experimenters. Schmeidler and McConnell (1958) found that believers in psi-phenomena (sheep) consistently scored higher than non-believers (goats) on tasks testing the paranormal. Non-believers often scored significantly below chance. Presumably, 'sheep' are more active than 'goats' in seeking cues from experimenters and acting on these cues. It is difficult to say which might come first, belief or experience, (i.e. do 'sheep' start off as non-believers and then experience leads them to believe, or does belief come first?). In either case the self-fulfilling prophecy would predict this cycle will be self-perpetuating.
- **Publication bias** – There is a tendency for positive paranormal research to be published, whereas studies that report no significance are rejected. This misrepresents the actual research that has taken place and produces a bias in favour of the existence of psi-phenomena. However, Honorton and Ferrari (1989) looked at over 300 forced-choice studies, finding a small but significant effect. They say this couldn't be due to selective reporting because, they calculated, one would have had to add a further 46 studies which reported no significance in order to reduce the significance effect.
- The James Randi Educational Foundation (JREF) has offered **$1 million** to anyone who can produce solid scientific evidence of psychic powers such as PK. To date no one has even passed the preliminary tests conducted in the claimant's own home.
- Randi (2003) has posed the question of why, if these special powers exist, have they **never been put to good use** and changed medicine or science?

Check out your own belief in the paranormal – take an online test at www.queendom.com and search for 'Paranormal Beliefs Test'. You could correlate the results of this test with tests of other factors, such as personality.

## Practice essays 15.1

(a)  Outline and evaluate studies of psychokinesis.          *(15 marks)*

(b)  Discuss issues related to scientific fraud.          *(10 marks)*

# 15.2 Factors underlying anomalous experience

*After studying this topic you should be able to describe and evaluate:*

- *cognitive, personality and biological factors underlying anomalous experience*
- *functions of paranormal and related beliefs, including their cultural significance*
- *the psychology of deception and self-deception, superstition, and coincidence.*

LEARNING SUMMARY

## Factors underlying anomalous experience

AQA A    U4

If claims about anomalous experiences are unfounded, how can we explain why some people are fervent believers? If such beliefs are not unfounded, why do some people continue not to believe?

### Cognitive factors

**Cognitive biases** – Thalbourne *et al.* (1995) suggest that low tolerance of ambiguity is associated with a fear of the paranormal.

**Thinking style (intuitive vs. analytical)** – Aarnio and Lindeman (2005) found an association between paranormal beliefs and tendency for intuitive thinking. They suggest that this might explain why more females believe in the paranormal – it is because they also prefer more intuitive approaches to thinking. However, other research has found a positive association between analytic thinking and belief in the paranormal (e.g. Wolfradt *et al.*, 1999) and some studies have found higher levels of paranormal belief in educated people (Farha and Stewart, 2006), although in the study by Aarnio and Lindeman psychology and medical students held fewest paranormal beliefs.

**Cognitive illusions** – Blackmore (1992) has explained psi-phenomena as a form of cognitive illusion. She argues that we are used to having explanations for everything and, if we haven't got one, we seek one. At least 'sheep' do; 'goats' accept that some things are simply random coincidences. 'Sheep' is a term used to refer to believers in anomalous experiences. 'Goats' are non-believers. Support of this was provided by Brugger *et al.* (1990) who found that goats were better at generating random numbers than sheep (they gave more consecutive repetitions of the same digit), i.e. they were able to cope with the nature of random occurrences better.

### Personality factors

Locus of control is also discussed on page 168.

**Locus of control** – Malinowski (1948) suggested that belief in the paranormal gives people an illusion of control. People who have an external locus of control (externals) believe that events are often explained by factors outside their own control, such as luck. Tobayck and Milford (1983) demonstrated a positive correlation between being an 'external' and having a greater belief in paranormal phenomena. However, not all research has supported this. One suggestion is that some forms of psi-phenomena (such as superstition and spiritualism) correlate positively with an external locus of control, whereas others (such as pk) correlate negatively (Wolfradt, 1997). Davies and Kirkby (1985) found a positive correlation between internality and belief in psi.

Piaget, in his theory of cognitive development (see page 81), suggested that young children are prone to magical thinking, for example, believing in Father Christmas.

**Psychopathology** – One element of some mental disorders is '**magical thinking**' (as seen in PK). This is a symptom of schizotypal personality disorder. Eckblad and Chapman (1983) found that people who scored highly on magical thinking also showed a predisposition to psychosis. Other research has found a link between holding paranormal beliefs and schizotypy (e.g. Thalbourne, 1994) and with manic-depressive experiences (Thalbourne and French, 1995).

**Neuroticism** is the tendency to experience negative emotional states such as anger, anxiety and depression.

**Neuroticism** may be linked to paranormal beliefs. Williams *et al.* (2007) found a link in 280 adolescents, and Thalbourne *et al.* (1995) found a significant positive relationship between neuroticism and paranormal beliefs (specifically belief in psi, witchcraft, spiritualism, precognition and traditional religion).

From the evolutionary point of view it can be argued that, if ESP does exist, it would have high adaptive value – or would it?

The **EEA** (environment of evolutionary adaptedness) is the environment to which a species is adapted. The selective pressures at that time explain the behaviours that we observe today. In humans it is suggested that our EEA was the period from 1.8 million to 11,000 years ago when humans lived on the plains in Africa.

However, other researchers (e.g. Lester and Monaghan, 1995) have found no such relationship. Auton *et al.* (2003) found that high believers also scored highly on aggression (related to neuroticism) and defendence (i.e. not readily accepting criticism).

## Biological factors

**Evolutionary explanations** – Paranormal beliefs are present in all cultures. This universality of paranormal beliefs suggests humans inherit a mental module which predisposes them to having such beliefs. If this is true then beliefs in the paranormal must be in some way adaptive, at least in the **EEA**. One suggestion is that such beliefs give comfort. In the face of uncertainty they stop people questing any further for answers and allow them to focus on more immediate concerns.

An alternative view is that it is a consequence of the adaptation of the human mind to seek explanations for events in the world. A desire to discover causes would be important in enabling humans to control their world. This desire leads to cognitive illusions, i.e. paranormal beliefs.

The significance of biological factors may be supported by universal similarities in paranormal beliefs. McClenon and Nooney (2003) analysed reports by anthropologists of anomalous experiences and found cross-culturally consistent features – belief in spirits, life after death and magical abilities.

The role of biological factors is further supported by genetic research on **religiosity**, which is related to anomalous experience. Koenig (2005) found that identical twins are more likely to have the same religious views than non-identical twins, which supports a genetic link.

**Brain biochemistry** – People with high levels of **dopamine** are more likely to regard coincidences as being meaningful and they pick out patterns where there are none. This was demonstrated in a study by Brugger *et al.* (2002) comparing people who either said they were believers ('sheep') or people who were skeptics ('goats'). The participants were shown both real faces and words, mixed together with jumbled up words; sheep were more likely to identify the jumbled words as more real than the goats. However, when the participants were given L-dopa, which increases levels of dopamine in the brain, both groups made the same errors. The drug did not increase the tendency of sheep to misinterpret the patterns.

### Evaluation of factors underlying anomalous experience

- Other research (e.g. Sparks *et al.*, 1997) suggests that **social factors** are more important, such as having friends who believe in the paranormal.
- One of the problems with research on factors related to paranormal beliefs is that all research **relies on tests that assess belief in the paranormal**. Some tests include items that may not be considered to be 'paranormal experiences'.

## Functions of paranormal and related beliefs

**Dealing with uncertainty** – The explanations outlined above lead us to suggest that paranormal and related beliefs provide answers in situations where there are no answers. They provide a means of dealing with uncertainty, though this is only true, as we have seen, for certain kinds of people (e.g. those who have intuitive ways of thinking or who tend towards neuroticism).

**Sense of control** – Watson *et al.* (2007) found an association between lack of a sense of control in childhood and tendency towards paranormal beliefs. This is linked to the explanation that paranormal beliefs provide an illusion of a sense of control.

**Cultural significance** – At a cultural level all beliefs perform an important function as part of shared cultural systems. A culture is defined as a shared set of values, norms and beliefs. Therefore, explanations of particular phenomena form a key part of what it is to belong to a community.

## The psychology of deception and self-deception, superstition, and coincidence

> Theory of mind (ToM) is the ability to understand what is going on in another person's mind, to 'guess' what they are thinking or feeling (see page 91).

### Deception

The ability to deceive someone else depends on possessing a **theory of mind** and is seen as a sign of intelligence in animals. **Machiavellian intelligence** (see page 75) refers to the ability to intentionally deceive another individual. In order to intentionally deceive another individual one has to have an understanding of what they know, or don't know.

Pinker (2004) suggests that religious and paranormal beliefs evolved because of the benefits for the leaders – the magician, crystal-ball gazer, and shaman. The ability to deceive others gives the deceiver power.

### Self-deception

> **Key points from AS**
> * Freudian explanations are explored in *Revise AS Unit 1.1, page 18.*

Self-deception can be related to the action of the unconscious and to Freudian explanations. According to Freud, thoughts that create anxiety are repressed into the unconscious to protect the ego (the action of **ego defences**). At a conscious level a person might believe that their reasons for action are, for example, honourable, but at an unconscious level the motivation may be quite different.

> **Key points from AS**
> * The accuracy of recall of paranormal events may be related to the study of eyewitness testimony, see *Revise AS Unit 2.2, page 35.* Memory is not always reliable. Some paranormal reports may be false memories.

In terms of belief in the paranormal, it may be that believers are deceiving themselves about the evidence. They may repress experience or repress evidence that runs counter to their beliefs. In addition, researchers who are believers may be deceiving themselves about the rigour of their investigations. Their wish to demonstrate psi-phenomenon means that some of their behaviours are repressed.

### Superstition

Superstitions are beliefs that may be linked to ritual behaviours, performed with the belief that they will deal with something beyond our control, such as wearing a particular shirt to ensure your football team wins. Such beliefs or behaviours help a person deal with the unknown.

> A **superstition** is a belief that is not based on knowledge or reasoned thinking, i.e. it is an irrational belief.

Skinner (1948) offered a behaviourist explanation for superstition. He suggested that the chance association of a behaviour with a reinforcer can produce a link between body movements (routines) and superstitious behaviour. The pigeons he used in his experiments sometimes learned unique sequences of body movement because they just happened to be performing them when they were given food.

People may acquire superstitions/superstitious behaviour through operant conditioning because in the past the behaviours have been associated with reducing the anxiety associated with uncertain events.

### Coincidence

> **Coincidence** is when two unrelated things happen together without any apparent causal connection.

When two unrelated things happen together it is a natural tendency to assume one has caused the other. For example, the presence of a spider and a person screaming leads to the assumption that the spider caused the scream. However, in some instances there is no cause yet some people prefer to impute a cause rather than be content with coincidence, a cognitive bias.

## Practice essays 15.2

(a) Describe and evaluate personality factors that underlie anomalous experience. *(15 marks)*

(b) Discuss the function of deception and self-deception in relation to anomalous experience. *(10 marks)*

# 15.3 Belief in exceptional experience

*After studying this topic you should be able to describe and evaluate:*

- *research into psychic healing*
- *research into out-of-body and near-death experience*
- *research into psychic mediumship.*

**LEARNING SUMMARY**

## Research into exceptional experience

AQA A    U4

> Psychic healing aims to help people recover from illnesses by channelling energy into their bodies to re-energise them.

> Skeptics suggest that psychic healing is no more than a placebo effect. **Placebos** are substances that have no pharmacological effects, but the person taking them thinks they are the real thing. This means you can separate the psychological from the physical effects of being given a drug treatment. A placebo effect occurs when someone thinks they are receiving treatment.

> If psychic healing is a real phenomenon then why is it not widely used to treat people?

> Another classic case of experimenter effects with animals is shown in the case of Clever Hans, the horse who could apparently add up. It was discovered, through objective testing, that Hans was merely responding to his owner's cues.

### Research into psychic healing

**Experiments** – Krieger (1979) studied the effects of one psychic healer (Oskar Estebany) on a group of physically ill patients. She found that the haemoglobin levels of the patients he 'touched' were significantly higher after being treated than those of a control group of patients, and that the levels were still significantly higher a year later.

**Distant healing studies** are conducted to rule out any subtle communication/placebo effects; the psychic just focuses on a photo of the patient. Braud and Schlitz (1988) tested the effects on patients' galvanic skin response (see page 37), which is evidence of activity in the sympathetic nervous system. The healer is instructed to focus their influence for one-minute periods and at this time the patient's responses are recorded. They found significantly changed GSR patterns during periods of influence. In such cases the placebo effect cannot be operating because the patient doesn't know when the influence is occurring.

**Studies with non-human animals** – Grad (1976) studied the effects that Estebany had on a group of iodine-deficient mice (the lack of iodine creates a condition called *goiter*). The psychic placed his hands on their cages for 15 minutes, 10 times a week. In the control condition the mice's cages were warmed to simulate the effect of hands. Grad found that the rate of goiter development was slower in the experimental mice.

### Evaluation

- Three explanations may account for **recovery from illness** (aside from psychic healing): it is spontaneous (people do recover spontaneously from many illnesses); it is temporary (a disabled person may walk again but relapses once out of the spotlight); it is due to a placebo effect (all physical disorders have a psychological element as demonstrated by the effectiveness of placebo therapies). Therefore, we cannot always be certain that recovery is due to psychic healing.

- The key question is the extent to which such studies were rigorously controlled – factors such as **experimenter effects and demand characteristics** may have acted as confounding factors, or the studies may have been fraudulent. However, the same criticisms are made of many psychological studies where, for example, the person who has designed the research also conducts it and may unwittingly communicate expectations. To deal with this we expect studies to be replicated; a practice not common in paranormal research.

- It is suggested that **non-human animals are not subject to unconscious suggestion** (placebo effects), but this is not true, as Rosenthal and Fode (1963) found in their classic study of experimenter effects on rats. Students were told they had to train rats to perform a task and were told that their rat was either dull or bright. The rats' performance was related to the students' expectations even though the rats had actually been randomly assigned.

- This research **has a serious side because some individuals make** considerable sums of money from claims of psychic healing.

Out of body experience (**OBE** or **OOBE**) involves a sensation of floating outside one's body and sometimes observing one's own body. It has been associated with near-death experiences (NDEs) which occur around the time of a person's death or potential death.

## Research into out-of-body experience (OBE) and near-death experience (NDE)

**Qualitative analysis** – Green (1968) analysed 400 first-hand accounts of OBEs and provided a classification of them. In **parasomatic** cases the observer has another body distinct from their normal physical body; in **asomatic** cases the observer is unaware of having a body; in a small number of cases (4%) there was a connecting cord between the bodies.

**Brain studies** – Blanke *et al.* (2005) showed that experiences similar to OBEs could be elicited in 'normal' people if a particular area of the brain was activated electrically – this area is the **TPJ** (the right temporal-parietal junction where the temporal and parietal lobes come together).

About 1 in 10 people claim to have had an OBE.

**Explanations** – OBEs may be the result of dream states (i.e. on the edge of consciousness) or related to taking certain drugs. In both instances consciousness is separated from the physical self. Blackmore (1982) suggests that OBEs occur when a person loses contact with their sensory input while remaining conscious. The person's perceptions are fed from elsewhere.

### Evaluation

- This research is **more credible** than other paranormal studies. The qualitative analyses have been verified by different researchers, supporting their validity. For example, Poynton (1975) analysed reports of OBEs in South Africa and found similar results to Green.
- The link to **possible explanations** is critical; phenomena do not make sense unless we can offer some account as to how they got there.

## Research into psychic mediumship

Schwartz *et al.* (2001) conducted a controlled test of five mediums. A woman unknown to them recorded details of six significant losses she had experienced in the previous 10 years. Each medium interviewed the woman, who was only allowed to answer yes or no. The mediums' average accuracy was 83% compared to control interviewers who were 36% accurate. O'Keeffe and Wiseman (2005) asked five mediums to give readings for five volunteer sitters (totalling 25 readings). Each sitter read all 25 readings and was asked to rate how much each statement was appropriate to them. The ratings were actually lowest for the statements relevant to them.

A **psychic medium** is a person who can communicate with the spirits of dead people. Mediumship may involve telepathy (reading someone else's mind), clairvoyance (information from distant objects/people) and communication with the spirit world.

Remote viewing involves an experimenter going to a remote location, and then the medium reports any images that arise. Afterwards a judge tries to match images with a set of possible target locations. Targ and Puthoff (1977) reported higher than chance findings, but Marks and Kammann (1980) couldn't replicate this and suggested that the transcripts contained clues about previous targets.

### Evaluation

- It is likely that psychic mediumship is impressive because **people only remember the things that were relevant to them**.
- The evidence above fits the common pattern – **believers obtain positive results**, non-believers don't. Gary Schwartz works with the research group VERITAS, investigating the continuity of life; Richard Wiseman is a skeptic.

Spiritualism has been brought into disrepute by the frequent cases of fraudulent activity.

## Practice essays 15.3

(a) Outline **one or more** research studies that investigated psychic healing and consider what these studies tell us about exceptional experience. *(15 marks)*

(b) Critically evaluate research into psychic mediumship. *(10 marks)*

# Chapter 16

# Psychological research and scientific method

## 16.1 The application of scientific method

*After studying this topic you should be able to describe and evaluate:*

**Science** is knowledge gained through systematic and objective observation of, and experiments with, phenomena.

- *the major features of science, for example replicability, objectivity*
- *the scientific process, including theory construction, hypothesis testing, use of empirical methods, generation of laws/principles (e.g. Popper, Kuhn)*
- *validating new knowledge and the role of peer review.*

**LEARNING SUMMARY**

## The major features of science

AQA A  U4
AQA B  U4

Popper (1969) argued that it was the possibility of **falsification** that separates science from pseudo-sciences.

There are several issues that can be debated:

- Is psychology a science?
- Is a scientific approach desirable in psychology? You can read more about these issues on page 186.

**Triangulation** is achieved by comparing the findings from a number of different studies or using different methods within one study. Close agreement confirms the validity of the findings.

Kuhn's conception was that science develops through pre-science, to science, and then to revolution. On the other hand, Palermo (1971) argued that, far from being a pre-science, psychology has already undergone several paradigm shifts, such as structuralism (introspection), behaviourism, and information processing. It is now in the revolution phase.

Look at a list of references at the back of any Psychology textbook and you will see the names of many journals.

The key concepts of a science are: objectivity, control and manipulation of variables, replication (to confirm validity), and falsification (being able to reject a hypothesis).

### The scientific process and the validation of new knowledge

The **hypothetico-deductive model** of science was proposed by Karl Popper (1935), suggesting that theories/laws about the world should come first and these should be used to generate expectations/hypotheses. These hypotheses can then be tested using experiments or other methods. This kind of science does not rely on chance observation but on deliberately organising opportunities to make observations.

1. Making observations, producing 'facts' (data about the world).
2. Constructing a theory to account for a set of related facts.
3. Generating expectations (hypotheses) from the theory. ←
4. Collecting data to test expectations.
5. Adjusting the theory in response to the data collected. ┘

The **laboratory experiment** is the best, but not the only means of hypothesis testing, e.g. naturalistic observations use the scientific method. Qualitative methods sometimes aim to be subjective in their collection of data but objectivity is also possible, for example, through **triangulation** where results from a variety of studies can be compared to enhance validity.

Kuhn (1962) claimed that psychology could not be a science because, unlike other sciences, there is no single **paradigm** (i.e. shared set of assumptions about human behaviour and the methods appropriate to its study). It may be that psychology has yet to identify its paradigm, i.e. it is a **pre-science**. Others argue that psychology is a science with a number of paradigms, such as behaviourism.

### The role of peer review

Scientists publish the results of their research in academic journals. These articles are subject to peer review (also called 'referring'), i.e. other academic psychologists read the article and judge whether the research is credible and valid. This ensures that a professional standard is maintained as well.

Some critics suggest that impartial review is an unachievable ideal, partly because research is conducted in a social world and social relationships affect objectivity. It is also not always possible to find a sufficiently knowledgeable person to conduct a review in a little-researched subject area.

# 16.2 Designing psychological investigations

### After studying this topic you should be able to describe and evaluate:

| AQA A | U4 |

**AS**

• This unit is covered in *Revise AS Unit 4.1 and 4.2, pages 75–91*.

• selection and application of appropriate research methods
• implications of sampling strategies, for example, bias and generalising
• issues of reliability, including types of reliability, assessment of reliability, improving reliability, assessing and improving validity (internal and external)
• ethical considerations in design and conduct of psychological research.

# 16.3 Data analysis and reporting

### After studying this topic you should be able to describe and evaluate:

**AS**

• Graphical representation is covered in *Revise AS Unit 4.3, pages 92–93*.

**AS**

• The analysis and interpretation of qualitative data is covered in *Revise AS Unit 7.3, page 94*.

• appropriate selection of graphical representations
• probability and significance, including the interpretation of significance and type 1/type 2 errors
• factors affecting choice of statistical test, including levels of measurement
• the use of inferential analysis, including Spearman's Rho, Mann-Whitney, Wilcoxon, Chi-squared
• analysis and interpretation of qualitative data
• conventions of reporting on psychological investigations.

## Data analysis

| AQA A | U4 |
| AQA B | U4 |

**Descriptive statistics** (such as the mean or standard deviation or a graph) describe a set of data.

**Inferential statistics** give us a different kind of information – they tell us how likely it is that the pattern in a set of observed data occurred by chance and whether we can *infer* that the same pattern exists in the general population.

Two samples may differ but what we are really interested in is knowing how likely it is that the populations from which the samples were drawn are different.

Type 1 and Type 2 errors were used to describe the results of Rosenhan's study (see page 97).

### Probability and significance

If we want to know whether men have better memories than women or vice versa, we might test the memories of a sample of men and a sample of women, and compare their scores. It is very unlikely that their scores will be identical, but what we want to know is whether the difference between the scores is **significant**, i.e. is the difference big enough to warrant a conclusion that men and women in the general population (as distinct from our sample) differ in their memory capacity? Or could the observed difference have occurred by chance and is, therefore, insignificant?

The idea of 'chance' is related to certainty. You can never be certain that an observed effect was due to chance or not, but you can state how certain you are. In general, psychologists use a **probability** of p≤0.05, this means that there is a 5% possibility that the results did occur by chance. In fact, what it really means is that there is a 5% probability of the results occurring if there is no real difference/association between the populations from which the samples were drawn. In some studies a more stringent level of significance is used, for example, if testing a new drug we want to be more certain. So researchers use p≤0.01 or even p≤0.001. This chosen value of 'p' is called the **significance level**.

### Type 1 and type 2 errors

A type 1 error is a correct assumption that is mistakenly rejected, for example, rejecting a null hypothesis that is true. This may occur when using a level of significance that is too high (or lenient, e.g. 10%). A type 2 error occurs when an incorrect assumption is mistakenly accepted, for example, accepting a null hypothesis that is false. This might occur when selecting a level of significance that is too low (or stringent, e.g. 1%).

## Factors affecting choice of statistical test

There are four statistical tests in the AQA A specification. The way to decide which one to use is to ask yourself the following questions:

1. Are your data in **frequencies** (i.e. nominal data)? If so, then you use Chi-squared.
2. **Are you looking to find out if your two samples are different or correlated?** If you are seeking to find out whether two samples are different you use a test of differences – either Mann-Whitney or Wilcoxon. If you are looking at a correlation then you use Spearman's rho.
3. **Experimental design** – Are your samples related (e.g. a repeated measures design is used) or are they independent (i.e. an independent groups design is used)? If they are related then you use Wilcoxon, if they are independent you use Mann-Whitney.
4. **Level of measurement?** There are four levels of measurement:
   **Nominal** – Data are in categories.
   **Ordinal** – Data are ordered in some way.
   **Interval** – Data are measured using units of equal intervals.
   **Ratio** – There is a true zero point.

## Inferential tests

**Spearman's Rho** is used when a hypothesis predicts a *correlation* between two variables. The two sets of data are pairs of scores from one person or an associated event (such as scores from twins), i.e. they are related. The statistic that is produced is called **rho**.

**Mann-Whitney test** is used when a hypothesis predicts a *difference* between two sets of data. The two sets of data are pairs of scores from two separate groups, i.e. they are *independent*. The statistic that is produced is called **U**.

**Wilcoxon test** is used when a hypothesis predicts a *difference* between two sets of data. The two sets of data are pairs of scores from one person (or a matched pair), i.e. they are *related*. The statistic that is produced is called **T**.

**Chi-squared test** is used when a hypothesis predicts a *difference* between two conditions or an *association* between variables. The sets of data must be *independent* (no individual should have a score in more than one 'cell'). The data are in frequencies (nominal level of measurement). The statistic that is produced is called $\chi^2$.

### Observed and critical levels of significance

A statistical analysis is applied to a set of data and produces an **observed value**. In order to determine whether this observed value is significant it is compared to **critical values**, which are given in a table of critical values for that statistic. On the left is an example of a table of critical values for the Wilcoxon T test. In order to use the table, you need to know: (1) whether you had a directional hypothesis (which is a one-tailed test) or a non-directional hypothesis (two-tailed test) and (2) the number (N) of participants or participant pairs. This information means you can locate the appropriate critical value for your test. For example, if you had a one-tailed test and 19 participants, the critical value would be for T 53 at the 5% level of significance.

For the Wilcoxon test and the Mann-Whitney test the observed value must be equal to or less than the critical value for significance to be shown.

For the Chi-squared test and Spearman's rho the observed value must be equal to or greater than the critical value for significance to be shown.

---

There are three main kinds of **experimental design** – repeated measures and matched pairs (which are both related) and independent groups.

The phrase '**levels of measurement**' refers to the different levels of detail that can be used when measuring something. Each level expresses more information about the thing we are measuring.

All of the tests in the AQA A specification are non-parametric tests, therefore, you do not need to further consider the question about the level of measurement that was used. However, you do have to know about the different levels of measurement.

AQA B requires an understanding of parametric tests and this is considered on page 187.

**Critical values of T at 5% level (p 0.05)**

| N = | One tailed test | Two tailed test |
|---|---|---|
| 5 | T 0 | |
| 6 | 2 | 0 |
| 7 | 3 | 2 |
| 8 | 5 ≤ | 3 |
| 9 | 8 | 5 |
| 10 | 11 | 8 |
| 11 | 13 | 10 |
| 12 | 17 | 13 |
| 13 | 21 | 17 |
| 14 | 25 | 21 |
| 15 | 30 | 25 |
| 16 | 35 | 29 |
| 17 | 41 | 34 |
| 18 | 47 | 40 |
| 19 | 53 | 46 |
| 20 | 60 | 52 |
| 21 | 67 | 58 |
| 22 | 75 | 65 |
| 23 | 83 | 73 |
| 24 | 91 | 81 |
| 25 | 100 | 89 |

## Conventions of reporting on psychological investigations

Written reports of psychological investigations are published in academic journals, as described on page 149. The convention is to divide such reports into the following sections:

- A short summary or **abstract** at the beginning, which provides key details of the aims, participants, research methods and procedures, findings and conclusions.
- An **introduction** or **literature review** outlining previous research (theories and/or studies) which have led the researcher to the **aims/hypothesis** for this study.
- A description of the **method/procedures**. These should be sufficiently detailed so that someone else could replicate the study and, thus, be able to confirm the findings. Any questionnaires or tests used, or other materials, may be included in an appendix.
- The **results** are described and a summary of the raw data given (the actual scores or data for individual participants, called the 'raw data', is not given). Other descriptive statistics (graphs, tables, measures of central tendency) are included, and finally, inferential statistics indicating the significance of the results.
- A **discussion** of the results, including reference to other studies/theories and suggesting alterations to existing theories or proposing new theories.

## Practice questions 16.3

A psychologist conducts a study into conformity to see whether gender differences vary with the kind of task undertaken. Two tasks are used in the experiment. Task one is a face-to-face conformity task, task two requires written answers.

Table 1  Results showing the number of people who conformed in each condition

|       | Task 1 | Task 2 | Total |
|-------|--------|--------|-------|
| Men   | 21     | 43     | 64    |
| Women | 31     | 33     | 64    |
|       | 52     | 76     | 128   |

Critical values of Chi squared ($x^2$) at 5% level ($p \le 0.05$)

| df | One-tailed test | Two-tailed test |
|----|-----------------|-----------------|
| 1  | 2.71            | 3.84            |

Observed value of $x^2$ must be EQUAL TO or GREATER THAN the critical value in this table for significance to be shown.

(a) Write a suitable directional hypothesis for this study. *(2 marks)*

(b) The Chi-squared value produced for this data is 3.36. Use the table of critical values to determine whether this would be significant at the 5% level (for a one-tailed test). *(1 mark)*

(c) Identify **one** factor that the psychologist had to take into account when deciding whether or not to use the Chi-squared ($x^2$) test. *(1 mark)*

(d) Sketch a suitable graph to display the results from this study. *(6 marks)*

(e) Describe **one** conclusion that you can draw based on the data in the table and the statistical significance. *(4 marks)*

(f) Outline the key features of the scientific method. *(6 marks)*

(g) Identify **one** strength and **one** limitation of the scientific method. *(4 marks)*

(h) The psychologist wanted to find out more about why men and women conformed in different situations and decided to conduct some follow-up interviews. Describe the design decisions that would be necessary, including some questions that would be used. Make sure you cover all the procedural details that he would need to plan. *(10 marks)*

## 1

"Research into schizophrenia shows there is a major genetic component but the fact that concordance rates between identical twins is never 100% means that there must be environmental contributions."

Discuss biological explanations of schizophrenia. *(25 marks)*

Schizophrenia is a psychiatric disorder involving loss of control with reality and a range of symptoms. There is considerable evidence that genetic factors are involved. This view considers that certain individuals possess certain genes that predispose an individual to schizophrenia. This means that it is inherited and we would expect to find that relatives have similar chances of developing the disorder. Indeed, research has found that first degree relatives of people with schizophrenia are 18 times more likely to be affected than the general population.

Identical (monozygotic, MZ) twins would be expected to have a similar chance of having schizophrenia since they carry the same genes. Research by Gottesman and Shields has found higher concordance rates (where both twins have the disorder) in MZ twins than DZ (dizygotic) twins who only share 50% of their genes. However, if schizophrenia was solely caused by genes then we would expect 100% concordance in MZ twins. Since this is not found then other factors must also be involved.

MZ twin studies have the advantage of controlling for genetics but the disadvantage of not controlling for environment. One way to get round this is to study MZ twins reared apart. Twin studies show similar concordance rates even when they have been reared apart, but the samples used in these studies tend to be rather small and family problems may have been the reason for the separation.

A genetic predetermination could lead to abnormalities in the brain. There is strong support for the idea that high dopamine levels are involved in schizophrenia. Dopamine is a neurotransmitter in the brain and post mortems have found higher levels than normal in the brains of schizophrenics. It has also been found that those drugs that are known to reduce dopamine (antipsychotic drugs) also reduce schizophrenic symptoms. However, this evidence tends to be correlational and we can't know whether the dopamine levels cause schizophrenia or schizophrenia causes high dopamine levels.

MRI scans have found that schizophrenics have enlarged ventricles in their brain and post-mortems have found that the brains of schizophrenics are lighter. This could reflect loss of cells in the brain and could explain the cognitive symptoms, such as poor attention, distractability and poor memory. This again could be a cause or effect of schizophrenia.

Viruses might also be involved as they could invade and disrupt brain development in the foetus. Research by Mednick has found a higher rate of schizophrenia in people exposed to flu in the second trimester of pregnancy, a time when there is greatest cortical development. Crow suggested that a retrovirus was incorporated into DNA and this was transmitted between generations. This would explain the fact that there is gradual brain damage and why schizophrenia spontaneously appears in families.

Adoption studies support the genetic explanation for schizophrenia. Tienari found that children who had been adopted away from a schizophrenic biological mother were still more likely to get it than a children adopted from non-schizophrenic parents, despite being raised in a different environment. Marcus also found that 22/50 children from 1 or 2 affected parents got it, and only 4/50 from healthy parents did. This supports the view that genetics has a strong role. However, not all high risk participants got it, indicating that other factors are involved.

See pages 9–11 for a breakdown of the marking criteria used to mark this question.

This student has wisely managed to avoid starting the essay with a description of the clinical characteristics of schizophrenia. You should only provide these if specifically required in the question, otherwise start immediately with a description of the explanations.

The answer shows a detailed and thorough knowledge of biological explanations for schizophrenia. The AO2/evaluation/ commentary points are scattered throughout the answer – paragraph 2 ends with an AO2 point and paragraph 3 starts with one.

The use of research throughout the essay could be credited as AO1 or AO2 – the studies have been presented as part of the descriptive content of the essay, but could have been turned into effective AO2 if key phrases had been used (e.g. 'this explanation is demonstrated by…') and/or if the conclusions from the studies were emphasised (e.g. 'This study indicates that…').

In the end the decision about whether to credit material as AO1 or AO2 is not of major significance here because there is sufficient of both. In some essays an examiner might choose to credit some material as AO2 because there is plenty of AO1 and not enough AO2.

This essay certainly has plenty of accurate and detailed AO1 (**9 out of 9 AO1 marks**). The AO2 contains reference to approaches since the topic of the essay is on the biological approach, therefore, **13 out of 16 AO2 marks**.

**The total mark is 22 out of 25 marks.**

See pages 9–11 for a breakdown of the marking criteria used to mark this question.

(a) In this part of the question there is a mixture of AO1 and AO2 marks. The student has given an accurate and detailed description of the Ganzfeld technique plus a reasonably accurate report of the findings of such studies, though key details are lacking (such as the actual percentages). However, there are only a few marks available for AO1 so this is sufficient for **4 out of 4 AO1 marks.** The evaluation is rather superficial and basic, tending towards 'rudimentary' rather than 'reasonable'. Therefore, **2 out of 6 AO2 marks.**

(b) The second part of this question contains a higher amount of marks and, therefore, more time should have been spent on this part of the answer, especially the evaluative component. There is some evaluation in paragraphs 2 and 4 but this is rudimentary. However, this is not a topic that lends itself to evaluation; research studies might have been used to comment on, for example, the individual differences.

There is also the question of synopticity – issues, debates and approaches. Determinism was thrown in right at the end, but not in a very meaningful way. It could be argued that humans tend to be determinist in their approach to understanding the world and, therefore, such an approach by scientists is a natural form of thinking. **5 out of 5 AO1 marks, 2 out of 10 AO2 marks.**

**The total mark is 13 out of 25 marks.**

**2**

(a) Outline and evaluate Ganzfeld studies of ESP. *(10 marks)*

(b) Discuss the functions of paranormal and related beliefs, including their cultural significance. *(15 marks)*

(a) Honorton first devised the Ganzfeld technique as a way to investigate ESP (extra sensory perception). This is the ability to perceive what is in another person's mind without direct contact. Honorton devised a way to cut out any signals – the participant who was receiving signals from someone else would be in a separate room and have no contact with anyone else. They also have ping pong balls taped to their eyes and cotton wool in their ears to cut out any extra sensory information. The sender concentrates on one of four pictures selected randomly by the experimenter and the receiver says which picture he thinks it is.

Honorton and other people used this technique to study ESP and concluded that people did demonstrate ESP because they did slightly better than chance with their identification of the image 'sent'. If it was chance then you would expect 25% 'hits' but people on average did better than this.

Some people don't believe these results and think that the experimenter influenced the choices in some way. However, Honorton repeated his studies using an automated technique and still found more hits than would be expected by chance. When Wiseman reviewed the evidence he found the opposite was true. The average result was poorer than chance. Both sides have argued back and forth and there really isn't a conclusion. It is possible that the results are related to the beliefs of the researcher – people who believe in ESP seem to find support, whereas people who don't believe don't find support.

(b) There are many reasons suggested about why people believe in ESP and other paranormal phenomena, and the function this serves for them. One such function could be related to a person's cultural background. Different cultures have different beliefs about ghosts and spirits, water diving, ESP and so on. Paranormal beliefs such as belief in spirits are embodied in your culture. Children learn abut the stories and explanations related to paranormal phenomena when they are young. They are part of things like fairy tales. The important thing is that such stories bind a group of people together and are an integral part of the culture. Culture is defined as the rules and customs shared by a group of people so it is just these stories that are a key part of what is meant by a culture.

Of course, on the negative side, this cultural importance may mean it is quite hard to stop people believing in such things as witchcraft or folk methods used to treat mental illness. And the knowledge people have today may not be accepted by the cultural group, which is not good for them.

Probably the most important function of beliefs in paranormal and related beliefs is it helps people deal with the unknown, with things that don't have an explanation. It makes some people feel very unsafe because they don't know why some things happen, such as seeing things in the sky, and no one can explain why those things are there. So people want an explanation and if there isn't one they will invent something or accept whatever explanation is offered.

There are individual differences in this because some people are more happy to accept uncertainty whereas others seek answers and, therefore, are more accepting of paranormal explanations. In fact the quest for explanations is a natural part of the way human minds work and this is adaptive. Humans seek explanations and their desire for such explanations means that they do find real explanations and this kind of scientific question enables them to find ways to control things in their world. This wish for explanations is an example of determinism.

See pages 9–11 for a breakdown of the marking criteria used to mark this question.

**3**

A psychologist wishes to investigate whether people in a group will decide on a riskier course of action than individuals making a decision on their own. In order to investigate this the psychologist gave participants a scenario to consider: A young man has decided to take a gap year before going to university and can't decide whether to (a) travel with a group of friends (the safer decision) or (b) travel on his own (the riskier decision). The psychologist sought participants for this study by advertising on the noticeboard at the university where he worked. He selected the first 40 students who volunteered and asked each participant to select one of the options after considering the scenario. Half of the participants were allowed to discuss their views with a small group of other participants before registering their opinion. The other half read the scenario on their own.

The results from the study are shown in the table below.

**Table 1 Decision made by participants in groups or on their own**

|  | Safer decision (choice a) | Riskier decision (choice b) |
|---|---|---|
| Participants who discussed the scenario in a group | 8 | 12 |
| Participants who made their decision on their own | 15 | 5 |

The psychologist decided to use a Chi-squared test to analyse the results. The Chi-squared analysis produced a value of 5.01.

**Table 2 Critical values of Chi-squared for a one-tailed test where $df = 1$**

| Significance level | 0.10 | 0.05 | 0.01 |
|---|---|---|---|
| Observed value of Chi-squared | 2.71 | 3.84 | 6.64 |

All of the answers given are fully correct, except for part (h).

In part (a) the answer would not receive full marks if it did not include mention of both levels of the IV.

(a) State an appropriate directional hypothesis for the above study       *(2 marks)*

People who discuss a scenario produce a riskier decision than people who do not discuss the scenario.

(b) Identify the target population in the above study.       *(1 mark)*

The target population is the group of people from which the sample was taken, which in this case would have been the students at that university who read the advertisement.

(c) Identify the type of experimental design used in the above study.       *(1 mark)*

It is an independent groups design.

(d) Identify **one** possible uncontrolled variable in the study and describe the effect it may have had.       *(3 marks)*

One possible uncontrolled variable would be the fact that students had taken gap years themselves and this would affect their judgement. This would affect the results if it happened that there was an uneven distribution of people who had taken gap years in one of the experimental conditions.

In part (e) the candidate has given two answers, both of which are correct and well explained. However, if the first answer had been wrong the candidate would have received 0 marks because, in the research methods section, only the first answer is marked. This is because you could give a range of answers, knowing that one of them is going to be correct.

(e) Describe how you would have dealt with this uncontrolled variable.       *(3 marks)*

To control this I would have allocated participants randomly to the two experimental conditions, which should mean that there should be no bias. Alternatively I could have asked people beforehand about their own travel experience and excluded anyone who had travelled.

The answer for (f) is fully correct; another possible reason is that a test of association was required.

The answer for (g) is fully correct; if the candidate had written 'the level of probability' this would be given only 1 mark.

The answer for (h) is only worth 2 marks because the full evidence has not been given – the answer should mention that it is significant at the 5% level because the observed value is 5.01, which is greater than the critical value at 5% (which is 2.71).

In part (i) there is sufficient detail for the full 5 marks.

The candidate has provided a detailed description of key design decisions that would need to be taken in extending the original project, so **12 out of 12 marks**.

The total mark is 33 out of 35 marks.

(f) Give **two** reasons why a Chi-squared test was used to analyse the results of the above study. *(2 marks)*

The data was nominal data, in other words it was in frequencies. And also the samples were independent – no person was represented in more than one category.

(g) What is meant in Table 2 by the phrase 'significance level'? *(2 marks)*

The phrase means that the probability that the results can be attributed to chance factors rather than the IV.

(h) Explain what conclusion could be drawn from the statistical results. *(4 marks)*

Chi-square is significant at the 5% level but not at the 1% level. The 5% level is adequate so there is a significant difference in whether people discuss things as a group or not, in that groups seem to produce a riskier result than a person just working on his/her own.

(i) Briefly describe the major features of science, with reference to the study described above. *(5 marks)*

Two of the key principles of science are replicability and objectivity. In this study it would be important for the psychologist to record his procedures in detail so that someone else could repeat the study. He would also aim to be objective, which is why he would get participants to note down their decision instead of discussing it with the psychologist, which might be subjective. The control of extraneous variables is also part of objectivity. Another feature of science is hypothesis testing. The aim is to see if you can falsify your hypothesis, in which case it is wrong.

(j) The psychologist was further interested in why people made the decisions they made and, therefore, decided to conduct a further study following the same procedures but interviewing the participants afterwards. This time the psychologist thought he would involve a wider target population. Describe in detail the procedures that would be involved in this follow-up study, including sampling methods, ethical issues, instructions to participants, and questions that might be asked. *(12 marks)*

In order to get a wider sample the psychologist might place the advertisement in a newspaper, which would mean you would get people of all ages and different occupations.

Once the main study is over the psychologist would ask each participant if they would be happy to discuss the scenario further. The psychologist should deal with ethical issues by explaining the aims of this part of the study (i.e. to find out the reasons behind their decisions) and remind the participants that all of their answers would be confidential and that they had the right to withdraw at any time from the interviews.

The psychologist should then take each participant one at a time to discuss the situation further. The psychologist might have a few questions fixed to start off the interview but would think of questions as the interview went along in order to respond to the answers that the participant was giving. This would allow the maximum amount of information to be collected.

The questions might start with 'What were the reasons behind the choice you made?' and 'What factors do you think were most important in that choice?'. It would be particularly important to interview the people who had been in a group discussion to see what effect the group discussion had on their final decision. If the participant had been in a group discussion it would be important to consider the effect of the other group members, so questions might be asked about the arguments presented by other group members. The psychologist might also ask people what their initial view might have been to see whether it had changed. It would also be important to ask people about what factors might have influenced their decision, such as personal experiences.

# Chapter 17

# Child development

## 17.1 Social Development

*After studying this topic you should be able to describe and evaluate:*

**AS**

- The first part of this unit (early relationships, attachment, privation and deprivation) is covered in *Revise AS Unit 3.1, pages 52–63*.

- *early relationships: attachment and the role of caregiver-infant interactions in the development of attachment, including reference to human and animal studies; function of attachment; secure and insecure attachments; measuring attachment; possible short-term and long-term consequences of privation and deprivation; Romanian orphan studies: effects of institutionalisation, age-related benefits of adoption (Rutter et al); the work of Bowlby, Schaffer, Ainsworth and van IJzendoorn*
- *later relationships: the development of friendship in childhood and adolescence; age-related change in friendship; sex differences in children's friendship; research into the causes and consequences of popularity and rejection.*

**LEARNING SUMMARY**

### Later relationships: the development of friendship in childhood and adolescence

AQA B    U3

A friend is more than a 'peer'; friendship implies an emotional aspect and includes elements of mutual trust, assistance, understanding, respect and intimacy.

#### Age-related change in friendship

Howes (1988) notes that toddlers have begun to form friendships – they direct more attention to one playmate and their friendships are characterised by sharing things like toys or food. After the age of 2 they develop more friendships and are able to distinguish between different types of friends.

Damon (1977) suggested three stages in the development of friendship based on interviews with children where he asked them about their friendships:

- Under 8 years: Children are egocentric in their thinking (see Piaget's theory, page 81), so friendships tend to be focused on the child's own needs. Friendships are rather short-lived and quickly formed and reformed.
- Between 8 and 11 years: Friendships based on mutual interests and kindness are valued.
- Over 11 years: More sharing of personal information, longer-lasting relationships.

Bigelow and LaGaipa (1975) confirmed the view that early friendships are based more on mutual activities, whereas later friendships are related to loyalty, similarity and acceptance. Selman (1980) used social dilemmas to investigate the development of friendships and empathy. He identified 5 stages, which are outlined on page 91.

#### Sex differences in children's friendship

Friendships are important in gender development where same-sex friends reinforce gender stereotypes (see page 65).

Waldrop and Halverson (1975) found a reversal in playmate choices in boys and girls around the age of 7. Up to this age boys have relatively 'intensive' relationships with same-sex peers whereas girls have 'extensive' relationships, i.e. relationships with a wider and mixed sex group. After the age of 7 girls foster a few best friends (intensive and same-sex), whereas boys become more interested in larger groups or gangs. Omark *et al.* (1973) report that this is found in other cultures, which suggests an innate basis for such behaviour, perhaps related to the roles boys and girls take on in adulthood. Girls focus more on friendship as a source of intimacy and confidantes, whereas boys' friendships tend to be more based on joint activities. This may be related to females' general orientation towards interpersonal matters (Eagly, 1978).

## Research into the causes and consequences of popularity and rejection

### Causes of popularity and rejection

**Social skills** – Dodge *et al.* (1983) observed 5-year-olds at play and noticed that popular children displayed more sensitive social skills than rejected children. If the children were watching others at play the popular children gradually joined in by making group-oriented statements, whereas the rejected children tended to barge in and behave aggressively. The rejected children were also uncooperative, self-serving and critical, all characteristics that led to their rejection. Other children were classified as neglected (they just watched) or average. Coie *et al.* (1982) describe another group, called 'controversial', who are aggressive but good at social skills.

**Cognitive skills** – Popular children have better **role-taking skills** and also tend to have higher IQs than rejected children (Shaffer, 2002). Inadequate social skills are associated with low IQ (Cartledge and Milburn, 1986).

**Parenting styles** – A number of studies have linked authoritative parenting style to popularity, where a parent is firm but fair (for example, Dekovic and Janssens, 2002). Highly authoritarian parenting, which relies on power assertion, tends to be associated with rejected children.

Sroufe *et al.* (2005) showed that securely attached children are more likely to be popular in school (the **continuity hypothesis**). Such children also go on to be good parents and form trusting adult relationships – as a consequence of secure attachment, not popularity.

**Physical attractiveness** – Vaughn and Langlois (1983) found a correlation between physical attractiveness and popularity in pre-school children.

### Consequences of popularity and rejection

**Mental illness** – Cowen *et al.* (1973) used longitudinal data from a study of 800 children in New York state. Those children who received negative ratings at age 8 were three times more likely to have sought psychiatric help in the following 11 years.

**Delinquency** – Dishion *et al.* (1991) suggested that 'rejected' children band together and form deviant cliques in adolescence. Kupersmidt and Coie (1990) used data from a longitudinal study to show that children identified as 'rejected' at age 11 were more likely to have been suspended from school later and three times more likely than normal children to have been in trouble with the police.

### Evaluation

- A lot of the data are correlational, though some studies have shown a causal link, for example, Ladd and Golter (1988) found that argumentative behaviour at age 3 predicted later unpopularity. Dodge (1983) found that rejected children continue to be rejected even when with unfamiliar peers, supporting a causal link.
- On the other hand the link between rejection and later consequences **may be due to common factors** such as poor social skills. In other words, mental illness may not be due to peer rejection but both are due to poor social skills.

The importance of social skills has led to social skills training programmes as a way to help rejected children improve their social relationships.

**Role-taking skills** refer to the ability to take the perspective of someone else, i.e. to 'stand in their shoes'. Such skills are related to social skills generally. Empathy and role-taking skills are discussed on pages 88 and 91.

The **continuity hypothesis** is based on Bowlby's theory of attachment, suggesting a 'continuity' between infant relationships and later adult relationships.

## Practice essays 17.1

(a) Suggest **one** way that researchers could investigate attachment in infants. *(3 marks)*

(b) Describe and briefly evaluate **one** cause of popularity. *(5 marks)*

(c) Describe and evaluate the development of friendship in childhood and adolescence. *(12 marks)*

# 17.2 Cognitive Development

*After studying this topic you should be able to describe and evaluate:*

Piaget's theory of cognitive development is covered on pages 81–82.

Vygotsky's theory of cognitive development is covered on pages 82–83.

- *Piaget's theory of cognitive development: schemas: adaptation, assimilation and accommodation; Piaget's stages of intellectual development; characteristics of these stages, including object permanence, conservation, egocentrism, class inclusion; Piaget's research, including the three mountains experiment and conservation experiments*
- *alternative approaches to children's cognition*
- *Vygotsky and cognitive development within a social and cultural context; Vygotsky's zone of proximal development; scaffolding; guided participation in sociocultural activity; nativist explanations and early infant abilities, including knowledge of the physical world (Baillargeon); the information processing approach: Siegler's research into problem-solving strategies.*

**LEARNING SUMMARY**

## Alternative approaches to children's cognition

AQA B    U3

**Nativism** is the view that abilities are innate. The nativist view of cognitive development suggests that infants are born with substantial knowledge about the physical world.

### Key points from AS

- There are two views of perception – one view says that we interpret what we see on the basis of expectations (Gregory's view) see *Revise AS Unit 2.4, page 46*). These expectations resolve ambiguities in perceptual data and incomplete data. The other view is that sensory input is sufficiently rich to explain our perceptions. This latter view was developed by James Gibson, see *Revise AS Unit 2.1, page 45*.

**Object permanence** is the realisation that objects continue to exist even when they cannot be seen. Piaget claimed that this developed after the age of 8 months.

Criticisms of research using infants can be found on page 26.

### Nativist explanations of cognitive development

Piaget's view was that the earliest stage of cognitive development was a perceptual stage (the sensorimotor stage). Therefore, theories of perceptual development are relevant to cognitive development. In Piaget's view sensory input is not sufficient on its own for perception of the world because such data is often ambiguous and incomplete and so infants have to learn to interpret their world through interactions with the world. In contrast, nativists believe that infants possess many innate perceptual and cognitive abilities. Gibson and Gibson (1955) developed this view in their **differentiation theory**, the view that perceptual (and cognitive) development is a process of learning to see the differences between objects, i.e. through a process called *differentiation*. As babies develop they can learn to make distinctions between objects and events that they were not able to make initially. Their early inabilities are not due to lack of cognitive skills; they simply lack the ability to differentiate.

**Renee Baillargeon** was another researcher who argued that infants know more about perception than Piaget claimed and she conducted research to demonstrate this. For example, Baillargeon and DeVos (1991) showed that infants aged 3–4 months demonstrated **object permanence** when tested on various tasks. In the rolling car task there was a large or small carrot sliding along a track and hidden at one point by a screen with a large window. The track is arranged so that the large carrot should be visible as it passes behind the window (but in fact doesn't appear), whereas the small carrot (not as broad) should remain hidden. The infants looked longer at the large carrot presumably expecting the top half to be visible behind the window.

Infants have also been shown to have other innate cognitive abilities. For example, Wynn (1992) assessed their arithmetic ability. 5-month-old infants were shown a series of pictures where, in one case, picture 1 shows a mouse placed behind a screen, picture 2 shows a second mouse placed behind the screen and then in picture 3 the screen slides down and either two mice or one mouse are shown. The infant should only show surprise at one mouse if he/she can add. Surprise was measured in terms of time spent looking at the picture. 5-month-olds showed rudimentary addition and subtraction abilities.

Gopnik and Meltzoff (1997) take an intermediate position with a **'theory' theory**, proposing that infants do have substantial innate knowledge, but cognitive development does require the construction of theories (hypotheses about how the world works), which are tested against reality.

The **information-processing approach** is based on computer analogies – input, output, storage, programmes, routines and so on. Information-processing theories assume that one person is more intelligent than another because they can process information more efficiently.

### Key points from AS

- For information on 'working memory' see *Revise AS Unit 2.1, page 29*.

The information-processing approach suggests that cognitive development is related to age-related changes in (1) what the brain can do (use of M space), and (2) the use of strategies. Piaget's theory has been viewed as an information-processing approach because it too focused on age-related changes to brain maturity and the development of more sophisticated strategies.

Piaget's theory suggested that children of different ages were typified by particular strategies.

The information-processing approach to explaining intelligence is presented on page 69.

## The information-processing approach

**Case's theory** – Case (1992) suggested that information-processing ability is related to **mental space** (M space), a concept rather similar to 'working memory'. There is a limit to the amount of information that can be held in M space at any one time, but processing efficiency increases with age:

- **The brain matures** – changes in the myelin sheath (a fatty protective layer around the nerves which increases), leads to faster neural transmission rates. Cowan *et al.* (1999) compared the abilities of children and adults to be able to recall digits presented in a way that prevented any rehearsal. Average span of apprehension (i.e. ability to hold information in mind without doing any operation on it) was 3.5 digits for adults, 3 for older children and 2.5 for 6 year olds.
- **Cognitive strategies** develop. As children get older the amount of M space needed for well-practised mental tasks is reduced, thus increasing the amount of available space. Chi (1978) tested M space by comparing the ability of child chess experts and adults who had no chess experience. The task was their ability to remember chess board positions. The children could recall more, presumably because they had developed relevant strategies through experience.
- **Metacognitive skills** (thinking about thinking) are important for efficient use of M space, for example, being aware of what words you don't understand when reading something, monitoring your own progress on a mental task, etc.

**Siegler's model** – There are also age-related changes to the quantity and quality of information-processing strategies. Siegler *et al.* (1996) formulated the **adaptive strategy choice model**, which suggests that at any one time a child has a variety of different strategies that can be used. With increasing age more sophisticated and powerful strategies develop, but a child will fall back on simpler strategies when faced with new tasks.

Siegler (1976) tested children on a Piagetian task where a child is shown a balance with a number of weights (different sizes) on either side. The child is asked to predict whether the scale will tip one way or the other. Siegler worked out four possible strategies that could be used to solve the problem, for example, number (the side with most weights will tip down) or distance (the side with weights further from the fulcrum will tip down). Siegler gave children a variety of problems and found that 5-year-olds used number strategy and were 89% correct when given the conflict-weight problem (one side has more weights and the other side has weights at a further distance), whereas 17-year-olds who tended to use the more sophisticated distance strategy were only correct 51% of the time on such problems, though they obviously did better on other types of problems. This shows that there is not a simple relationship between strategies and success on solving problems.

Siegler *et al.* (1996) looked at children's arithmetic strategies. Very young children use a *sum strategy* (when adding 5 + 3 counting every number singly, i.e. 1 and 2 and 3 and 4 and 5 and 6 and 7 and 8), older children use a *min strategy* (start from 5 and add one at a time, i.e. 6 and 7 and 8). The most sophisticated strategy is 'knowing' the answer, called *fact retrieval* (i.e. they just know that 5 + 3 is 8).

## Practice essays 17.2

(a) Describe what Vygotsky meant by the zone of proximal development.
*(3 marks)*

(b) Outline and evaluate **one** method used by Piaget to investigate cognitive development.
*(5 marks)*

(c) Describe and evaluate nativist explanations of cognitive development.
*(12 marks)*

# 17.3 Moral development

*After studying this topic you should be able to describe and evaluate:*

- *Piaget's stages of moral development: pre-moral judgement, moral realism and moral relativism*
- *Kohlberg's pre-conventional, conventional and post-conventional levels; the stages of moral reasoning within these levels; ways of investigating moral development, including the use of moral comparisons and moral dilemmas*
- *alternatives to Piaget and Kohlberg*
- *Eisenberg's model of pro-social reasoning, including hedonistic, needs, approval, self-reflective and internalised orientations*
- *Gilligan's ethic of care: differences between boys and girls; Gilligan's three levels of moral development*
- *Damon's research into distributive justice*
- *psychodynamic explanations of moral development; the role of the superego.*

Kohlberg's theory of moral development is covered on pages 87–88.

Eisenberg's model of pro-social reasoning is covered on pages 88–89.

**LEARNING SUMMARY**

## Piaget's theory of moral development

AQA B ▶ U3

Both Piaget and Kohlberg's theories are cognitive-developmental theories, characterised by identifying innately-determined stages of development.

Children in the stage of moral relativity recognise that morals are not absolute, for example, there are some situations where it is acceptable to lie.

Piaget (1932) proposed a stage theory based on investigations with children and moral stories (see research evidence).

| age (approx) | stage | rules |
|---|---|---|
| 0–5 years | Pre–moral judgement | Rules not understood |
| 5–9 years | Moral realism | Rules exist as real things (**realism**). Actions evaluated in terms of **consequences**. Punishment in terms of **atonement**: make up for damage done (**expiatory**). |
| 9+ years | Moral relativity | Rules mutually agreed and changeable (**relativism**). Actions evaluated in terms of **intentions**. Punishment in terms of **principle of reciprocity**, where punishment fits the crime. |

### Research evidence

Piaget believed that moral development was in part due to maturation, but also due to exposure to the views of others that cause the child to question his/her own values.

An example of Piaget's paired moral stories was one boy who accidentally broke lots of plates whereas another boy deliberately threw one plate down and broke it. Which one should be punished most severely?

**Realism vs. relativism** – Piaget (1932) played a game of marbles with a group of children and asked questions about the rules. Children under 3 used no rules at all. By the age of 5 rules were seen as 'untouchable' and from some semi-mystical authority. By the age of 10 children understood that people had invented the rules and they could be changed but only if all players agreed. Linaza (1984) found the same sequence of development in Spanish children, supporting the universal nature of such stages.

**Intentions vs. consequences** – Piaget presented pairs of moral stories to children where one story had greater consequences but the intentions were good. He asked who was naughtiest and why. The **heteronomous** younger child could distinguish between intentional and unintentional actions but based their judgment on the severity of outcome. The **autonomous** older child used the motive/intention as the means for judgment. However, Nelson (1973) found that even 3-year-olds can make judgments about intentions if the information is made explicit.

Hartshorne and May (1928) found little consistency in moral behaviour. A child who cheated in one situation didn't in another. They also found that immoral behaviour was more governed by the probability of being caught than any principles of morality.

## Evaluation

- The game of marbles is a **rather insignificant** example of morals.
- The moral stories **confound intentions and consequences**, making it difficult for younger children. Armsby (1971) manipulated the stories so there was a small amount of deliberate damage or a large amount of accidental damage. He found that younger children did take intention into account.
- Piaget **introduced the idea of stages**, which are related to cognitive maturity.
- This account does not explain moral inconsistency (see Hartshorne and May on the left and Gerson and Damon on the next page), and ignores emotional influences.

# Alternatives to Piaget and Kohlberg

AQA B    U3

Eisenberg's model of pro-social reasoning is an alternative approach to that of Piaget and Kohlberg. It is described and evaluated on pages 88–89.

Gilligan entitled her book '*In a different voice*' because she argued that women were not inferior – just different – to men.

## Gilligan's ethic of care

Carol Gilligan (1982) suggested that Kohlberg made the error of assuming there was only one moral perspective, one of justice and fairness, whereas women tend to operate an ethic of care. Gilligan based her stage theory (below) on interviews with women facing real-life dilemmas (about abortions).

Gilligan explained why women were more 'caring' – she suggested that their **'interconnectness'** stems from identifying with their mother. In contrast, men have to separate early from their mother in order to form a separate masculine identity. This separation heightens boys' awareness of the power differences between themselves and adults, and so makes them more concerned with inequality (justice).

| stage | justice perspective | care perspective |
|---|---|---|
| 1 | Uphold moral standards and withstand pressure to deviate | Concern with what others say and how choices might affect relationships. |
| 2 | Justice plus mercy. Principles are most important but one should consider others' feelings. | Sacrificing one's own concerns to the welfare of others. Relationships are more important than conventional rules. |
| 3 | Everyone is best served by universal laws, though there are some exceptions to the rule. | Aiming for a balance between valuing the individual and trying not to hurt anyone. |

## Research evidence

Gilligan and Attanucci (1988) asked a group of men and women to produce accounts of their own moral dilemmas. Overall, men favoured a justice orientation and women favoured a care orientation.

Garmon et al. (1996) tested over 500 people and found that women were more likely to refer to care issues.

Eisenberg et al. (1987) found that girls aged 10–12 gave more caring responses than boys, although this may be because girls mature earlier.

## Evaluation

- The findings may be due to **demand characteristics**. Eisenberg and Lennon (1983) found that, if participants knew researchers were looking at empathetic behaviour, they portrayed themselves more like that.
- Walker (1984) reviewed 79 studies and found **variable support**; some studies found no gender difference and some found that males were more caring.
- If a man's moral perspective was assessed using Gilligan's stage theory, he might appear to be morally inferior to women – so Gilligan's approach might also be seen as **gender-biased**.

## Psychodynamic explanations of moral development

Freud suggested that moral development is related to the **phallic stage** and emergence of the **superego**. Around the age of 3 years a child's sexual interest focuses on their genitalia and they feel desire for their opposite-sex parent (the **Oedipus complex**). This makes them see their same-sex parent as a rival. The child feels unconscious hostility, resulting in guilt. The child also feels anxiety and fear of punishment should his true desires be discovered. Resolution occurs through identification with the same-sex parent. **Identification** is the process of 'taking on' the attitudes and ideas of another person.

Freud explained the strong bonds between dominant parents and their children as the result of a threatening parent producing a greater fear of punishment, which leads to a stronger sense of identification.

The Oedipus complex only explains moral development in boys. Freud proposed that girls go through a similar conflict – they recognise they haven't got a penis and blame their mother, thus, their father becomes their love-object and the girl substitutes her '**penis envy**' with a desire to have a child. This ultimately leads to identification with her mother. However, the resolution of penis envy is less satisfactory than resolution of the Oedipus conflict and therefore, according to Freud, girls have inferior moral development compared to boys.

**The internalised parent** – The ego-ideal rewards you when you behave in accordance with parental moral values. It is the source of feelings of pride and self-satisfaction, acting as the 'rewarding' parent. Your conscience punishes you when you do something wrong. It is an internal representation of the 'punishing' parent and is composed of prohibitions imposed on you by your parents. The conscience appears at age 5 or 6 and is a source of 'guilt feelings'.

Unsatisfactory resolution of the phallic stage results in problems such as amorality, homosexuality or rebelliousness.

### Research evidence

Freud predicted an inverse relationship between guilt and wrongdoing: the more guilt a person experiences the less likely they are to do wrong. MacKinnon (1938) gave nearly 100 participants a test and left them alone with the answer book. Of those who cheated (about 50%) most said they did not feel guilty, which confirms the inverse relationship between guilt and wrongdoing.

Inconsistency of moral behaviour – Freudian theory suggests that moral behaviour should be consistent because of the conscience, though there is the possibility of some inconsistency because of irrational behaviour by the id. Hartshorne and May's study (see previous page) found little consistency in moral behaviour.

Another example of inconsistency can be seen in Damon's research into distributive justice. Gersen and Damon (1978) showed that children don't distribute rewards as fairly as they said they would. In a pretend situation children gave an average of 18% of candy bars to themselves. In a real test a few months later, this rose to 29%.

### Key points from AS

- Freud's view of moral development is part of his psychodynamic theory see *Revise AS Unit 1.1, page 19.*

The phallic stage and the process of identification that occurs in that stage are also important for gender identity.

Erikson's theory of social development (see page 39) is also a psychodynamic theory. He de-emphasised the unconscious and emphasised the social world. Each stage of life is marked by a crisis, which must be confronted and resolved. Both parents influence the development of moral behaviour, which is a product of the superego (determining what is acceptable or not) and the ego (inhibiting undesirable impulses of the id). Since the ego is the rational component of the personality, morality must be related to cognitive development generally.

### Key points from AS

- General criticisms of Freud's theory of personality development can be used to evaluate this account, see *Revise AS Unit 1.1, page 19* and also *AS Unit 7.1, page 153.*

Damon's research on distributive justice shows that children are capable of more sophisticated moral judgments than Kohlberg had predicted in his theory.

## Practice essays 17.3

(a) Explain what Piaget meant by the terms 'moral realism' and 'moral relativism'. *(4 marks)*

(b) Outline and evaluate **one** method that was used by Kohlberg to investigate moral development. *(4 marks)*

(c) Describe and evaluate Gilligan's approach to explaining moral development. *(12 marks)*

# Chapter 18

# Applied Psychology

## 18.1 Cognition and law

*After studying this topic you should be able to describe and evaluate:*

Face recognition is covered on pages 29–30.

### AS

• Research on eyewitness testimony is covered in *Revise AS Unit 2.2, pages 35–37*.

• *recognising and remembering faces: processes involved in recognition of faces; explanations for face recognition, including feature analysis and holistic forms; the construction of likenesses using composite systems; identification procedures: simultaneous and sequential line-ups*
• *recalling events: factors affecting the reliability of eyewitness accounts and eyewitness identification, including post-event contamination; improving eyewitness recall, including features of the cognitive interview; children as eyewitnesses; flashbulb memory: memory for shocking events*
• *the false memory debate: controversy surrounding the recovery of repressed memories; the existence of false memories; evidence relating to repression and false memory; ethical and theoretical implications of the false memory debate.*

LEARNING SUMMARY

## The false memory debate

AQA B      U3

A **false memory** is a memory for something that did not happen, but which feels as if it is a true memory. **False memory syndrome (FMS)** refers to a memory of a traumatic experience, such as sexual abuse, which rules a person's entire life, disrupting normal functioning.

### Key points from AS

• Repressed memories and motivated forgetting are discussed in *Revise AS Unit 2.3, pages 41–42*.

The ethical implications relate to the extent to which psychiatrists should encourage recovered memories, and, thus, might be instrumental in creating them.

The theoretical implications relate to the extent to which this evidence can be seen as supporting or challenging the concept of motivated forgetting.

### Controversy surrounding the recovery of repressed memories

FMS advocates, such as Elizabeth Loftus, believe memories are confabulations, i.e. reconstructed memories put together from fragments of real and imaginary events that might include stories seen on TV or suggestions made by therapists. The danger of FMS is that it has resulted in wrongful accusations and lawsuits – both by those who have been accused, and also by those who thought they had recovered memories during therapy but later realised these were false memories.

Others, such as Dallam (2002), argue that repression is an unconscious strategy for dealing with traumatic experiences, well documented by research. This supports the view that false memories are real.

### The existence of false memories

#### Evidence for FMS

Loftus and Pickrell (1995) conducted a study referred to as 'lost in the mall'. They interviewed participants about childhood events, implanting a memory about having been lost in a shopping mall when younger (they were told a close relative had reported the incident). About 20% of the participants came to believe in their false memories to such an extent that they still clung to them even after being debriefed.

#### Evidence against FMS

Pezdek (1995) suggested that people may accept relatively innocuous memories (such as the ones above) but they may not accept suggested traumatic memories. In a similar study she found that no participants remembered an innocuous memory (of receiving a painful enema as a child from their parent).

### Practice essay 18.1

Discuss evidence relating to repression and false memories.          *(20 marks)*

# 18.2 Schizophrenia and mood disorders

**After studying this topic you should be able to describe and evaluate:**

Schizophrenia is discussed on pages 95–104.

Unipolar depression is discussed on pages 105–110, including seasonal affective disorder.

- *classification of schizophrenia, including sub-types; symptoms and diagnosis; explanations, including biological and cognitive; sociocultural explanations: labelling and family dysfunction; treatments of schizophrenia, including anti-psychotic drugs, behavioural treatments and psychotherapy; the role of community care; evaluation of these treatments*
- *mood disorders: unipolar and bipolar depression; seasonal affective disorder (SAD); symptoms and diagnosis of mood disorders; explanations, including biological, cognitive, behavioural and psychodynamic; treatments of mood disorders, including biological and cognitive; evaluation of these treatments.*

## Biological explanations of bipolar disorder (BD)

AQA B ▸ U3

**Bipolar disorder** is also referred to as manic-depression because many sufferers oscillate between mania (being hyperactive, elated, making grandiose plans) and depression. There are often long periods of normal behaviour in between the manic or depressive phase, though in some sufferers the episodes alternate even within one day. Bipolar I disorder refers to full manic and depressive episodes; bipolar II disorder refers to milder manic episodes that alternate with depression over time.

About 1% of the population experience bipolar disorder.

The manic phase of bipolar disorder has been related to creativity and charismatic leadership, and, therefore, would be an adaptive trait. Many artists and famous leaders have been manic-depressives (e.g. Winston Churchill, Abraham Lincoln, Vincent Van Gogh, Robbie Williams, Stephen Fry). However, for most it is a crippling disorder that ruins their lives.

### Genetic explanations

Individuals may inherit a gene or genes that cause BD. Such genes predispose individuals to develop the disorder – this is the **diathesis-stress model** described on page 54.

### Research evidence

**Gene mapping** – Egeland *et al.* (1987) studied the Amish, an American religious sect who have a high incidence of BD, and a cluster of genes on chromosome 11, which were present in 63% of those with the disorder. However, subsequent research (e.g. Hodgkinson *et al.*, 1987) failed to find any common marker on chromosome 11. Continuing research has identified other possibilities. Recently, Gurling *et al.* (2006) found evidence that the '**Slynar' gene**, on chromosome 12, may be implicated. It is present in about 10% of cases. Some studies also show links between BD and schizophrenia, pointing to a shared genetic cause.

**Twin studies** – Durand and Barlow (2000) report a concordance rate of 80% for identical (MZ) twins, as compared to only 16% for non-identical (DZ) twins, showing a high genetic component for BD.

**Adoption studies** – Gershon (1983) looked at adopted individuals with manic depression. 2% of their adoptive parents had the disorder whereas 30% of their biological parents had it.

**Family studies** – In families of individuals with BD, first-degree relatives (i.e. parents, children, siblings) are more likely to have a mood disorder than the relatives of those who do not have BD (Davis and Palladino, 2000). This suggests a genetic basis for mood disorders generally.

### Neuroanatomical explanation

Zubieta *et al.* (2000) studied the brains of 16 people with BD using PET scans and found 30% more brain cells in certain areas of the brain – areas containing signaling cells that release the brain chemicals dopamine, serotonin and noradrenaline.

### Biochemical explanation

The **permissive amine theory** of mood disorder (see page 105) has also been used to explain BD. When serotonin is low noradrenalin fluctuates wildly causing highs and lows (serotonin and noradrenalin are biogenic amines).

## Psychological explanations of bipolar depression

AQA B  U3

### Key points from AS

- General evaluations for biological and psychological explanations of abnormality can be found in *Revise AS Unit 7.1, pages 151–155.*

### Behavioural explanations

The fact that BD runs in families can be explained in terms of environmental rather than biological factors. It may be that such families reward particular behaviours, for example, praise or attention is given for grandiose plans so that such behaviours are encouraged. It may also be that family members with the disorder act as role models; having a parent with a tendency towards manic behaviour could influence a child.

### Psychodynamic explanations

One psychodynamic suggestion is that bipolar depression results from alternating dominance of the personality by the superego (depression) and the ego (elation).

Freud in fact placed BD under the heading of 'psychosis', along with schizophrenia, i.e. a disorder where the patient does not have insight into their condition.

### Cognitive explanations

#### Linear schematic processing model

Beck (1976) extended his concept of the negative triad, which is an explanation of depression (see page 107). He suggested that mania was the opposite of depression. In the case of mania, sufferers had a positive cognitive triad of self, world and future, and positive cognitive distortions. For example, they saw themselves as extremely attractive and powerful, saw the world filled with wonderful possibilities, and the future with unlimited opportunities. Typical cognitive distortions include underestimating risks, minimising problems, and seeking immediate gratification.

#### Integrative model

Beck (1996) recognised the failure of his earlier model of BD to take biological factors into account; given the research evidence it is clearly important to include such factors. Therefore, his new model includes two key additions: the concepts of 'modes' and 'charges'. **Modes** are methods of responding to specific demands or problems, for example, 'primal modes' have evolved from prehistory as survival reactions (and are therefore biological). When a mode is activated this leads to increased physiological activity and the person becomes 'charged'. **Charges** are energy levels.

### Socio-cultural explanations: life events

Psychological factors are important as a trigger for the onset of the disorder. It is likely that people inherit susceptibility for BD but the disorder only appears as a consequence of stressful life events, such as the death of a close family member or friend, or the loss of one's job. Once the disorder has developed it then seems to have a life of its own, which may suggest that certain neurotransmitter dysfunctions have been triggered.

#### Evaluation

- The importance of psychological explanations is supported by the fact that **drug therapy on its own is not effective.**
- Not all individuals who inherit a genetic susceptibility develop BD, therefore, **psychological factors must be important in triggering** the disorder, as described by the diathesis-stress model (see page 54).

## Therapies for bipolar depression

ECT may be used in the treatment of bipolar disorder, especially for the depression component (see page 102).

### Biological therapies: drugs

The most commonly prescribed drug for BD is **anti-manic drugs**, especially *lithium*. It is often referred to as a 'maintenance treatment' because patients must continue to take the drug even when apparently recovered in order to prevent further episodes. Lithium relieves the depressive episodes as well as the mania, though to a lesser degree. **Anti-depressants** are prescribed for depressive episodes, as well as **anti-psychotic drugs** for acute mania episodes to slow the individual down.

### Evaluation

**Key points from AS**

- General criticisms of drug therapies and psychological treatments are included in *Revise AS Unit 7.2, page 156*.

- The effectiveness of lithium depends on getting **the correct dosage** – too low a dose will have little effect, whereas too high a dose results in lithium intoxication (or poisoning).
- As long as patients continue taking **lithium the results are impressive**. For example, Viguera *et al.* (2000) report that more than 60% of patients with mania improve with lithium. Stuppes *et al.* (1991) found that relapse was 28 times greater when patients stopped taking lithium so it is important to continue taking the medication even when the symptoms have stopped.
- On the other hand, drug therapies are **not totally effective**. Kulhara *et al.* (1999) report that 30% of patients do not improve when taking lithium (which may in part be due to receiving the wrong dosage or not taking their medication).

### Psychological therapies

**Cognitive therapy** – Basco and Rush (1995) list some of the aims of cognitive therapy: to facilitate acceptance of the disorder and the need for treatment; to help the individual recognise and manage psychosocial stressors and interpersonal problems; to improve medication adherence; to teach strategies to cope with depression and hypomania; to teach early recognition of relapse symptoms and coping techniques; to improve self-management through homework assignments; and to identify and modify negative automatic thoughts.

**Family focused therapy** (Miklowitz and Goldstein, 1997) recognises the role of the family in the care of people with BD. The treatment lasts over 9 months and involves education (family members are taught about treatments for BD, how to recognise the onset of episodes and to develop a relapse prevention plan); patient and family are taught communication skills and are given help with how to deal with specific family problems.

### Evaluation

- **STEP-BD** (Systematic Treatment Enhancement Program for BD) is a large-scale US longitudinal study. In 2007 they reported that 64% of the cohort followed had recovered after psychotherapy, compared to 52% of a control group getting just case management, and they did it an average of 110 days faster. Family focused therapy (FFT) made for the best outcomes.
- **Psychotherapy alone is rarely effective** in treating BD (Klerman *et al.*, 1994), but the same is true for using lithium therapy alone.

## Practice essays 18.2

(a) Explain the differences between unipolar and bipolar disorder. *(4 marks)*

(b) Briefly describe **one** treatment for bipolar disorder. *(4 marks)*

(c) Describe and evaluate **at least one** biological explanation of bipolar disorder. Refer to empirical evidence in your answer. *(12 marks)*

# 18.3 Stress and stress management

*After studying this topic you should be able to describe and evaluate:*

- *stress and illness: the role of the autonomic nervous system (ANS) and endocrine system functions in mediating and responding to stress*
- *ways of measuring stress, including physiological, behavioural and self-report techniques; the role of personal variables, including behaviour types A, B and C, locus of control and hardiness in mediating responses to stress*
- *stress management: problem-focused and emotion-focused strategies, the role of defence mechanisms in coping with stress, including repression, regression, rationalisation and denial*
- *techniques of stress management: behavioural approaches, including biofeedback and systematic desensitisation; cognitive therapy; the role of social factors in coping with stress: social support, including types of social support.*

**LEARNING SUMMARY**

**AS**

- Most of the topics on stress and stress management are covered in *Revise AS Unit 5.1 and 5.2, pages 98–110.*

## Extra stress topics for AQA B

AQA B    U3

The **ANS** (autonomic nervous system) controls our response to stress; the sympathetic branch of the ANS is aroused by a stressful situation.

**Key points from AS**

- The Daily Hassles and Uplifts Scale, and other scales, are discussed in *Revise AS Unit 5.1 pages 101 and 102.*

Locus of control can be measured using Rotter's Locus of Control Scale.

Taking control is a way to reduce levels of stress.

### Ways of measuring stress

**Physiological** – The **galvanic skin response (GSR)** indicates stress arousal by measuring activity of the ANS. When the ANS is aroused the electrical conductivity of the skin is altered and this is measured by attaching electrodes to the skin.

**Behavioural** – Signs of ANS activity include sweating, rapid pulse, raised heart rate, flushed face – so stress can be measured by assessing these behavioural signs.

**Self-report techniques** – There are a vast array of questionnaires that can be used to assess stress, including SRRS (Holmes and Rahe, 1967) and also the Daily Hassles and Uplifts Scale (DeLongis *et al.*,1982).

### Locus of control in mediating stress responses

Locus of control (Rotter, 1996) refers to where you place the responsibility (or blame) for things that happen to you.

- **Internals** have an internal locus of control, i.e. they believe they are responsible for the things that happen to them.
- **Externals** have an external locus of control. This can make one feel comfortable because when things go wrong, you blame someone or something else ('a bad workman blames his tools'). On the other hand this makes an individual feel that things 'happen to them'. Life is simply a matter of luck or fate.

Individuals who have a high internal locus of control feel less stress and are less disrupted by it. For example, Kim *et al.* (1997) found that children who were 'internals' showed fewer signs of stress when their parents divorced. Cohen *et al.* (1993) found that participants were more likely to develop a cold if they felt their lives were unpredictable and uncontrollable; the likelihood to become ill is linked to a weaker immune system, which is a sign of stress. Rodin and Langer (1977) found that residents in a nursing home were likely to live longer if they were given a greater sense of control (e.g. how they arranged the furniture in their rooms, when they could receive visitors).

## The role of defence mechanisms in coping with stress

Freud (1910) suggested that we unconsciously deal with anxiety by means of ego defence mechanisms, such as:

- **Repression** – placing uncomfortable thoughts in the unconscious, e.g. you might forget that a favourite pet had died because you failed to feed it.
- **Regression** – a person behaves in a way that in the past may have brought about relief from the anxiety-provoking situation.
- **Rationalisation** – things that create anxiety are dealt with in a rational or logical manner in order to avoid the emotional content.
- **Denial** – simply denying the existence of something that is threatening. However, denying the existence of the thing does not make it go away.

Such ego defences can be effective in protecting the individual from overwhelming anxiety in the short-term, but in the long-term may be counterproductive. One study found that the use of denial following an HIV diagnosis was associated with more rapid disease progression in HIV-seropositive gay men (Ironson *et al.* 1994).

## The role of social factors in coping with stress

**Social support** – Research has shown that social support has a significant effect on stress. For example, Kamarck *et al.* (1990) recruited 39 female psychology student volunteers to perform a difficult mental task (stressful) while their physiological reactions were monitored. Each participant attended the lab session alone or they were asked to bring a close same-sex friend who was told to touch the participant on the wrist throughout the mental task. In general the participants who were with a friend showed lower physiological reactions than those who were alone.

Kiecolt-Glaser *et al.* (1984) looked at **T-cell activity** (an indicator of immune system activity) in the blood of students before and after taking exams. They also gave students a questionnaire at the beginning of the study, which looked at psychiatric symptoms, loneliness and life events. Levels of T-cells were higher during the month before the students took exams, and dropped during the examination period itself. What is notable is that the effect was strongest in those students who said they were lonely/lacked friends. This indicates the importance of social support in enhancing the functioning of the immune system and, thus, resisting stress.

Nuckolls *et al.* (1972) studied 170 pregnant women. The women with high life stress and low social support had more early pregnancy complications than those with high life stress and high social support (91% vs. 33%).

Brown and Harris (1978) interviewed 400 women living in Camberwell, London. Some of them had experienced a stressful event in the preceding year, yet not all developed any serious psychological problems, such as depression. Those who did develop such problems shared one important factor, the absence of a close, supportive relationship.

**Types of social support** – Family and friends provide social support. Social support may also be provided in self-help groups.

## Practice essays 18.4

(a) Explain **one** method that could be used to measure stress. *(3 marks)*

(b) Distinguish between *problem-focused* and *emotion-focused* strategies for coping with stress. *(5 marks)*

(c) Describe and evaluate **one** stress management technique. Refer to evidence in your answer. *(12 marks)*

# 18.4 Substance abuse

After studying this topic you should be able to describe and evaluate:

Explanations of substance abuse (addiction) are discussed on pages 133–136.

Treatments of substance abuse (addiction) are discussed on pages 137–140.

- *use and abuse: distinctions between addiction and physical dependence; psychological dependence, tolerance and withdrawal; solvent abuse, tobacco and nicotine, alcohol, stimulants and depressants; explanations for substance abuse: hereditary factors; personality characteristics and social factors, including peer influences*
- *treatment and prevention: psychological treatments and their effectiveness, including aversion therapy and self-management; prevention techniques; identifying and targeting 'risk' groups; use of fear-arousing appeals; social inoculation; health promotion/education in treatment and prevention; the stages of behaviour change proposed in the Prochaska model.*

LEARNING SUMMARY

## Use and abuse

AQA B    U3

### Distinctions between addiction and physical dependence

Many substances are *used* for genuine medical purposes. The term *abuse* refers to the harmful use of such substances.

**Addiction** refers to *psychological* dependence on a drug, which is separate from the *physical* dependence.

**Physical dependence** refers to the effects of abrupt discontinuation of a drug. This can be the result of long-term use of a legal or an illegal drug. Characteristics of physical dependence include:

- **Tolerance or habituation** – The body increasingly adapts to the substance and needs larger doses to achieve the same effect. These increases eventually level off.
- **Withdrawal** – When the substance is discontinued the person may experience symptoms such as anxiety, cravings, hallucinations, nausea and 'the shakes'.

### Psychological dependence

Addiction and psychological dependence relate to feelings of well-being, whereas physical dependence relates to a physical craving.

Psychological dependence is related to the reinforcing properties of substance abuse – using such substances creates a sense of pleasure and this is positively reinforcing; not taking the drug is a negative experience, which acts as a punisher. Thus, addiction is maintained. In addition, as we saw on page 134, addiction can be explained in terms of faulty cognitions and also in terms of psychological vulnerabilities such as low self-esteem or dependency needs.

It has recently been recognised that addictions to physical substances (such as drugs) and psychological activities (such as gambling) share many of the same symptoms. Substance abuse may appear to be solely physical, whereas the psychological elements may be equally or even more critical in dealing with the problems. Conversely, something like gambling may appear to be solely psychological, whereas the activation of reward circuits in the brain may create a dopamine addiction.

Griffiths (1995) has listed six components of addiction:

The physical effects experienced by gamblers may be explained in terms of the role of dopamine in addictive behaviours, see page 133.

- **Salience** – The addiction is highly important to the individual.
- **Euphoria** – The addictive behaviour makes the individual feel 'high'.
- **Tolerance** – Over time, a drug user increases the dosage; a gambler increases the stakes to gain the same 'high'.
- **Withdrawal** symptoms are experienced by gamblers as well as drug addicts.
- **Conflict** with others and with themselves.
- **Relapse** is always likely even after giving up for a long period, the individual is always vulnerable and must resist key triggers.

## Examples of substance abuse

A solvent is a substance that dissolves other substances. Water is a solvent, however, solvent abuse refers specifically to volatile solvents (i.e. solvents that evaporate rapidly) such as dry cleaning fluids, nail polish remover, butane gas, glue or turpentine (paint solvent).

### Solvent abuse

Solvent abuse involves sniffing or breathing in solvents. The effect is similar to drinking – initial euphoria followed by a lowering of inhibitions. The after-effects may be like a hangover, however, long-term use can include kidney and liver damage and even death; over 1,000 people have died in the UK in the last 20 years (Ives, 1999). Unlike most drugs, solvents are not addictive in themselves; it is a purely psychological addiction.

Research has identified certain vulnerability factors such as children in the care of local authorities ('looked after' children). Melrose (2000) also identifies two other groups: young offenders and school excludees. He also notes that children are likely to come from unstable or abusive family backgrounds.

Research on alcoholism is included on pages 133–134.

### Alcohol

Alcohol abuse (alcoholism) is classed as a chronic disease (American Medical Association). The distinction between alcohol use and abuse is that the latter involves physical and social harm, including problems with tolerance, withdrawal and an uncontrollable urge to drink. It is included in the DSM classification of mental disorder.

DSM is explained on page 96.

Current evidence suggests that there is a considerable genetic component (Dick and Bierut, 2005). Addiction to alcohol is a mixture of physical and psychological dependence.

**Stimulants** are drugs that increase alertness either by increasing activity in the autonomic nervous system (ANS) or central nervous system (CNS), or both.

### Stimulants

**Amphetamines** increase alertness and concentration, as well as heart rate and blood pressure. They stimulate the CNS and the sympathetic branch of the ANS and also increase levels of dopamine. They are prescribed for narcolepsy (see page 24) and major depression.

Research on cocaine abuse is described on pages 133, 138 and 139.

**Cocaine** is primarily prescribed for its anaesthetic properties, but it is also a stimulant. It too increases levels of dopamine in the brain.

**Nicotine** is the chemical associated with smoking addiction (see page 135). It is a stimulant and leads to physical dependence because of its capacity to release dopamine, which then may also lead to sensations of reward and relaxation. Research suggests that some people are predisposed to smoking because they have a mutation in a gene (**CYP2A6**) that helps to rid the body more rapidly of nicotine (Pianezza *et al.*, 1998).

**Caffeine** is found in coffee, tea, many soft drinks and, to a lesser extent, in chocolate. Drinking coffee is a common way to keep awake and many people avoid it because of its stimulant properties. It reduces levels of the neurotransmitter adenosine in the brain, which leads to increased dopamine activity. It is regarded as highly addictive and leads to a physical dependence. People quickly develop a tolerance and also experience symptoms of withdrawal.

Depressants have a calming effect on the CNS. They increase the activity of the neurotransmitter GABA, which is the body's natural means of reducing anxiety.

### Depressants

**Barbiturates** are prescribed as anti-depressants and also for sleep. Common names include 'purple hearts' or 'blue heavens'. They are abused as a form of anxiety relief and because they reduce inhibitions. Their use has declined dramatically because even a slight overdose can be fatal and also because they are highly addictive and withdrawal symptoms can be life-threatening.

Alcohol is also a depressant.

Benzodiazepines (BZs), such as Valium, are also used as anti-depressants. BZs reduce anxiety levels and are, therefore, relaxing. They can be dangerous when taken with alcohol but on their own they are relatively harmless. They have replaced barbiturates because they are less addictive but they are not without psychological and physical dependence. They also produce unpleasant side effects such as slurred speech and difficulty breathing. Long-term use has been linked to anorexia.

## Treatment and prevention

AQA B    U3

Some aspects of treatment and prevention are discussed on pages 137–140.

### Prochaska's spiral model of behavioural change

Prochaska *et al.* (1992) proposed a model that explained both professionally-motivated and personally-motivated changes in health behaviour:

- **Precontemplation** – The person is unaware of a problem and, therefore, has no intention to change their behaviour.
- **Contemplation** – The person is thinking about doing something in relation to the problem. People may stay in this stage for a long period of time (even several years).
- **Preparation** – The person has decided to take action and may have begun to make some minimal changes. They may, for example, have started to reduce the number of cigarettes they smoke.
- **Action** – The person has made changes to their behaviour or environment for a significant period of time (ranging between 1 day and 6 months). Many people focus on this stage as being critical, whereas the early stages are equally important in bringing about change.
- **Maintenance** – Continued action in maintaining change, most importantly focused on preventing relapse. A person can be said to be in the maintenance stage if they have been able to remain free of their addiction for more than 6 months.

The model is a spiral because people are usually not successful at the first attempt so they have to repeat these steps several times, each time getting further towards action and maintenance. Prochaska *et al.* suggested that smokers usually have to make three or four attempts before they reach the maintenance stage. People also may not go through the stages in a linear fashion.

### Effectiveness

- This model incorporates **behaviour as well as attitudes**, and is realistic about the need to repeat the steps several times before behaviour change can be accomplished.
- DiClemente *et al.* (1982) provided **evidence to support the model** in a study of about 1500 smokers (white American females who started smoking at about 16 years of age). Those who were in the preparation stage at the beginning of the study were more likely to have tried to quit smoking or actually succeeded when assessed 6 months later as compared to those in earlier stages.

## Practice essays 18.4

(a) Explain the difference between *addiction* and *physical dependence*.

*(4 marks)*

(b) Describe **one** method used to treat alcohol addiction.     *(4 marks)*

(c) Describe and evaluate explanations of substance abuse that are related to inherited factors. Refer to evidence in your answer.     *(12 marks)*

# 18.5 *Forensic psychology*

*After studying this topic you should be able to describe and evaluate:*

- *offending behaviour: problems in defining crime; measuring crime, including official statistics and alternatives (victim surveys and self-report measures); offender profiling, including typology and geographical approaches; theories of offending; physiological approaches: atavistic form and somatotype theories; biological explanations, including genetic transmission; psychodynamic and learning theory explanations, including social learning; Eysenck's theory of the criminal personality*
- *treatment of offenders: the role of custodial sentencing; effectiveness of custodial sentencing, including recidivism; alternatives to custodial sentencing; treatment programmes: behaviour modification; social skills training and anger management; evaluation of these treatment programmes.*

## Offending behaviour

AQA B    U3

> Crime is the breach of a rule or law that has been created by a governing authority.

> In order for any society to function effectively, it is necessary to prohibit certain behaviours, especially those that harm other people or their property.

### Key points from AS
- Self-report techniques are discussed in *Revise AS Unit 4.1 page 78.*

> Offender profiling is a method of identifying the perpetrator of a crime based on an analysis of the nature of the offence and the manner in which it was committed.

> Typology means the study of types.

### Problems in defining crime

Crime is defined with reference to a particular society's rules, therefore, there is no single definition of crime that isn't circular – crime is what is designated as criminal by the relevant authorities. Certain offences are universally regarded as criminal, such as murder. However, murder may be classified according to intention (the French have *crime passionnel* – crime of passion – which results in a lesser sentence). Another issue is the consideration of 'how much' (for example, stealing one sweet may not be regarded as a criminal act) and also what counts as a mitigating factor (for example, murdering someone who has injured your child).

### Measuring crime

**Official statistics** – The Home Office publish *Criminal Statistics* containing a record of the number and types of crimes recorded by the police in England and Wales. One drawback with this is that many crimes go unreported so it is not an accurate picture, yet it is important in forming public perceptions, changes in law and policing policy.

**Victim surveys and self-report measures** – The *British Crime Survey* is conducted every two years in the UK of people over the age of 16, asking about their experiences of victimisation in the previous year. This permits access to unreported crimes. However, questionnaires have problems in obtaining reliable data.

### Offender profiling

**Typology** – The FBI was the first to use offender profiling and the typology approach. The process involves:
(1) assimilation (information including the crime scene, victim and witnesses).
(2) classification (integrating the information and classifying the type of criminal e.g. as organised or disorganised – an organised criminal is skilled and leaves few clues, a disorganised criminal is impulsive and lacks social skills).
(3) construction of a behavioural sequence (reconstruction of the crime).

**Geographical approaches** are relevant to serial crimes and focus on making geographical links between various crimes to help catch the criminal. Ideally, a minimum of five crimes is required to build up a geographic profile that will help track the criminal. Geographic profiling complements the typological approach.

## Theories of offending

AQA B  U3

### Physiological approaches

**Atavistic form** – Lombroso (1876) proposed that some people are born with a strong, innate predisposition to behave anti-socially. This is essentially a 'throwback' to an earlier human type (which he called *homo delinquens*). Individuals actually look different: a narrow sloping brow (low in intellect), prominent jaw (strong in passion), and extra nipples, toes and fingers. They were adapted to survival in the wild but could not cope with social living and could not distinguish right from wrong.

> **Atavism** is the tendency to revert to ancestral type.

#### Evaluation

- Goring (1913) reported a study comparing the physical features of 3000 convicts with 3000 non-criminals and found **no significant differences** in any features.

**Somatotype theories** – Sheldon *et al.* (1949) proposed that there were three basic body types: **endomorphs** (fat and soft), **ectomorphs** (thin and fragile) and **mesomorphs** (muscular and hard). Mesomorphs are also aggressive and insensitive to other people's feelings and, thus, potentially criminals. Sheldon rated people on a scale of 1 to 7 according to the amount of each of the three components they showed and used this to rate criminals and normal people, demonstrating that criminals tended to be mesomorphs.

> 'Soma' means 'body', so somatotype means 'body type'.

#### Evaluation

- This explanation has **received some support**, for example, Cortes and Gatti (1972) conducted a study of 100 delinquents and found that 57% were mesomorphic, whereas only 16% were ectomorphic compared with 19% and 33% respectively for controls. Most research, however, has not been supportive.
- Even if there is a correlation between physique and criminality this **doesn't demonstrate a cause**; there may be some common factor, which causes both physique and criminality, such as home environment.

### Biological explanations

> Eysenck's theory (on page 175) is a biological explanation of offender behaviour.

Various studies have looked at the link between genes and criminality as evidence of the genetic basis of aggression (see page 44).

### Psychodynamic explanations

**Key points from AS**

- Freudian concepts are explained in *Revise AS Unit 1.1, page 19.*

Criminality can be explained in terms of the superego, which develops during the phallic stage when a child identifies with their same-sex parent. Some children develop a weak superego because their same-sex parent is absent or unloving, which results in selfishness and uncontrolled aggression. Alternatively, criminality may be explained by identification with a deviant parent, resulting in a deviant superego. Freud called this phenomenon **pseudoheredity**, i.e. non-genetic inheritance.

> The superego is important in moral development, see page 163.

Bowlby (1946) proposed that certain delinquents (**affectionless psychopaths**) were unable to feel empathy for other people and that is why they commit crimes. Bowlby suggested that affectionless psychopathy was caused by attachment bonds being disturbed in early life. This was supported by Bowlby's study of delinquents (Bowlby, 1944); 86% of the affectionless psychopaths had experienced frequent early separations.

**Key points from AS**

- Bowlby's research is discussed in *Revise AS Unit 3.1, page 53.*

#### Evaluation

- Psychoanalysts do not claim to account for all types of crime in terms of unconscious conflicts. For example, Kline (1987) suggests that white collar crimes and even **some aggressive crimes are rational** rather than irrational.
- This approach **does address the importance of emotional factors** in criminal behaviour.

## Learning theory explanations

Classical and operant conditioning are explained on page 72.

- **Classical conditioning** involves learning to associate one thing with another, so a child may learn to associate stealing sweets with excitement.
- **Operant conditioning** involves learning by the consequences of your actions; criminal behaviour is learned and maintained by the rewards it brings.
- **Social learning theory** – we learn from observing others and model the behaviours that are rewarded (due to **vicarious reinforcement**).

**The theory of differential association** – Sutherland (1947) argued that criminal behaviour, like all behaviour, is learned through social interactions. Social groups are defined in terms of the norms they share and for some social groups there are norms that are favourable towards criminal activities as well as norms that are unfavourable. The term **differential association** reflects the ratio of favourable to non-favourable definitions of crime.

### Evaluation

- This theory **explains why crime rates are higher in some neighbourhoods** than in others, and not just poor neighbourhoods. 'White collar crimes' are committed by professional middle classes who view such behaviours as acceptable.
- The theory does **not explain more impulsive, emotional crimes**.

## Eysenck's theory of the criminal personality

Eysenck (1977) proposed that criminality is produced by an interaction between personality (which is genetically based) and the environment. Eysenck's theory of personality identified three dimensions: extraversion-introversion (E); neuroticism-stability (N); psychoticism-normality (P). Criminality is associated with **extraversion** – extraverts are impulsive, have a high need for excitement and danger, and lose their temper easily. Extraverts are also harder to condition and, therefore, less affected by reinforcement and punishment. Eysenck proposed that the dimension of extraversion-introversion is based on activity of the **reticular activating system (RAS)**, a part of the brain responsible for arousal levels. In extraverts, the RAS inhibits incoming sensations and, therefore, the person seeks arousal.

Sensation seeking has also been associated with addictive behaviour. (See page 136.)

According to Eysenck **neuroticism** may also be linked to criminality, a trait which is also biologically based. People who score highly on neuroticism have a more reactive ANS, they tend to be high on emotionality, are jumpy and anxious, and find it very difficult to cope with stress. Finally, **psychoticism** involves a hostile and uncaring attitude to others, cold cruelty and a lack of empathy.

**Neuroticism** is the tendency to experience negative emotional states such as anger, anxiety and depression.

### Evaluation

- There is **poor evidence that extraversion is consistently linked** to the traits suggested by Eysenck. For example, Zuckerman *et al.* (1988) didn't find sensation seeking was related to extraversion.
- Some **studies have found support** – criminals score more highly than non-criminals on the scales of extraversion, neuroticism and psychoticism, as measured by the Eysenck Personality Questionnaire (EPQ). However, important variables (such as socioeconomic class, cultural background and intelligence) were not controlled (Dwyer, 2001).
- Many other **studies have not been supportive**. For example, Bartol *et al.* (1979) compared EPQ scores of 400 male prisoners with controls and did find that robbers were high on extraversion, but overall the criminals were less extravert than the control group.
- The theory **does recognise that both biology and the environment** may be important determinants of criminality.

## Treatment of offenders

AQA B  U3

### The role of custodial sentencing

A **custodial sentence** is a punishment where a person is kept in custody, i.e. some form of prison.

There are four main functions that prisons serve:

- **Incapacitation** to protect other members of society.
- **Rehabilitation** through education and/or treatment.
- **Punishment** to decrease the probability that a behaviour will be repeated.
- **Deterrence** to discourage people from committing crimes in the first place.

### Effectiveness of custodial sentencing

**Recidivism** refers to repeating criminal behaviour.

**Recidivism** rates suggest that prison does not act as an effective punishment or deterrent. In the US rates stand at about 60% compared to 50% in the UK (BBC, 2005). One possible explanation for the difference is the greater emphasis on education and rehabilitation in UK prisons.

**Type of criminal** – Glaser (1983) concluded, from a review of evidence, that supervision in the community is better for new offenders since prison often encourages and reinforces criminal behaviour. This is particularly true for 'low risk' offenders.

Two judges, Davies and Raymond (2000), argue that a longer jail sentence does not deter others, nor does it discourage the criminal himself; sentences are often imposed as a result of public demand. Many crimes are committed under the influence of alcohol or during an emotional rage, therefore, the perpetrator is not making rational choices based on the likelihood of punishment.

**Length of sentence** – Walker and Farrington (1981) found that the length of sentence made little difference to rates of reoffending among habitual offenders. Some argue that a short sentence has the greatest effect, especially for first offenders.

### Alternatives to custodial sentencing

Alternatives include being given a caution, a fine, a community order, or a community order with an unpaid work requirement.

### Treatment programmes

**Behaviour modification** is a form of operant conditioning where a person is rewarded for desirable behaviours in order to increase such behaviour.

**Social skills training (SST)** – Since criminals often lack appropriate social skills, programmes may focus on the acquisition of such skills, which involves modelling the behaviour of someone else and/or role play.

One example of behaviour management is token economy, which is discussed on page 103.

**Anger management** – Impulsive people may need to learn to become desensitised to disconnect anger and fear arising in frustrating situations. Therapeutic approaches usually include frustration tolerance training as well as meditation and relaxation techniques.

### Evaluation of these treatment programmes

One issue for any treatment programme is the longevity of the effects – often changes are just short-term or do not transfer to the real world.

- Goldstein (1986) reviewed 30 studies of SST with delinquent teenagers and found **participants had acquired certain skills,** such as how to negotiate with a probation officer. However, not many could transfer these skills to everyday life.
- Blackburn (1993) suggests SST may be useful with criminals who have serious social difficulties, but it **does not have much value for the majority of offenders**.
- Anger management courses have had **mixed success**. For example, Ireland (2000) assessed the effect of an anger management course on 50 prisoners and found considerable improvement in most of the prisoners as measured by questionnaires, although 8% showed a deterioration after completing the course.

## Practice essays 18.5

(a) Describe and evaluate **two** methods used to measure crime. *(8 marks)*

(b) Discuss biological explanations of crime. *(12 marks)*

**1**

(a) A group of psychology students are going to replicate Piaget's study of conservation in young children.

(i) Describe a suitable sample of children that should be used in order to demonstrate age differences in conservation. *(2 marks)*

(ii) Identify suitable materials that might be used to test the children's ability to conserve. *(2 marks)*

> (i) They could use some children under the age of 7 and some over the age of 7 because around the age of 7 is the age when children become able to conserve. They wouldn't use very young children because they couldn't cope.
>
> (ii) You could use counters to show conservation of number, clay for conservation of mass, and beakers of water for conservation of volume.

(b) Outline the nativist approach to explaining cognitive development. *(4 marks)*

> Nativists are people who believe in nature rather than nurture. So the nativist approach is one where psychologists have suggested that infants are more capable than Piaget suggested. Piaget suggested that children acquire schemas through the processes of assimilation and accommodation. At first infants have very few innate schemas but these develop through interactions with the world. Nativists like Baillargeon suggest that children are more capable than Piaget suggested.

(c) Describe and evaluate Vygotsky's theory of cognitive development. *(12 marks)*

> Vygotsky's view of cognitive development was that the main driving force was social interactions. A child is led through the ZPD (zone of proximal development) because experts lead them through it. Experts are people with greater knowledge. Experts are one kind of social interaction. The other kind is culture more generally. We are surrounded by cultural things such as language and the internet, and these things provide us with the stimulus to develop cognitively.
>
> Vygotsky suggested that there are two kinds of mental functions: elementary ones and more complex ones (higher functions). All children are born with elementary mental functions, and animals have these too — things like attention and perception. Through social interactions these functions are transformed into higher level cognitive abilities.
>
> Vygotsky's theory has been used to develop the idea of scaffolding in education where a child is guided in the learning process but not told what to do except when the child is floundering. The expert essentially provides a scaffold for the learning and this helps them through the ZPD.
>
> There is some research evidence to support Vygotsky's theory, but not as much as Piaget's because Vygotsky's theory is less easy to test. Research on scaffolding has shown that it is an effective way to learn, for example, a study by McNaughton and Leyland. There is also evidence from other cultures which shows how cognitive development is different and this is related to the culture surrounding the child.
>
> Vygotsky's theory can be contrasted with Piaget's theory, which is more representative of European capitalist society and which focuses on the importance of the individual. Piaget felt each child should invent knowledge through his/her own self-discovery whereas Vygotsky felt knowledge should be socially constructed. In fact, both of their theories recommend active learning so in some ways the theories have similarities. They may be appropriate to different cultures.

---

1. (a) (i) A reasonable answer but should mention why the age of 7 has been selected e.g. explain the age divide for pre-operational/concrete op. stages. **1 out of 2 marks.**

1. (a) (ii) The answer would be better if the student had referred to the actual task, but there is sufficient for **1 out of 2 marks.**

1. (b) This is a competent answer; the candidate makes three clear points and, therefore, gains **3 out of 4 marks.**

1. (c) This answer provides a reasonable amount of description and evaluation, however key details are missing, for example there is no explanation of the ZPD (what it means). There is also no mention of the different speech shown by children as they develop cognitively and this is important to Vygotsky.

The evaluation (final two paragraphs) also contains some useful points but these could have been further explained in order to score top marks, for example, providing more understanding of the active learning strategies recommended by both approaches.

The evaluation carries more weight than the description so only **6 out of 12 marks.**

**2**

(a) Distinguish between the concepts of privation and deprivation.     *(4 marks)*

Privation refers to the lack of any attachments whereas deprivation refers to the loss of attachments. It is suggested that privation has more serious consequences whereas children may recover from early deprivation.

(b) A psychologist intends to study the attachment behaviours of young children when playing with their father. Describe **two** behaviours that might be studied and how they could be measured.     *(4 marks)*

The psychologist might look at reunion behaviour. When the father comes into a room the way the child greets his/her father is related to how securely attached the child is. Another behaviour that might be studied is the distance between the child and his/her father while the child is playing. Secure children are not so clingy.

(c) Describe and evaluate Bowlby's work on early relationships.     *(12 marks)*

Bowlby's first research looked at the effects of deprivation on a child's emotional development. He proposed the maternal deprivation hypothesis, which stated that children who experience frequent early separations from their mother figure will later become maladjusted. Bowlby said that there was a critical period for this development – children under the age of 2 would be affected. He supported this with his study of juvenile delinquents. He showed that the children who became affectionless psychopaths had experienced frequent early separations. However, Rutter said Bowlby was wrong in claiming that this is true of all children and also Bowlby overlooked the fact that there is a difference between privation and deprivation.

Bowlby further developed his original hypothesis and it became a theory of attachment. This theory focuses more on the benefits of attachment rather than on the consequences of deprivation. It is an evolutionary theory because it is concerned with the way that attachment is something that is adaptive – attachment increases the likelihood that an animal or baby will survive. This is similar to the process of imprinting that Lorenz documented in his study of goslings that imprinted on a goose or on Lorenz depending who they saw first.

Bowlby suggested that this early attachment relationship forms the basis for later relationships in a person's life. The kind of attachment relationship the infant has with its mother figure leads them to expect the same, for better or worse, from relationships later in life, like with their romantic partners or with their own children.

It's always difficult to get evidence to support evolutionary explanations but one piece of evidence is from Hazan and Shaver who did find a link between the kind of attachment a child experiences early in life and their later relationships. They found that children who are securely attached go on to form more trusting relationships. However, this study was a questionnaire where people had to recall their early childhood so the data may not be entirely reliable. Bowlby's theory of attachment also included the concepts of primary and secondary attachments. Children are attached most to one person in terms of emotional development. This is most likely to be a child's mother but could be their father or someone else. This attachment is probably related to the quality of the contact with the other person. Children also develop secondary attachments that are also important.

2. (a) The answer to this question is brief regarding privation and deprivation, but enough for **2 out of 4 marks**. In the second sentence an example of the serious consequences should have been given for an extra mark and the difference between them is not explained enough.

2. (b) The first sentence is sufficient for 1 mark but does not go on and say how this can be measured. The other behaviour mentioned is not explained sufficiently for 1 mark and again this does not say how it can be measured. **1 out of 4 marks**.

2. (c) This is a competent and thorough answer. It provides a clear description of Bowlby's theories showing sound and accurate knowledge and understanding.

There are good references to other studies that back up Bowlby's theory. There are also evaluative comments throughout the essay, however, the evaluation is perhaps not as full as the description – and it is critical to focus on evaluation as more weight is placed on AO2 marks. **10 out of 12 marks**.

# Chapter 19
# Approaches, debates and methods in psychology

## 19.1 Approaches in psychology

*After studying this topic you should be able to describe and evaluate:*

**AS**

- A discussion of all six approaches is presented in *Revise AS Unit 1.1, pages 13–21.*

Classical and operant conditioning are explained on page 72.

- *the biological approach: assumptions and application of the biological approach; the role of the central and autonomic nervous system in behaviour; the genetic basis of behaviour; strengths and limitations of the biological approach*
- *the behaviourist approach: assumptions and application of the behaviourist approach; key concepts including stimulus, response and reinforcement; types of reinforcement; classical and operant conditioning as applied to human behaviour; strengths and limitations of the behaviourist approach*
- *the social learning theory approach: social learning theory as a bridge between traditional behaviourism and the cognitive approach; assumptions and application of social learning theory; the role of mediational processes in learning, motivation and performance of behaviour; observational learning and the role of vicarious reinforcement; strengths and limitations of social learning theory*
- *the cognitive approach: assumptions and application of the cognitive approach, including the idea that thoughts influence behaviour; information processing and how this applies to human behaviour and thought; use of computer analogies in understanding behaviour; strengths and limitations of the cognitive approach*
- *the psychodynamic approach: assumptions and application of the psychodynamic approach; Freud's approach to personality structure and dynamics; unconscious mental processes; psychosexual stages of development; Freud's use of case studies to highlight concepts; post-Freudian theories including Erikson and at least one other; strengths and limitations of the psychodynamic approach*
- *the humanistic approach: assumptions and application of the humanistic approach; the person-centred approach of Rogers and Maslow; rejection of the traditional scientific approach and experimentation; the importance within humanistic psychology of valuing individual experience, promoting personal growth, the concepts of freewill and holism; strengths and limitations of the humanistic approach*
- *the extent to which different approaches overlap and complement each other. The value of individual approaches and the merits of taking an eclectic approach to explaining human behaviour and in the application of psychology.*

**LEARNING SUMMARY**

On the next page there is a table comparing the approaches in terms of the various debates listed on page 181. The discussion of each of the debates (pages 180–186) provides useful information related to the value of each approach and the merits of an eclectic approach.

## Comparison of the approaches

AQA B    U3

| | The biological approach | The behaviourist approach | The social learning approach | The psychodynamic approach | The cognitive approach | The humanistic approach |
|---|---|---|---|---|---|---|
| Causes of behaviour | Internal, physical | External, psychological | External (observational learning) and internal (cognitive representations) | Internal, biological/ psychological | Internal, cognitive | Internal, psychological |
| Determinism / free will | We are determined by internal factors and/or inherited factors, both of which are outside our control. | Environmental determinism: we are controlled by external factors. | Reciprocal determinism: a person's behaviour both influences and is influenced by personal factors. | Psychic determinism: causes of behaviour are unconscious and hidden from us. | Thoughts determine behaviour, therefore, the individual has control (free will). | Each individual is responsible for making their own choices. |
| Nature and nurture | Biological systems are innate (nature) but experience may modify them (e.g. changed hormone levels when stressed). | All behaviour is learned (nurture), though the capacity to be conditioned is innate. | Behaviour is learned through direct and indirect reinforcement, but biological factors are not ignored. | Behaviour is driven by innate systems, but outcome is the result of an interaction with experience (nurture). | Faulty thoughts may be innate or due to experience. They may be a cause or effect of mental disorder. | Behaviour is affected by life experiences, which shape self-esteem, and also by an individual's self-determination. |
| Reductionism and holism | Reduces behaviour to basic biological components. | Reduces behaviour to stimulus-response units. | Reduces behaviour to effects of learning. | Reduces behaviour to a set of hypothetical mental structures and processes. | Reduces behaviour to thoughts, beliefs and attitudes. | Emphasises the importance of the whole person. |
| Idiographic / nomothetic | Nomothetic. | Nomothetic. | Idiographic and nomothetic (reciprocal determinism). | Idiographic, though also produced generalisations. | Nomothetic. | Idiographic. |
| Scientific status | Lends itself to experimental study. Often uses non-human animals because of ethical objections. | Highly objective and experiment-based approach. | An experimental approach. | Relied on case studies and subjective interpretation; may better reflect the complexity of human behaviour. | Highly experimental approach. Propositions can be easily tested. | Qualitative research (e.g. unstructured interviews), but this can be a scientific approach. |

# 19.2 Debates in psychology

## Free will and determinism

AQA B    U4

Behaviour can be determined by internal or external forces.

**Key points from AS**

• Psychological explanations of stress are given in *Revise AS Unit 5.1 page 98.*

This view of behaviour may be more applicable to non-human animals where learning has less influence on behaviour.

**Key points from AS**

• Prejudice is discussed in *Revise AS Unit 6.3 page 143.*

Where do you think a cognitive psychologist would stand on the free will–determinism debate?

At any time, would your behaviour have been different if you had willed it? Believers in free will say 'Yes'.

### Kinds of determinism

**Biological determinism** – Behaviour is determined by internal (biological) factors, e.g. physiological explanations of stress and genetic explanations of gender development (see page 59).

**Environmental determinism** – The behaviourist view is that we are controlled by external forces. Skinner said that freedom was an illusion, maintained because we are unaware of the environmental causes of behaviour. The social learning approach suggests that our behaviour is controlled by vicarious/indirect reinforcement (environmental), but also by direct reinforcement.

**Psychic determinism** – Freud also thought that freedom was an illusion, because the actual causes of our behaviour are unconscious and, therefore, hidden from us.

**The scientific emphasis on causal explanations** – Science is based on the assumption that one thing causes (determines) another. Scientific research can be used to predict behaviour and manipulate it, e.g. reducing prejudice. Free will denies such relationships.

### Issues related to determinism

**Moral responsibility** – When a person commits an anti-social act, the cause of their behaviour may be due to biological (inherited) or social (e.g. the media) causes. We cannot hold individuals legally responsible for their actions if the causes were outside their control. Criminals have used this argument to 'excuse' their behaviour – their actions were not their fault and, therefore, they shouldn't be punished. Free will, on the other hand, suggests that we are each morally responsible for our actions.

**Lack of determinism** – Both Heisenberg's **uncertainty principle** (1927) and Hilborn's **chaos theory** (1994) suggest that even in a hard science such as physics there are no purely deterministic relationships. The uncertainty principle states that the act of making an observation changes the observation, thus no objective research is ever possible. Chaos theory proposes that very small changes in initial conditions can result in major and unpredictable changes later.

## Free will

Individuals have an active role in determining their behaviour, i.e. they are free to choose.

**Humanistic psychologists** (such as Maslow and Rogers) believe we exercise choice in our behaviour. Rogers believed that it is only by taking responsibility for all aspects of your own behaviour that an individual can be well-adjusted and capable of self-actualisation. Maslow also used the concept of self-actualisation and regarded it as the highest form of motivation.

Sartre, an existentialist philosopher, said that we are 'condemned to be free'; freedom is a burden because we must each be totally responsible for our behaviour and we must each respect each other's views. The law embodies this view.

## Reconciling determinism and free will

> Soft determinism offers a way to make determinism compatible with moral responsibility.

### Hard versus soft determinism

William James (1890) proposed a way that the determinism–free will debate can be resolved, which he called 'soft determinism'. He suggested that we can separate behaviour into a physical and mental realm. It is the physical that is determined, whereas the mental realm is subject to free will.

Elizabeth Valentine (1992) proposed a different form of 'soft determinism'. She described it as the view that behaviour is always determined, it just sometimes appears to be less determined. Behaviour that is highly constrained by a situation appears involuntary; behaviour that is less constrained by a situation appears voluntary.

Westcott (1982) conducted a study to demonstrate the validity of this view. University students were asked to indicate the extent to which they 'felt free' in 28 different situations. They reported that they felt most free in situations requiring self-direction, absence of responsibility, performing a skilled behaviour, or when behaviour would result in escape from an unpleasant situation (i.e. where there was little constraint). They felt least free in situations characterised as 'prevention from without', 'diffuse unpleasant affect', 'conflict and indecision' and when they recognised that there were limits on their behaviour, for example having to take their abilities into account when selecting course options (i.e. where there was most constraint).

### Freedom within constraints

Absolute free will means that behaviour is not determined in any lawful way. However, even humanistic psychologists believe that behaviour is governed by conscious decisions, which have some regularity. Heather (1976) resolved this by suggesting that much of behaviour is predictable, but not inevitable. Individuals are free to choose their behaviour, but this is usually from within a fairly limited repertoire.

# The nature–nurture debate

AQA B    U4

**Nature** refers to behaviour that is determined by inherited factors, whereas nurture is the influence of environmental factors such as learning and experience.

This debate is sometimes called the 'heredity versus environment debate'.

**Key points from AS**

• Bowlby's theory is discussed in *Revise AS Unit 2.1, page 53*.

'Empirical' means to discover something directly through one's own senses. Empiricists argue that all behaviour is acquired directly through experience

**Key points from AS**

• Gregory's theory of perception is discussed in *Revise AS Unit 2.4, page 46*.

Nature versus nurture was once a heated philosophical debate, but now it is accepted that our genetic blueprint provides certain limitations through which the environment can express itself

The diathesis-stress model (page 54) is a similar concept where potential is modified to produce phenotype.

Both Piaget and Freud suggested that development is 'driven' by biological changes. Adult characteristics are the consequence of the interaction between these biological factors and experience (nature and nurture).

**Key points from AS**

• Theories of perception cover both nature and nurture, see *Revise AS Unit 2.4, pages 43–48*.

IQ is a classic example of the nature–nurture debate (see page 78–79).

## Nature

The 'nature' position is sometimes called 'nativism' or 'heredity'. It is the belief that human characteristics are largely inherited or native to an individual, a view espoused by the Greek philosopher Plato and later notably by the French philosopher Rousseau who believed that children were noble savages, and they should be allowed to follow their natural inclinations and inherent sense of goodness. This European view led to, e.g. Piaget's concept of the child actively engaged in his cognitive development.

Some examples of explanations where inherited factors are seen to be uppermost: evolutionary explanations of behaviour (e.g. Bowlby's theory), and biological accounts of aggression (page 43), mental illness (e.g. page 98) and gender development (page 53).

## Nurture

The 'nurture' position is sometimes referred to as 'empiricism' or 'the environment'. Locke, a 17th Century philosopher, suggested that all babies are born alike; their minds can be described as a blank slate (*tabula Rasa*). Their development is passively moulded by empirical, sensory experiences. This view developed into the behaviourist view of environmental control.

Some examples of explanations in terms of environmental factors include Gregory's theory of perception, learning theories of aggression (page 40), gender development (page 61) and mental disorder (e.g. page 100).

## Nature or nurture? An interactionist approach

Hebb (1949) pointed out that the question of 'nature or nurture' is like asking whether a field's area is determined more by its length or by its width. However, we can still consider the contributory factors.

Gottesman (1963) described a **reaction range**, e.g. our potential height is inherited but actual height is determined by factors such as diet. Potential is your **genotype** (the actual genes that an individual has) and realised potential is your **phenotype** (an individual's observable characteristics).

**Phenylketonuria** (PKU) is given as the classic example of gene-environment interaction. It is an inherited metabolic disorder where phenylketones build up and cause brain damage unless the child is given a diet (nurture) low in phenylalanine. Nature interacts with diet to produce the final phenotype, which may or may not be brain damage, depending on the child's diet.

## Practical implications

If behaviour is entirely due to heredity then intervention would have little effect on the development of children. Herrnstein and Murray (1994), the authors of *The Bell Curve*, argue that we can't significantly change IQ and, therefore, intervention programmes are a waste of money. If intelligence can be boosted by experience then intervention programmes make sense. The evidence suggests that such programmes have a positive effect, supporting the 'nurture' position (page 79).

If behaviour is learned it can be manipulated by others. Skinner (1948) wrote a novel, *Walden Two*, describing how an ideal environment could be created to engineer human behaviour. If behaviour is learned it can be unlearned. Behaviourist principles are used to shape the behaviour of prisoners and mental patients, assuming that their behaviour is learned rather than innate. However, if such behaviours are biological then we should treat them with drugs.

## Holism and reductionism

AQA B ▶ U4

**Holism** is the view that systems as a whole should be studied rather than focusing on the constituent parts, and suggests that we cannot predict how the whole system will behave from a knowledge of the individual components.

**Reductionism** is any attempt to reduce a complex set of phenomena to some more basic components.

### Examples of reductionism

**Environmental reductionism** – Reducing behaviour to the effect of environmental stimuli, as in behaviourist explanations of gender development (page 61) and mental illness (e.g. page 100). This approach overlooks innate influences and has potential for abuse through social manipulation.

**Biological reductionism** – Explaining behaviour in terms of physiological and genetic mechanisms, for example, biological explanations of gender development (page 59) and mental illness (e.g. page 98). However, this diverts attention from other, more social explanations and can result in over-use of biochemical methods of control (e.g. for mental illness or treatment of jet lag).

**Machine reductionism** – Explaining behaviour in information-processing terms. However, interconnectionist networks have been described by Penrose (1990), which are holist insofar as the network behaves differently than the individual parts.

**Experimental reductionism** – Use of controlled laboratory studies to understand similar behaviours in everyday life, may lack ecological validity.

Most determinist explanations are reductionist, and vice versa.

**Key points from AS**

- Perception is discussed in *Revise AS Unit 2.4, page 44.*

### Examples of holism

**Gestalt** psychologists argued that the whole does not equal the sum of the parts. They applied these principles to perception.

**Humanistic** psychologists (e.g. Rogers, 1951) believe that the individual reacts as an organised whole, rather than a set of stimulus–response (S–R) links.

**Cognitive systems** like memory and intelligence are examples of the value of a holistic approach. They are complex systems whose behaviour is related to the activity of neurons, genes and so on; yet the whole system cannot be simply predicted from these lower level units.

### An eclectic approach

Relevant data is gathered together from various sources and disciplines, e.g. understanding the causes of schizophrenia involves both reductionist and holist explanations, or using data from brain scans to understand cognitive processes (see page 114).

### Strengths and limitations

You can work out the strengths and limitations of holistic explanations by reversing the reductionist arguments.

#### Strengths of the reductionist approach

- Reductionism may be a **necessary part** of understanding how things work.
- Reductionist arguments are **easier to test empirically.**
- Reductionist explanations may be correct or appropriate; they are incomplete because **psychological research has yet to identify all the facts.**

#### Limitations of the reductionist approach

- Reductionist explanations may **oversimplify complex problems** that have no single answer, taking attention away from other levels of explanation so that we fail to usefully understand behaviour.
- Reductionist explanations **may not answer the question.** Valentine (1992) suggests that physiological explanations focus on structures, whereas more holist explanations are concerned with process (see 'levels of explanation' on the next page).

### An interactionist approach

Rose (1976) suggested that the controversy over reductionism is due to a semantic confusion.

If psychologists attempt to 'explain away' psychological phenomena using reductionist concepts, the result is unsatisfactory. However, if one accepts that there is a hierarchy of **levels of explanation**, then it is possible to see that reductionist explanations are one form of discourse and contribute to explaining behaviour. Rose proposed that physical explanations are at the bottom, moving through chemical, anatomical-biochemical, physiological, psychological (mentalistic), social psychological and, finally, sociological explanations.

## Idiographic and nomothetic approaches

AQA B    U4

The **idiographic approach** is an approach to research that focuses more on the individual case as a means of understanding behaviour, rather than aiming to formulate general laws of behaviour (the nomothetic approach).

'Nomos' means 'law'.

The **idiographic approach** involves the study of individuals and the unique insights each individual gives us about human behaviour. It is the approach favoured by humanistic psychology and also the approach taken by Freud in his case histories. Case studies focus on individuals, such as the study of Jenny undertaken by Allport as a means to study personality. He analysed 300 letters written by 'Jenny', arguing that this idiographic perspective could tell us more about human behaviour and personality than could the use of personality tests, which provide statistical information.

The idiographic approach typically uses qualitative methods such as unstructured interviews, case studies, introspection, etc. Such techniques allow new insights to be presented. The approach is typical of humanistic and psychoanalytic psychologists.

The **nomothetic approach** involves the study of a large number of people and then seeks to make generalisations or develop laws/theories about their behaviour. This is the goal of the scientific approach. The biological, behaviourist and cognitive approaches are concerned with general laws of behaviour. In fact, most psychological research focused on generalisations, for example, research on gender focuses on the way that men on the whole and women on the whole differ from one another.

### Strengths and limitations

You can work out the strengths and limitations of nomothetic approach by reversing the idiographic arguments.

#### Strengths of the idiographic approach
- Recognises the **uniqueness** of each person.
- Sees the world from the **perspective of the individual**.
- A more **holist approach** to understanding behaviour, rather than reducing it to particular elements.

#### Limitations of the idiographic approach
- Tends to be **less scientific** insofar as the approach does not aim to make generalisations. However, qualitative methods are not unscientific in that they seek verification through empirical evidence.
- Makes it **more difficult to produce predictions** about how people will behave. Such predictions can be useful, for example, in producing drugs to treat mental illness.

### An interactionist approach

A number of approaches actually combine the two approaches. Freud used idiographic methods to study people, but also used those insights to make generalisations about human development in his theory of personality.

Bandura's concept of reciprocal determinism embraces the uniqueness of each person and the laws of behaviour and the environment. He proposed that our behaviour is determined by the environment (conditioning) but our behaviour also shapes the environments we are in.

185

## Psychology and science

AQA A ▶ U4
AQA B ▶ U4

> The features and principles of the scientific approach and the role of peer review are presented on page 149.

### The subject matter of psychology

Psychology has been defined as the science of behaviour and experience, which points out the two strands of interest:

(1) psychologists seek to study overt behaviour and use objective, nomothetic methods to do this
(2) they also seek to understand subjective, private experience and tend to use more idiographic and qualitative methods.

### Strengths and limitations of the scientific approach

> The word 'science' refers both to the body of knowledge and the methods used to obtain that knowledge.

#### Strengths

- The scientific method enables **theories to be constructed and tested** through the collection of objective, verifiable data. Without a scientific approach we are easily beguiled by pseudoscientific explanations.
- The scientific approach enables us to **make generalisations** about people and **apply this knowledge constructively** in, for example, reducing prejudice and treating mental disorders. The applications themselves can then be evaluated using the scientific method.

#### Limitations

- The problems of bias in science are especially problematic in psychology where the object of study is active and intelligent. Experimental artifacts, such as **experimenter bias**, **demand characteristics**, and **sample bias** mean that it may be impossible to conduct objective and repeatable research.

> **Key points from AS**
> - These concepts are explained in *Revise AS Unit 4.2, pages 82 and 84.*

- Science may be an **impossible ideal** even in the 'hard sciences' such as physics. No investigator is ever truly objective and no observations are unaffected by the process of being observed, as indicated by Heisenberg's uncertainty principle (page 181).

> **Social representation theory** emphasises the way that we represent *social* knowledge and how this knowledge is unconsciously shaped by *social* groups, i.e. such representations are social in two ways.

- **Social representation theory** suggests that scientific knowledge is not a timeless concept, but a feature of a particular group of people at a particular time in history. Scientific beliefs are subject to the same group pressures of other groups, i.e. not objective.
- Even if one accepted that psychology was scientific, we must ask what **relevance** this approach has to the understanding of human behaviour.
- The scientific approach is both determinist and reductionist. This means that scientific experiments may not have **ecological validity** because what is studied is very divorced from everyday life (i.e. it lacks **mundane realism**).

> **Mundane realism** refers to things that are similar to everyday activities.

- All scientific research is based on **restricted samples**. In psychology these are culturally and socially biased, producing theories that are not universally valid.
- Humanistic psychologists feel that objective data can tell us little about subjective experience. It has statistical, but **not human, meaning**. New research methods are needed to properly investigate human behaviour, such as qualitative methods.

> **Key points from AS**
> - Qualitative data is discussed in *Revise AS Unit 4.3, page 94.*

## Practice essays 19.3

(a) Outline what is meant by the terms 'hard determinism' and 'soft determinism' in psychology. *(4 marks)*

(b) Explain the idiographic approach to the study of human behaviour, using examples in your answer. *(4 marks)*

(c) Discuss the nature–nurture debate in psychology, with reference to **at least one** topic area in psychology. *(12 marks)*

# 19.3 Methods in psychology

*After studying this topic you should be able to describe and evaluate:*

In addition to the topics listed on the right, candidates are expected to draw on topics studied in the AS course, such as research methods and design.

**Inferential statistics:**

- statistical inference: the concepts of probability and levels of significance; hypothesis testing: null and alternative (experimental or research) hypothesis
- one and two tailed tests, Type I and Type II errors; positive, negative and zero correlation; limitations of sampling techniques and generalisation of results
- statistical tests: use of non-parametric and parametric tests; statistical tests of difference: the sign test, Wilcoxon signed ranks test, Mann-Whitney, related (repeated measures) and independent tests; statistical tests of association: Spearman's rank order correlation, Pearson's product moment correlation, the Chi-squared test; factors affecting the choice of statistical test, including levels of measurement, type of experimental design; criteria for parametric testing: interval data; normal distribution; homogeneity of variance.

Students should have experience of designing and conducting informal classroom research using a variety of methods. They will be expected to analyse data collected in investigations and draw conclusions based on research findings. They will be required to draw on these experiences to answer questions in the examination for this unit.

**Issues in research:**

- strengths and limitations of different methods of research; strengths and limitations of qualitative and quantitative data
- reliability and validity applied generally across all methods of investigation; types of reliability and validity; ways of assessing reliability and validity
- critical understanding of the importance of ethical considerations within the social and cultural environment; ethical considerations in the design and conduct of psychological research.

**LEARNING SUMMARY**

### AS

- These are covered on pages 151–152 and also in *Revise AS Units 4.1, 4.2 and 4.3*, pages 75–94.

### AS

- These topics were covered in *Revise AS Units 4.1 and 4.2*, page 75–91.

## Inferential tests: Non-parametric and parametric tests

AQA B    U4

The inferential statistical tests described on page 151 are all non-parametric tests. Another group of inferential tests are called **parametric tests**. These are distinguished by the fact that they have been developed based on certain assumptions about the data they test. The assumptions are that:

1. The level of measurement is **interval** or **ratio** (levels of measurement are described on page 151). '**Plastic interval scales**' are also acceptable – these are scales where the intervals have been arbitrarily determined, such as on a rating scale. We can assume, for the purpose of analysis, that the intervals are equal.

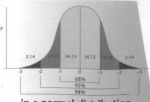

In a **normal distribution** 34.13% of the data scores are 1 standard deviation below the mean and an equal number are 1 standard deviation above the mean, i.e. 68.26% are within 1 standard deviation of the mean. 95% of the scores are within 2 standard deviations of the mean.

The **standard deviation** is calculated by working out the difference between each score and the mean and calculating the mean of these differences.

2. The data are drawn from a population that has a **normal distribution**. Note that it is not the sample that must be normally distributed but the **population**. A normal distribution is a bell-shaped distribution, where most scores cluster around the mean with an equal number of scores above and below the mean, as illustrated on the left. We expect many physical and psychological characteristics to be normally distributed, such as IQ and shoe sizes.

3. The **variances** of the two samples are not significantly different (i.e. they are homogenous or the same). The variance is related to the **standard deviation** of a set of data – it is the standard deviation squared. When looking at related samples, differences in variances should not distort the result (Coolican, 1996). Therefore, we do not need to be too concerned about variance when dealing with related measures. When looking at independent samples, the best way to ensure similar variances is to collect samples that are similar in size.

However, parametric tests are quite robust – they are reliable unless the parametric assumptions are met quite poorly. The reason for preferring to use a parametric test is that they are more powerful, i.e. they can detect a significant difference when the actual difference/relationship between the data is smaller.

## Which test should be used?

| Design/Data | Non-parametric | | Parametric |
|---|---|---|---|
| | Nominal data | Ordinal data | Interval data |
| Association/ Correlation | Association: Chi-squared test | Correlation: Spearman's rank order correlation correlation | Correlation: Pearson's product moment |
| Independent samples | Chi-squared | Mann-Whitney | Independent t-test |
| Repeated measures (and matched pairs) | Sign test | Wilcoxon signed ranks | Related t-test |

## Looking up the critical value for each test

For some tests a statistical result is significant if the observed value is greater than the critical value. Sometimes it is significant if the observed value is less than the critical value. The letter 'r' can sort this out for you!

The observed value should be greater than the critical value for:

Spearman, Pearson, Chi-Squared, Related t-test, Unrelated t-test (each test name, like the word 'greater' has a letter 'r' in it).

The observed value should be less than the critical value for:

Wilcoxon, Mann-Whitney, Sign test (there is no letter 'r' to be found!)

## Practice questions 19.3

See practice questions on page 152.

**1**

(a) Describe **two** methods used by biological psychologists to investigate human behaviour, and give examples for each. *(4 marks)*

One method used by biological psychologists is twin studies. This is used to see whether a particular trait, such as schizophrenia is genetically inherited or not. Another method is brain scans which are used, for example, to see what part of the brain is active when a person is engaged on a particular task or to see if the brain of a schizophrenic is different to a normal person's brain.

(b) Outline **two** strengths of the behaviourist approach. *(4 marks)*

One strength is that it is easy to conduct experiments to show whether certain behaviours are acquired through reinforcement. A second strength is that this approach has led to many applications, such as therapies for treating mental disorders.

(c) Discuss the psychodynamic approach in psychology. Refer to **at least one** other approach in your answer. *(12 marks)*

The psychodynamic approach is associated with Freud's theory of psychoanalysis. This theory proposes that our personalities develop as a result of interactions between biological forces and life events. The personality is divided into three elements. The id is the primitive self, driven by the pleasure principle. The second element, the ego, develops towards the end of a baby's first year and is driven by the reality principle. The id and ego are inevitably in conflict because the id wants what it wants, whereas the ego takes reality into account. Around the age of four the superego develops. The superego is your ideal self and your moral self. The id and ego are in conflict and this creates anxiety. In order to protect itself from anxiety the ego has certain ego defences such as repression, where any thought or event that creates anxiety is repressed into the unconscious mind. Another ego defence is projection where a person projects their anxious feelings onto something else.

Freud also suggested that there are stages of psychosexual development. These stages are biologically determined (all children go through the same stages) but the outcome of each stage depends on individual experiences and these experiences shape adult personality. The first stage is the oral stage, in the first year of life when pleasure is derived from the mouth. A baby who experiences too much or too little pleasure in this stage will be fixated on it later in life and is described as having an oral personality. This may mean that they like to do things such as chew on a pencil or smoke, or it may mean they are pessimistic (frustrated in the oral stage) or optimistic (overindulged in the oral stage). The next stage is the anal stage followed by the phallic stage where focus is on the child's genitals. In this stage a boy goes through the Oedipus conflict where he desires his mother and, therefore, sees his father as a rival. Eventually, the conflict is resolved, which leads the boy to identify with his father and, thus, develop important moral values. Lack of identification will affect moral development. Girls go through a different conflict and their resolution isn't as strong so Freud said this explains why girls have a less well-developed sense of moral values.

Freud has received lots of criticisms because his theory is based on a small group of neurotic Viennese Victorian women and may not really apply to other people. He has also been criticised because his theory was too focused on sex and Erikson proposed a similar psychodynamic theory which had social instead of sexual conflicts.

**2**

(a) Explain what is meant by the terms 'nomothetic' and 'idiographic'. *(4 marks)*

Nomothetic refers to making generalisations about people, whereas idiographic is when you just study one individual.

(b) Outline why some psychologists favour reductionist explanations of human behaviour. *(4 marks)*

Reductionist approaches are desirable because they are simpler and mean that you identify individual factors and can then conduct experiments to look at causes and effects.

(c) Discuss the nature and nurture debate in psychology. In your answer, refer to **at least two** topics that you have studied in psychology. *(12 marks)*

It is agreed by psychologists that behaviour is not simply all nature or all nurture. There is some interaction or relationship between these two. Hebb made the point that trying to separate them was like trying to decide whether the length or width of a rectangle contributed more to its area. This shows that it cannot be an either/or question. They interact.

The nature-nurture issue has been studied in many areas of psychology: perception, mental illness and probably most notably in the area of intelligence. Aspects of perception are hard-wired, such as our ability to see colour and perceive form. But a considerable amount of perception is affected by expectations because much sensory input is incomplete. We fill in the gaps using expectations. This means that there are cultural differences in perception because of different experiences. For example, Segall et al. (1963) suggested that people who live in carpentered environments are more likely to be fooled by visual illusions based on depth cues.

Mental illnesses such as schizophrenia have been explained in terms of the diathesis-stress model which again expresses this interaction between nature and nurture. The principle is that some individuals are born with genes for a mental disorder, but the disorder only surfaces when there are triggers (stressors). This explains why the concordance rates in twins is not 100%, but does not explain why few schizophrenics report stressful episodes in the months leading up to the initial onset of the disorder (Rabkin, 1980).

In the case of intelligence much research has looked at twins. If an individual's intelligence is entirely due to nature then we would expect identical twins, even those reared apart, to have identical intelligence. They don't (e.g. Pederson et al., 1992). However, they do have greater similarity in IQ (and many other personality variables) than non-identical twins. It is better to compare identical and non-identical twins because one presumes that each pair has more similar nurture experiences than brother and sister who are genetically as similar as non-identical twins but there are age differences. However, recently the idea of micro-environment has been raised. Each individual creates their immediate environment and this effect of the environment is related to aspects of their genetic self. For example, if they are an innately attractive baby then people treat them better and this attractiveness creates a halo effect – people who are attractive are seen as possessing many other desirable qualities. Such effects can be self-fulfilling. In the case of identical twins they will create more similar micro-environments than non-identical twins who look and behave more differently. Thus, we can see that genes interact with environment such that environmental influences are at least in part genetic.

2. (a) The question asks for an explanation but the answer only gives a brief description of each term. **2 out of 4 marks.**

2. (b) Even though the question only asks for an 'outline' there is insufficient detail in the answer. The student should have expanded on the fact that such approaches are simpler (in what way) and gone on to say what factors can be experimented on. **2 out of 4 marks.**

2. (c) The answer contains a very good descriptive element, as is common in student answers. At least two topics are referred to, as required in the question, but there is no clear explanation of what is meant by nature or nurture.

The evaluation is weak because there is not much reference to the debate in the essay, nor are nature and nurture compared. The part of the essay that referred to twin studies and intelligence is muddled.

**7 out of 12 marks.**

See page 155 for a student answer to a research methods question.